Guidebook to the

Aransas

National Wildlife Refuge

Wayne H. and Martha K. McAlister

Mince Country Press

Victoria, Texas

This guidebook is dedicated to the late E. Frank Johnson, Manager of the Aransas National Wildlife Refuge, 1973-1986.

Published by:
Mince Country Press
Rt. 1, Box 95C
Victoria, Texas 77901

First Edition   9 8 7 6 5 4 3 2 1

Library of Congress Card Catalog Number: 87-060510

ISBN 0-9618448-0-9

Printed in the United States of America.

Table of Contents

List of Illustrations

Photographs

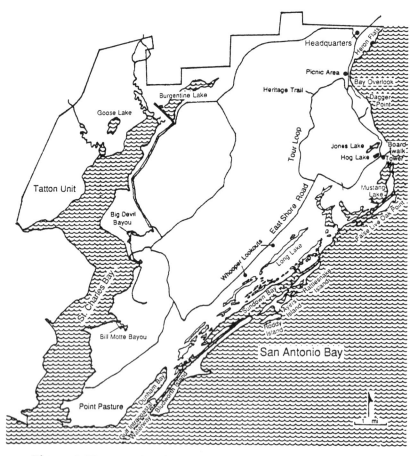

Figure 1 The mainland portion of the Aransas National
Wildlife Refuge.

Preface

It is easy to extol Nature on the Aransas National Wildlife Refuge: the oblate sun clearing the dawn mists over San Antonio Bay; a bright crimson and yellow roadside ribbon of Indian blankets; the faint norther-tossed gabble of Canada geese reckoning on instinct in a dark sky; the poetic poise of a white-tail buck with head up and ears flared; the rugged mix of sand, oak and sea--all so different from the straight-edged and shiny civilized world.

Yet, for all its sublimity, Nature alone does not make a refuge. The plants and the animals and the vagrant breezes simply survive and exist. They do not comprehend themselves or each other. Only people do. Today it takes people to insure that these wild things have the opportunity to persist in their wild way. Wherever a wildlife refuge exists, it stands in evidence that someone cares.

"We the people" have dictated that this particular lonely stretch of Texas coastline shall remain forever untamed. Our collective concern is as vital to the Aransas Refuge as is the haunting bugle of the giant white birds that have for ages made it their winter home.

In 1903, appalled by the wholesale slaughter of waterbirds for the millinery trade, President Theodore Roosevelt designated three-acre Pelican Island in Florida a Federal bird sanctuary. This was the beginning of the nation's wildlife refuge system, which today numbers over 400 units and encompasses some 90 million acres.

The Aransas National Wildlife Refuge was established on December 31, 1937. It is one of ten such Federal sanctuaries in Texas. All are administered by the U.S. Fish and Wildlife Service, Department of the Interior, for the purpose of protecting and conserving the nation's wildlife resources.

In today's busy world every wildlife refuge is a critical meeting ground of demands which are frequently contradictory. The wildlife requires a complicated fund of natural resources including food, shelter and freedom to roam and rest unmolested by humans. The people desire access to observe and enjoy the wild creatures in their natural haunts. For some that enjoyment derives from the simple liberty to stroll. Others use binoculars or camera. Yet others employ a rifle. Sometimes there are demands of other sorts. The Gulf Intracoastal Waterway which slices through a critical portion of the Refuge is an example. The privilege of the prior landowners to retain and exploit the mineral rights on the Refuge is another. The USFWS attempts to conciliate these demands by subtly managing both wildlife and people. People management is by far the more difficult task.

First priority is given to wildlife by the protection of vital habitat. This means designating and patrolling refuge boundaries and letting natural events transpire within. But because even a large refuge is only a relatively small and isolated segment of Nature and because many kinds of wild creatures exist in precariously small populations, the habitat must usually be manipulated to some extent. Vegetation is managed to insure ecological stability. Some animal populations are necessarily culled while others are given subtle support. Soil erosion is checked. Air and water pollution are monitored. All of this without upsetting the enormously varied natural cycles or significantly altering the natural appearance of the area.

People are necessarily manipulated on a wildlife refuge by restricting their access and by exposing them to a vigorous program of environmental education. Visitors contact wildlife in native habitat on designated walking and driving routes and through closely scrutinized hunting and fishing programs. Everything from brochures and films to guided tours and special visitor centers are used to inform the public about both the delight and the plight of our wildlife heritage.

In addition to its general charge of protecting and conserving the native creatures within its bounds, each wildlife refuge assumes certain special responsibilities. The Aransas Refuge was originally established for the benefit of migratory waterfowl passing along the Central Flyway, and in fact it was initially called the Aransas Migratory Waterfowl Refuge. The $463,500 purchase price came from the sale of migratory bird stamps. Management of habitat for ducks, geese and shorebirds remains a primary local objective.

Shortly after World War II the impending extinction of the whooping crane was fully appreciated, and it was then realized that by happy coincidence the last significant wintering ground of this large crane lay in the tidal flats on the Aransas Refuge. Since that revelation the fate of the bird and the renown of the Refuge have been inextricably joined.

Besides waterfowl and whooping cranes, the Aransas Refuge hosts a lengthy list of endangered and threatened animals. Equally important, the Refuge is endowed with a generous sampling of the wonderful diversity of common kinds of plants and animals representative of the wild biota of the Texas Gulf Coast. In accord with the enlightened habitat approach to wildlife management (so very different from the predator eradication concept of the Roosevelt days and from

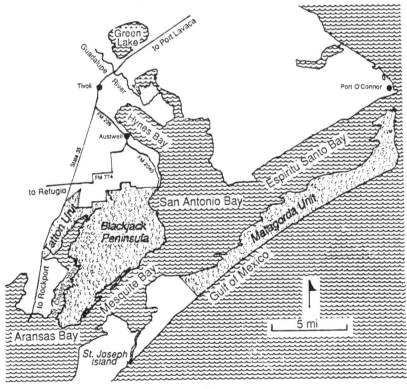

Figure 2 The 74,000 acre Aransas National Wildlife Refuge is composed of the Tatton Unit, Blackjack Peninsula and the Matagorda Unit.

the notion of a game animal farm prevalent until only a decade ago), all of these creatures--the seen and the seldom seen, the rare and the commonplace, the beneficial and the pestiferous and the indifferent, the game and the nongame, the great and the small--deserve and get their place in the Texas sun.

The Aransas National Wildlife Refuge consists of three units. As originally established in 1937, the Refuge encompassed the 47,261 acres on Blackjack Peninsula. This neck of land, 16 miles long and from 2-7 miles wide, is bounded by St. Charles Bay on the west and San Antonio Bay on the east. In November, 1967, the contiguous 7,568 acre Tatton Unit was added along the west shore of St. Charles Bay. The combined 54,829 acre tract constitutes the mainland portion of the Refuge.

In December, 1982, the 19,000 acre Matagorda Unit on Matagorda Island 10 miles across San Antonio Bay from the mainland became a part of the Refuge, boosting the total area to over 73,000 acres. In December, 1986, negotiations were completed which will eventually transfer ownership of 11,502 acres at the southern end of Matagorda Island to the Federal Government, thereby putting the entire barrier island in either State or Federal hands. This tract should ultimately become part of the Aransas National Wildlife Refuge.

USFWS jurisdiction covers an additional 13,000 acres of bay waters established by presidential proclamation as a buffer zone around the margin of Blackjack Peninsula.

The major public access to the Aransas National Wildlife Refuge is the 5,000 acre wildlife interpretive area on the

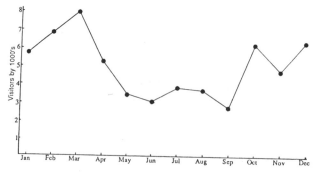

Figure 3 In 1985, 60,575 people visited the Aransas National Wildlife Refuge. The monthly pattern of visitation is typical of most years.

northeastern portion of Blackjack Peninsula, 7 miles southeast of Austwell. Despite its relative isolation this site lies within a four-hour drive for over 2.5 million people, and it hosts about 70,000 visitors annually.

Facilities include the Headquarters complex, a well-designed Visitors Center, an Observation Tower overlooking Mustang Lake and a Boardwalk across the adjacent tidal flat, a picnic area, a Youth Environmental Training Area, a 16-mile paved vehicle loop and numerous interpretive foot trails, overlooks and sites of special interest. There are no concessions or gasoline stations on the Refuge, and no camping is allowed except by special arrangement for eductional groups.

The registration and information desk is in the Visitors Center. The Refuge gate is open from sunrise to sunset the year round.

The bulk of Blackjack Peninsula and the entire Tatton Unit are devoted to the management of wildlife.

The northern two-thirds of Matagorda Island--some 44,000 acres--is jointly owned by the Department of the Interior and the State of Texas. All of this public land is administered by the Texas Parks and Wildlife Department as a collective unit called the Matagorda Island State Park and Wildlife Management Area. The wildlife management section (37,000 acres) is open for limited recreational use. The state park section (7,000 acres) has a year round visitation program. Access to Matagorda Island is by private or charter boat only. Facilities on the island are limited. Information can be obtained at the manager's office in Port O'Connor on the adjacent mainland.

This guidebook is intended to provide a general orientation for the routine visitor to the mainland portion of the Aransas National Wildlife Refuge. (Although it is given passing mention, a detailed description of the ecology of Matagorda Island is beyond our scope.) The guidebook has been written with an ecological theme that not only names the various species of resident plants and animals but offers insight into their natural relationships. Space has been allotted to various creatures according to their general interest and their ecological significance: an entire chapter to the whooping crane; several paragraphs to the live oak tree; only a passing mention of the sooty-winged skipper.

We must stress what this guidebook is **not**. It is not a definitive identification manual. The task of field identification is adequately handled by an array of well written and illustrated fieldguides. Some of these are available for purchase at the Visitors Center. Others can be obtained at any well stocked bookstore. Most come in paperback format. We have limited our presentation to ecological commentary and remarks about the life history of the included biota.

Admittedly, this approach puts the burden of identification on the visitor. To take fullest advantage of your visit to the Aransas it is best to read beforehand the section of the guidebook that interests you. All creatures are referred to by their accepted common names. (For invertebrates and plants the Latin names are given as well.) Look these up in the appropriate fieldguide. Check their fieldmarks and study their pictures. Then when you visit the Refuge you will be as prepared as you can get for a rewarding outdoor experience.

And if, after all your diligent homework, the first creature you see on the Refuge is completely unknown to you and is nowhere mentioned in this guidebook--welcome to the intrigue and the challenge of the Texas out-of-doors!

We believe that the staff of the Aransas National Wildlife Refuge is outstanding. From maintenance man to manager, all have courteously and enthusiastically assisted us in the preparation of this guidebook. This willing team effort is doubtless in large part a result of the instruction and example set by the late E. Frank Johnson, former Refuge Manager, who extended us every assistance and many solicited and unsolicited personal favors. Ken Schwindt, Assistant Manager, and Tom Stehn, Refuge Biologist, willingly shared their professional knowledge with us. Melvin Maxwell, Outdoor Recreation Planner, extended us every courtesy. Without the generous cooperation of these and the rest of the Aransas staff, this guidebook could not have been written.

We thank members of the Refuge staff and Mark and Sharon Terry for reviewing the manuscript. Of course, the authors assume ultimate responsibility for its content.

Introduction

The Aransas National Wildlife Refuge lies in the center of the Texas Coastal Bend about 50 miles north of Corpus Christi. Because of its inherent value to both wildlife and man, and especially because of its crucial role in the struggle to save the stately whooping crane, the Aransas is known worldwide.

Whether you are a newcomer or an old friend, the mood of the Aransas creeps up on you enroute. You will have traveled for miles across the flat Coastal Plain, threading highways busy with automobile and truck traffic in this most densely populated sector of the state. When you get onto the midsection of State 35, the picturesque hug-the-coast highway, the congestion eases. Finally you are among small towns, occasional chemical plants and grain elevators and welcome voids of pastureland and grain fields. By this time you will feel the insistent nudge of the steady southeast breeze against the front of your vehicle, and you will probably be treated to a magnificent display of billowing Gulf clouds. The clouds supply a generous third dimension to the monotonous local topography.

Coming from the south, turn coastward on FM 774. From the north take FM 239. Either way, just follow the Refuge signs. Both routes eventually join FM 2040 for the final seven miles to the Refuge gate.

The rows of the enormous grain fields flash by. Then the land turns sandy and the fields give way to mottes of scrubby live oaks and widespread mesquite trees. Thickets of groundsels and dark mounds of Gulf cordgrass guard the roadside ditches. A flock of great-tailed grackles bats the wind. A great egret startles up. All of these are harbingers of what lies just ahead.

Finally you crest a low sandy ridge and suddenly behold San Antonio Bay spread out to the horizon. Before you can catch

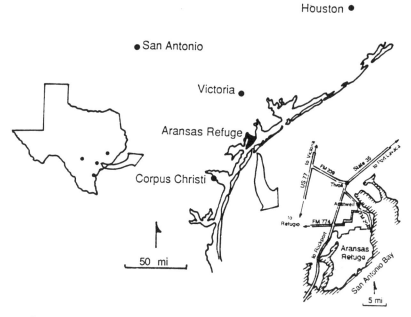

Figure 4 Location of the Aransas National Wildlife Refuge in the Coastal Bend of Texas.

your breath you are through the Refuge gate and you will likely immediately spot your first tourist-wise white-tailed deer and admire the grove of wind sculptured live oaks.

By the time you have registered at the Visitors Center the full impact of the Aransas should be upon you. It fosters a paradoxical mix of relaxation and exhiliration; of wanting to sit quietly in one place while feeling the urge to trek about so you do not miss anything. Hopefully you will have time to do both. And while you pleasantly exhaust yourself you will come to appreciate that the Aransas is not only a refuge for harried wildlife. It is a haven for harried people as well.

The Land: How It Came To Be

An inquisitive person can hardly gaze across San Antonio Bay from Dagger Point or marvel at the mighty live oaks along the Big Tree Trail without falling into a reflective frame of mind. How and when did this tangled web of nature come to be? By what forces? What came before?

Good questions. They impel us to put our scattered observations into an orderly scheme. Good also because if we can fathom how this land came about, then we will be in a better position to insure its continued well-being.

GEOLOGY

Since early Cretaceous time, over 100 million years ago, this area has been beneath the sea much more than it has been above. The margin of the Cretaceous sea lay along the present-day Balcones Escarpment in the central part of the state, and it can be traced from San Antonio through Austin and northward past Waco and Dallas. At this early time the arc of the current coastline was an undistinguished part of the shallow sea floor.

Whenever deep tectonic forces elevated the land, the sea drew back. The low Bordas, Reynosa and Oakville escarpments which lie in a crescent about midway between the Balcones and the present coastline, mark significant pauses during the recession of the sea. Rivers pursued the retreating shoreline, spilling their loads of sediment across the recently exposed marine shelf and laying the foundation for the gently tilted modern Coastal Plain. But the Aransas area remained submerged.

Ice Ages

One million years ago the first of the four major glaciations of the Pleistocene Epoch began. Although no glacier pushed as far south as Texas, these great ice sheets had two important

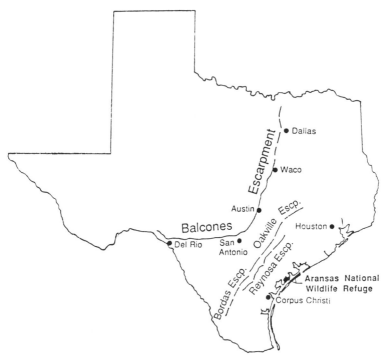

Figure 5 The Balcones Escarpment marks the shoreline of
the Cretaceous Sea in Texas. Smaller escarpments, some
bold, eastward facing cliffs, some only subtle variations in
the local topography, indicate retreating shorelines.

impacts on local landforms. First, when the glaciers built up
they caused a drop in sea level. An enormous quantity of
water was incorporated into ice shields that spanned the
northern third of the continent with a burden of ice and snow
nearly two miles thick at their centers. Second, the retreat of
the glaciers not only caused a compensating rise in sea level,
it initiated widespread flooding and erosion as the surge of
meltwater drained off the continent.

Throughout the early Pleistocene the locale of the Aransas
Refuge was alternately exposed and submerged according to
the vagaries of the ice sheets and the tectonic forces that
affected the elevation of the Coastal Plain. All the strata
formed at this time lie bent deep beneath the surface. They are
the platform upon which the modern stage is set.

In late Sangamon time (120,000 years ago, just before the
final push of the glaciers) the local shoreline lay
approximately where it does today. Events which transpired
at that time formed the modern surface substrate for the
Aransas Refuge and its environs.

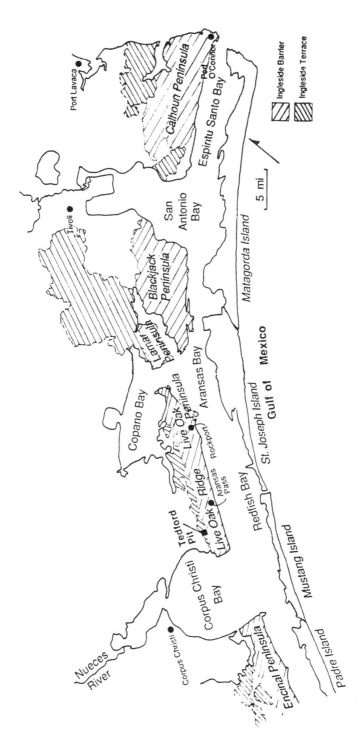

Figure 6 The Ingleside Barrier, remains of a late Pleistocene sand bar, and the Ingleside Terrace were deposited about 120,000 years ago. The Terrace was marshland that backed the bar. Note the Tedford Pit on Live Oak Ridge, from which many mammalian fossils have been recovered.

The Sangamon was a period of deposition of sediments eroded from the highland interior of Texas. Large primordial rivers already identifiable as the ancestors of the modern Nueces, Aransas/Mission, San Antonio/Guadalupe, Lavaca/Navidad and Colorado were heaping their burdens of sand, mud and silt across the flat land and into the local marine embayments. Each river system created a broad delta complete with meander loops, oxbows, leeves, lakes and fresh, brackish and saltwater marshes. Vast splays of muddy sand were shoved about, buried and disinterred, sorted and resorted as the streams cut new channels and reoccupied old ones.

These late Pleistocene fluvial deposits eventually compacted into the black waxy Beaumont Clay which the local grain farmers till into mile long furrows. The final approach to the Refuge passes through such darkland fields.

Ingleside Barrier

Sea level oscillated continually during the late Pleistocene. During one of its prolonged high phases in the Sangamon, the sea pushed the shoreline inland several miles from its modern position. Waves, longshore currents, tidal surges, storms and the omnipresent coastal winds began to rework the recently submerged deltaic sediments. The water smoothed out the finer silts and muds across the continental shelf, and it heaped the coarser sand into windrows along the shore. The wind piled the dried sand into a long ridge parallel to the shoreline.

The resultant Pleistocene sandbar averaged three miles across and ranged from 10-25 feet above sea level. Locally portions of this relict strandplain are exposed as the Encinal Peninsula (Flour Bluff), Live Oak Ridge (Aransas Pass), Live Oak Peninsula (Rockport), Lamar Peninsula (Goose Island), Blackjack Peninsula (the Aransas Refuge) and the Calhoun Peninsula (Port O'Connor). The same stratum has been traced from Alazan Bay south of Corpus Christi around the margin of the Gulf until it disappears in the bowels of the great delta of the Mississippi River.

Geologists named this unassuming ridge of sand the Ingleside Barrier. Some workers contend that the barrier was actually an island, fronting the sea and backed by a continuous inland lagoon. If so, then the Ingleside Barrier was quite comparable to modern barrier islands like Matagorda and St. Joseph.

Recent interpretation suggests that the Ingleside Barrier was a strandplain--a windrow of sand heaped up directly on the unprotected shoreline, cut across by the major river drainages, and backed with a broken series of marshes, lakes and brackish bays. Either way, the Ingleside environment must have been quite similar to that on our modern barrier islands.

Whether continuous or fragmented, the 8-10 mile wide swath of rich sediment that accumulated just inland of the Ingleside Barrier is called the Ingleside Terrace. It too crops out along the local coastline.

One hundred thousand years ago the last of the Pleistocene glaciers began to build and the sea necessarily embarked on its final significant retreat. By the time the Wisconsin ice shield had reached its peak the local shoreline had moved nearly 50 miles Gulfward of its present position. The Ingleside Barrier was left high and dry. The several rivers were obliged to gouge their valleys through the exposed continental shelf to gain access to the sea. In order to reach grade level some of these streams scoured basins and channels 80 feet below the level of the Ingleside strata and on out across the Pleistocene Coastal Plain. At this time the local area must have resembled the modern terrain as it appears near Beeville and Goliad, but with deeper drainage channels and a somewhat more broken topography.

Then, 18,000 years ago, the Pleistocene Epoch ended with the melting of the Wisconsin glaciers and the final advance of the sea. With the onset of this last geological epoch called the Holocene, natural forces began to erase much of their late Pleistocene work. The sea advanced into the river valleys and scour basins, turning them first brackish and then marine. Wave and current action caused the submerged valley walls to cave in and fill the old channels. All the while the rivers, swollen with their latest surge of meltwater, were building new deltas and unloading huge burdens of sediment into the advancing sea.

The resulting mix of marine and fluvial deposition, action of wave and current and general compaction and subsidence of the malleable coastal margin finally produced the modern landform. Ten thousand years ago the outlines of the local bays were becoming recognizable as the sea filled the old scour basins. At the same time the several fragments of the Ingleside Barrier achieved the status of peninsulas protruding into the inland margins of the bays. The modern river deltas and estuaries stabilized.

Three thousand years ago the coastline reached its current level and the coastal margin began to form into its modern aspect. Continued submarine erosion and deltaic filling reduced the depth of the bays to less than twenty feet. The flow of the several river systems was reduced to current level. Typical coastal vegetation secured the land.

As the Gulf waves moved shoreward across the shallow shelf they pushed a load of sand into submarine bars paralleling the shoreline. Eventually the major shoals coalesced and broke the surface. The wind piled the dried sand higher. Once begun, the accretionary process rapidly compounded. Smoothed by the wind and profiled by waves and longshore currents, the progenitors of the modern barrier islands came into being.

These islands took the brunt of the energy of the sea on their surfsides, leaving the leeside tidal flats, bays and estuaries in relative serenity. Narrow passes, originally cut by the major river mouths, allowed a mixing of the two aquatic systems and the development of a gradient of salinity and temperature from estuary to Gulf.

So we find Blackjack Peninsula, a surviving fragment of the old Ingleside Barrier, situated about ten miles from the open Gulf of Mexico. It is lapped by the shallow waters of St. Charles, Aransas and San Antonio bays, themselves flooded river basins. These bays lie behind the protective influence of Matagorda and St. Joseph islands.

Although this brief survey brings the geological story of the Aransas to date, it certainly does not mean that the tale is finished. Any seacoast exists in dynamic equilibrium, with phases of accretion and degradation separated by intervals of relative stability. Locally the Texas mainland shore is relatively fixed, although the barrier islands and passes exhibit changes on a perceptible scale. Storm breach, wind erosion and the damming of rivers and erection of marine breakwaters are the significant factors affecting local cycles of erosion and accumulation of sand. Generally speaking, we live in a fairly quiet interglacial period. The level of the sea has not changed significantly for 3,000 years.

You might be interested in seeing firsthand some evidence of the development of Blackjack Peninsula. Although not dramatic, clues lie everywhere. Perhaps the most telling of these is a handful of soil. Regardless of where you scoop it up it is likely to be sandy. Often it is nearly pure sand. Those much abraded grains of silicon dioxide will have had a long and tortuous history, pummeled by water, driven by wind, dragged by gravity, buried and exposed thousands of times until you hold them in your palm. Dribble them back and they will continue on their endless journey.

Walk the Dagger Point Trail. Follow the Yellow Route toward the bayside. On the way you will gain one of the highest points on the Refuge, a less-than-dizzying elevation of 45 feet. You will be standing atop a huge wind-deposited sandpile.

As the late Pleistocene sea drew back the coastal breeze heaped up successive parallel bands of Ingleside sand. Over two dozen of these northwest-southeast trending folds have been charted across the peninsula. (As you drive the Tour Loop you will occasionally be aware of the peninsula's subtly corrugated ridge-and-swale topography.) These ridges get progressively younger eastward. The Dagger Point Trail meanders across the most recent exposure of the Ingleside Barrier, rendered the more impressive by its wave cut eastern face.

Continue on the Yellow Route down to the point. Here, where Blackjack Peninsula absorbs the brunt of norther and storm-driven waves off San Antonio Bay, erosion of the shoreline has been rapid. To see geology in action, watch one wave leave its ripple mark amid the wrack and sediment on the shore. Then let your imagination ramble backward across the centuries of accretion and erosion.

For some time Dagger Point has been in an erosive phase. Since 1860, this promontory has lost an average of 5-10 feet to the sea each year. Most of this depletion occurs catastrophically during storms, but the wear-and-tear never ceases. Look southward along the shoreline and you can observe live oak and red bay trees in all stages of demolition along the calving cliffside. The rubble of trunks and branches at the water's edge helps suppress the erosive action of the waves.

In 1961, Hurricane Carla pounded and scoured Dagger Point into its present conformation and destroyed a residence that stood just inland of the group of live oak trees that crouches on the current shoreline. (The rockwork just offshore is the remains of a low seawall which protected a pier and boat dock associated with the residence.) In 1967, heavy machinery was employed to shove the concrete rubble from the house to the bayside of the oaks. Then soil was packed over the rubble and the mat of exposed oak roots. Rye grass was sown to hold the patch in place. So far both the fill and the oaks have survived several more hurricanes and Dagger Point has endured as one of the most picturesque sites on the Refuge.

Examine the shoreline between the picnic area and the Bayfront Overlook. Here a concrete bulwark had to be poured to protect the margin from the persistent erosive action of waves coming in off the open bay. Again, geology in action.

A rare outcrop of natural sandstone is exposed along the bayshore just south of the Environmental Training Area. The waves are already busy grinding this stratum back into sand.

Try sampling the soil along the first half of the Heron Flats Trail. It will be more difficult to scrape up, and it will contain more organic matter as well as abundant oyster shell. The shell originated from offshore Holocene reefs and was thrown into several low ridges by storm tides. The firm limey base allowed a unique assemblage of woody and herbaceous growth to become established. Decay of the plants enriched the substrate to provide one of the Refuge's few significant soil profiles.

You can get a feel for what the early Ingleside Barrier must have been like by visiting one of the modern barrier islands. Mustang Island State Park and Padre Island National Seashore afford easy access. Or you might arrange a boat trip to Matagorda Island. And as you leave the Aransas Refuge, watch for the local change from blackland to sandyland as your route takes you across exposures of the Ingleside Barrier, the Ingleside Terrace and lobes of the Pleistocene river deltas.

ANCIENT LIFE

What weird and wonderful creatures roamed Blackjack Peninsula in bygone ages? Such a question is always steeped in intrigue, but before embarking upon visions of Coal Age scale trees and of lumbering dinosaurs, recall one salient fact. The Ingleside Barrier is only 120,000 years old. By the time this low mound of sand was ready for occupancy much of the early drama of the evolution of life had already transpired, and many spectacular species had already become extinct.

What might you have seen if you had visited the local Coastal Plain in the late Pleistocene some 75,000 years ago? The sparsely vegetated Ingleside sand ridge would front the sea. Behind the sand there would be a maze of fresh and brackish marshes and lakes--the Ingleside Terrace. River deltas would interrupt these coastal features. The Coastal Plain which stretched inland would look much as it does in less trammeled spots today: a bountiful prairie of knee-high grasses dotted with clumps of oaks and glades of sedges and supporting a dendritic pattern of rich forestland along the drainage courses.

To any but the professional eye, all of the plant life would appear quite modern, although everyone would notice that the greenery was more lush than it is today. Partly this is because it was pristine, but probably the climate was warmer and more moist at this time. The forests, for instance, would remind us of those we now see in East Texas.

What of the animal life? Most of it would already be disappointingly modern. The insects, the shoreline crustaceans, even many of the backboned creatures were essentially as we find them today. You could have found a thoroughly updated specimen of bullfrog, watersnake, alligator, seagull, sparrow, vulture, white-footed mouse, coyote, bobcat, cottontail, raccoon, opossum, striped skunk and white-tailed deer in this Pleistocene landscape. Here and there, however, you would encounter a creature which definitely belonged in the weird-and-wonderful category. Most of the ones that caught your eye would be mammals.

Our best insight into the late Pleistocene mammalian fauna of the local area derives from the fossil site called the Tedford Pit situated 25 miles down the coast near the town of Ingleside. Here paleontologists from the University of Texas unearthed the remains of 42 species of vertebrates, including a remarkable diversity of now extinct mammals.

What did they find? A rich array of large plant eaters: 17 mammalian species compared to the current four. Among them were everyone's favorites, the Columbian mammoth and the American mastodon. The mammoths were huge elephants standing 14 feet at the shoulder, while the mastodons were shorter, extremely stocky cousins with flat-browed heads carried high on nearly neckless forequarters. The many-tiered grinding teeth of the grazing mammoths were very different from the high-cusped molars of the mastodons which browsed on woody vegetation.

A third species of elephant occurred at Ingleside, this one with a curious spiral twist in its long tusks.

Judging from the abundance of their remains, herds of wild horses of several species were common on the Pleistocene prairie. These resembled wild asses in body size and probably in general behaviour as well.

Small groups of camels browsed on the edge of the prairie. Although larger, they resembled modern dromedaries. The camels had a more prolific cousin that ranged out across the grassland in fleet-footed flocks. These alert cameloids resembled llamas with exceptionally long necks.

No North American Pleistocene prairie would be complete without its nomadic herds of bison. The Ingleside boasted the ponderous, shaggy-coated *Bison antiquus*, which carried more beef than two modern bison and a hornspread of three feet. Doubtless they influenced the ecology of the land just as the American bison did during its heyday.

Some herbivores were restricted to the forest. One of the most spectacular of these was the giant ground sloth. Two species of these ox-sized, bear-like creatures were recovered from the Tedford Pit. The powerful forelegs and strong claws of these docile ground sloths were used to rake a tangle of vegetation into their maws, but these same appendages could mount a telling defense against predators.

One of two species of armadillos that occupied the early forests closely resembled our current one and it probably led the same sort of snuffling existence. The second species was something else. The glyptodont was an animated tank with a massive domed shell nearly five feet high and nine feet long. The rigid roof of the shell was composed of hundreds of interlocking bony scutes and it accounted for most of the animal's weight, which exceeded a ton. The passive glyptodont apparently spent its time chomping through streamside vegetation where it was more in danger of bogging down than of being attacked by any would-be predator.

The forest during Ingleside time also supported foraging groups of flat-headed peccaries, an occasional tapir and a herbivorous bear that resembled the modern black bear.

Where there are herbivores of such variety, there will be carnivores geared to take them. Certainly the most devasting meat-eater of the region was the dire wolf. With a wolf build, wolf wile, wolf endurance and better than wolf size plus a fearful hyena-like turn of mind, this animal was made to order to terrorize the hooved fauna of the land. It was the dire wolf that perfected the art of hunting in packs, of cutting one prey animal aside and hamstringing it and of eating it from one end before it had fully expired on the other.

Prides of lions stalked the big game of this late Pleistocene Coastal Plain. They resembled the modern African lion so closely that only a paleontologist can detect skeletal differences between the two.

The tapirs and the peccaries were surely aware of another predator which laid silent ambush beside their forest trails. Even young mastodons were regularly pulled down by the sabertooth cat. This was an especially powerful, stump-tailed animal with enlarged canines, bulging neck muscles and heavy forequarters geared to its particular mode of assassination. The sabertooth was the master of the patient stalk, the swift leap and the dagger thrust into the neck accompanied by a bulldog grip and raking, disemboweling hind claws.

What happened to them all? Even the paleontologists are not sure. Widespread extinction swept through all of the large North American mammals in the late Pleistocene. Some investigators suggest a nebulous shift in climate and vegetation as the cause, but there is little evidence to support their contention. Lately a less pleasing but very credible disruptive force has been proposed: the coincidental appearance of early man with his cunning and his hunting technology. It is a sobering suggestion.

What evidence can you find of ancient life on the Aransas? Probably none. Despite the yield at the Tedford Pit, the coastal sands are not particularly fossiliferous. Mostly this is because the surface strata are too young and ill-suited to mineralizing organic remains. You might be alert for a fossil horse tooth deposited on the shoreline of the bay, but your chances of success are so slight that it is better to observe the display of fossils in the Visitors Center. Of course, most of the fragmented oyster shell along the Heron Flats Trail dates to the late Pleistocene or Holocene, but it is hardly inspiring to observe.

The Land: Where It Fits

The Aransas National Wildlife Refuge occurs at 96° 48' west longitude and 28° 16' north latitude and occupies portions of Aransas, Refugio and Calhoun counties in the state of Texas.

The position of the Refuge has much to do with its ecology. It lies at the southern end of the Great Plains which sweep down across the continent from Canada. It straddles the critical transition zone along the east-west moisture gradient across the state, and it is near the middle of the north-south shift from tropical to temperate temperature regimes.

Because of its proximity to the Gulf of Mexico the Aransas harbors a fluctuating combination of communities across a salinity gradient, from fresh through brackish to marine and even hypersaline. The fact that the refuge lies directly in the geographical arc--the Coastal Bend--of the Gulf shoreline has implication for the water circulation in the surrounding bays, the degree of wind-generated sand erosion and the subtle thinning of the coastal vegetation.

And of course, its position relative to the Gulf of Mexico makes the Aransas one of the most critical sites along the great Central Flyway, the ages-old route for millions of migratory birds.

This coincidence of geography and ecology has prompted biogeographers to regard the Aransas and its environs as a veritable biological crossroads where a wonderful diversity of plants and animals meet, mingle, migrate and reside.

GEOGRAPHY

The Aransas Refuge lies on the outer perimeter of the Gulf Coastal Plain, that vast outwash of imperceptibly tilted land which stretches south and east of the Balcones Escarpment and which encompasses over a third of Texas. Much of this

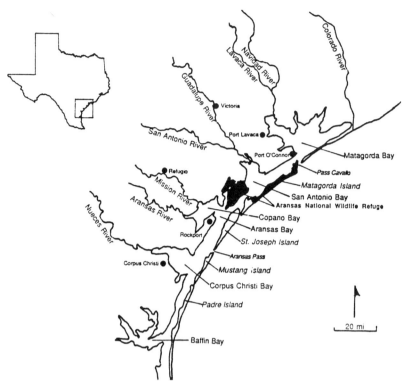

Figure 7 Geography of the Texas Coastal Bend.

area is open country, and it originally supported unbroken prairie or a thin hardwood savannah.

The subdivision designated the Coastal Prairie, which includes the Aransas Refuge, is a strip of land parallel to the coastline and spreading inland for about 40 miles.   It stretches from the Louisiana border to Baffin Bay below Corpus Christi. Although it is interrupted by riparian forests and indented by marshland, this flat coastal sector is basically grassland. The mile or so of immediate shoreline and the offshore barrier islands are under the direct influence of the Gulf of Mexico.

PHYSIOGRAPHY

The Coastal Prairie changes from north to south. The most noticeable shift occurs in the Coastal Bend at the mouth of the Guadalupe River just north of the Aransas Wildlife Refuge. Here the curve of the coastline alters the angle at which the prevailing southeasterly winds strike the landmass. This affects the pattern of rainfall. North of the Guadalupe the

Coastal Prairie is wetter so it supports a sward of tall grasses and luxuriant salt marshes. South of the river the Coastal Prairie is drier, and there it can muster only short grasses and the salt marshes give way to low tidal flats. With its more sparse vegetation the southern sector is also subject to more severe wind erosion. The Refuge lies directly in this transition zone.

The major bodies of water surrounding the Aransas are San Antonio Bay, Aransas Bay and St. Charles Bay. All contribute to the well-being of the tidal flats which fringe the peninsula, and St. Charles Bay has tidal access into Burgentine Lake and both Big and Little Devil bayous on the west side of the Refuge.

These bays are shallow and of variable turbidity. Salinity averages about 25 parts per thousand (water in the open Gulf has a salinity of about 33 ppt.), but it can fluctuate from virtually fresh to hypersaline. At the height of the drought in 1956, the lower part of San Antonio Bay registered a devastating 50 ppt. When the drought broke in 1957, the salinity of the bays plunged to less than 1 ppt--fresh enough for human consumption but lethal for most marine organisms.

Water temperature in the bays is equally changeable and occasionally extreme. Sometimes the shallows are hot enough to drive out nearly all dissolved oxygen. Occasionally they freeze. All of the peninsular food chains are closely linked to these surrounding bodies of water.

The presence of Matagorda and St. Joseph islands about five miles at sea renders the bays a somewhat independent marine system. As far as the Aransas Refuge is concerned, the principal freshwater input into the bays is from the Guadalupe River. Saltwater flushes in through Pass Cavallo 30 miles up the coast at the northern end of Matagorda Island and at Aransas Pass 25 miles down the coast at the southern end of St. Joseph. Cedar Bayou is a narrow cut between the two islands directly opposite the Refuge. Although it can be an important exchange point, it is commonly filled with sand. This natural pass has been artifically cleared several times and is currently scheduled to be opened again in 1987.

Primarily because of the influence of the Guadalupe River, there is a tendency for water in the local bays to flow southward past the Aransas Refuge and there is always a marked salinity drop in the direction of the river.

Although tides along the Texas coast routinely range only 1-2 feet, they are important in maintaining the tidal flats and in promoting a flushing of the bays through the passes. At certain times of the year the fickle Texas tides may hold high or low for a week or more. Strong winds are often more significant than ordinary tidal action in moving the water in the shallow bays.

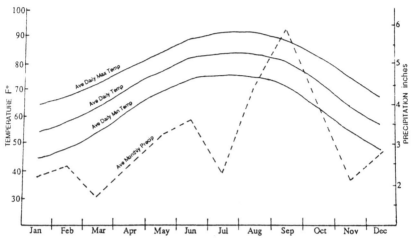

Figure 8 Average monthly temperature and precipitation on the Aransas National Wildlife Refuge. (Data from Climatological Summary, National Weather Service and Bureau of Business Research, Univ. of Texas.)

CLIMATE

The term "weather" refers to short-term meteorological conditions. "Climate" refers to long-term trends in weather patterns. Texas weather is notoriously capricious, but the climate of the state can be reliably described. Figure #8 summarizes pertinent climatic data collected on the Aransas over the past four decades.

Although it is easy enough to describe the main components of the climate of the Coastal Bend, these only take on ecological significance when considered in concert. We have tried to indicate some of this interaction as each component is briefly described.

Precipitation

Rainfall is of outstanding importance to the biota of any region. It can make the difference between a desert and a swamp, between a good year and a disastrous one. Adequate rainfall affects animals in a multitude of direct and indirect ways: drinking water, reproductive sites, hunting grounds, soil texture, ease of navigation, incidence of parasites, abundance of prey. Too much rain or untimely rain can drown plants and animals or cancel their reproductive efforts.

More fundamentally, both the total amount and the annual distribution of rainfall dictate the type and quantity of vegetation and this in turn determines what animals can find shelter and food in the region.

A routinely dry spring on the Aransas Refuge usually promotes the nesting success of turkey, quail and prairie chickens. However, a dry spring followed by a dry summer rapidly draws down the waterholes. Hatchling mottled ducks and black-bellied whistling ducks are exposed to excessive predation and everything from javelinas to alligators is forced into a constant search for freshwater. The stress of dehydration is especially hard on newborn animals and seedling plants.

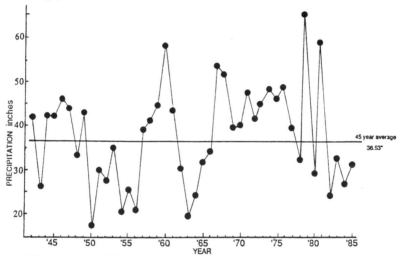

Figure 9 Rainfall on the Refuge in the years from 1942 to 1985. (Data from Refuge Files.)

Of course, timely rainfall benefits vegetation and animals alike, and good fall rains are vital for the well-being of winter waterfowl, but excessive, prolonged or unseasonal precipitation can wreak havoc: drowned upland bird nests, flooded rodent runways, poor fawn survival, hoof disease among the deer and swine, reduced acorn crop, poor yield of grass seeds, lowered salinity in the tidal flats, hordes of voracious mosquitoes.

Figure #9 indicates the sort of wet and dry cycles that have occurred on the Aransas Refuge. Because of abundant moisture from the Gulf of Mexico and because of its very porous sandy substrate, the area is prone to oscillate between drought and flood conditions, often over an interval of only a few months. The average annual rainfall is 36.81". In the wettest year on record (1979) 64.20" of rain accumulated; in the driest (1950), only 17.36" were received.

Although Hurricane Beulah (1967) inundated the Refuge with a record 20.44" rainfall, the heaviest single cloudburst came from an unnamed tropical depression in October, 1974, which dropped 14.25" in six hours. Notable droughts occurred in 1950-56 and 1962-65. A string of wet years spanned 1968-75. The combination of hurricanes Beulah and Candy left much of the Refuge under standing water during 1967-70.

You can see the annual pattern of rainfall on the Refuge in Figure #8. A moderate amount of rain falls each month with an increase in the spring and a peak in late summer-early fall. But what you cannot see is that even when the Aransas receives its average annual dole of rain, it actually suffers from a chronic deficiency of freshwater.

Despite the uncomfortably high humidity (an annual average of 89% at dawn only decreasing to 60% by noon), the omnipresent wind causes rapid evaporation. The prevailing high air temperature increases the water-drawing capacity of the atmosphere. Finally, the nonabsorbant sand allows rapid percolation of rainwater below the root zone. Because of the sand, even relatively large bodies of water like Jones Lake and Hog Lake are rapidly drawn down when the rains fail. Despite numerous input channels and a restraining dike, Burgentine Lake, the largest inland body of water on the Refuge, sometimes goes bone dry.

Average annual rainfall decreases southward down the Texas coast. This decrease takes a dramatic jump in the Coastal Bend. On the Aransas Refuge an open pan of water would lose 12" more fluid to evaporation in a year than it would gain from rainfall. No wonder, then, that most of the plants and animals have water conserving adaptations some of which rival those of desert dwellers.

Temperature

Temperature has as pervasive an impact on a region as rainfall, and the effects of the two work together. We know that cold/wet does not feel the same as cold/dry, nor is hot/dry so uncomfortable as hot/wet. Plants and animals have comparable responses.

Figure #8 reflects the fact that the annual temperature on the Aransas is dominated by the moderating influence of the Gulf of Mexico. The summertime peak is smoothed by the afternoon and evening coastal breeze while the wintertime trough is constrained by the heat contained in the vast body of saltwater.

The average annual temperature on the Refuge is 70.8° F. The coldest month (January) averages 64.5° F; the warmest months (July and August) average 84.0° F. During a normal year the temperature climbs to 90° F or above on 77 days and drops to 32° F or below on 10 days. But averages can be deceiving. In 1983, for instance, the summer was a scorcher with the temperature reaching or exceeding 90° F for weeks in succession. Then in December the mercury hovered at or below freezing for 10 consecutive days and dipped to a low of 13° F, freezing the bays.

Because of its subtropical position and the sweep of open country to the north, the Texas Coastal Plain is liable to wildly fluctuating wintertime temperatures. One can easily go from sweating to shivering in a few hours. The shifts play havoc with both temperments and immune systems.

Whereas the average monthly temperatures dictate the well-being of the plants and animals that live on the Aransas, it is the extremes, especially the duration of the extremes, which determine what kinds of creatures can permanently reside in the area. A meaningful way to express the low temperature extreme for plants and for cold-sensitive animals is the average number of frost-free days in a year. This so-called growing season for the Aransas Refuge is a generous 312 days. The average date of the first fall frost is December 16; of the last spring frost, February 7. Freezing temperatures usually occur for only an hour or two before sunrise about ten times a year.

Despite short, mild winters, temperature drops are often rapid and wind chill on the bays can be brutal. Occasionally the bays develop a light crust of ice. On the other hand, the dogdays of July can shrivel fruit on the vine and drive oxygen from the water. They take their toll of creatures which lack the appropriate escape behaviour. The all-time recorded temperature extremes on the Refuge are 11° F (Jan, 1962) and 103° F (June, 1953; Aug, 1955).

Extremes of heat or cold wreak a culling effect which eradicates pioneer colonies of organisms that have entered the region during benign intervals. Ultimately such selective elimination produces what we recognize as the natural biota.

Wind

To the casual visitor the chief importance of the wind is probably how efficiently it holds down the mosquitoes. As a matter of fact, many of the larger animals on the Refuge enjoy the same benefit. (For instance, deer sometimes succumb to what can only be called "mosquito stress"--a chronic malaise brought on by the continual harrassment and debilitation caused by clouds of these ravenous insects.) But there is more than that to wind as a coastal climatic factor.

Wind (routine air currents; we consider storms below) has two kinds of influences on a region. One is its direct mechanical impact. The persistent force of the wind can sculpt a live oak tree, provide lift to a turkey vulture, tumble a grain of sand, misdirect a moth into a spiderweb, waft a pollen grain and puff a milkweed seed out of sight. Likewise the wind can move water, piling it into waves and streaming it into currents; and the waves and currents will have telling effects of their own.

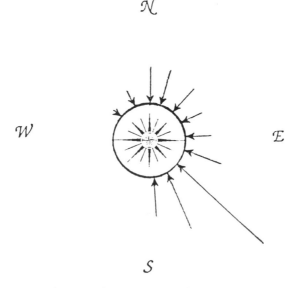

Figure 10 Surface winds at Corpus Christi, Texas. Direction is shown by arrowhead and average annual frequency by length of line.

Wind also has an indirect impact through its influence on temperature and moisture: evaporative cooling, wind chill, and the passage of weather fronts.

The Aransas Refuge experiences two annual wind regimes: persistent, moderate southeasterlies from March through November and brief, gusty northerlies from December through February. The direction and strength of these winds is shown by the wind rose in Figure #10, which is actually based on records for Corpus Christi, 50 miles down the coast.

The prevailing southeasterly breezes keep man and beast from gagging during the sultry coastal summer.

Because of their abrupt arrival and their high energy and associated low temperature, the "northers" have special impact on the coast. Most animals simply hunker down during the worst of the blow. Tardy fall migratory birds use the early northers as welcome tailwinds, while spring migrants encounter late northers as strong energy-sapping headwinds. The cool air often sets off valuable winter rainfall.

A strong norther commonly drives the water in the bays against the southern and western shores where it causes significant bankside erosion. At the same time the water level may drop by as much as two feet on the north shore. This recession of the water can be rapid enough to expose and kill tidal flat fauna. The bays churn brown during northers, and much of this sediment is flushed out the passes on high ebb currents. Most northers blow through in 48 to 72 hours.

Storms

Violent tropical depressions and full-blown hurricanes regularly wheel out of the Gulf of Mexico and slam into the Texas Coast. Historically the sector of the Coastal Bend which includes the Aransas Refuge has experienced a hurricane landfall once every five years. These great cyclones can be expected any time from late June through early November, with peak frequency in August and September.

Over the past two decades the Aransas has weathered its share of hurricanes. Carla (1961) sent a 10-foot tidal surge over the barrier islands and across San Antonio Bay, pounding the mainland shoreline and inundating all low-lying areas with saltwater. Beulah (1967) brought 6-foot tides and torrential rains. The prolonged runoff from this hurricane freshened the bays and swamped the Refuge for months. Before the accumulation from Beulah drained away Hurricane Candy (1968) dropped a 20-inch downpour on the soggy Refuge. Celia (1970) left 12 inches of rain and blew the weather record book away. Paradoxically, ominous Hurricane Allen (1980) was accompanied by moderate winds and tides and a much needed 5-inch rainfall.

A hurricane can wreak more havoc in a few hours than quieter natural forces could effect in years. Direct battering by cyclonic winds, torrential rainfall and tidal surge are the principal elements of devastation. Much wildlife is killed outright and much more is displaced. Plants may be torn asunder or killed by flooding or saltwater incursion. The bays may be fresh for weeks on end from heavy runoff, and the marine fauna suffers and is dislocated. Massive amounts of sand are heaved about. Some areas undergo severe erosion while others experience accretion. Tidal passes are routinely occluded or reopened during storm passage.

Despite the evident misery and destruction that attend the passage of a hurricane, it is a fact that Nature suffers less lasting damage than do man and his accouterments. Hurricanes are, afterall, natural phenomena to which the coastal biota is adapted. Resident populations soon resurge, often with renewed vigor. Aside from standing water and a scattering of debris, several weeks after a hurricane the most evident damage on the Refuge is to the roadways and buildings.

And it is indeed an ill wind that blows no good. The rapidly shifting, violent cyclonic air currents act like huge egg beaters as they whirl across the shallow bays, whipping up sediments and pollutants and eventually heaving them into the Gulf. When conditions settle down the recently flushed bays take on a fresh surge of marine life which eventually works into the inland food chains. Many a hurricane has been a boon to the parched Texas coast when it brought life-giving rather than life-threatening rains.

Even the manifest death which a severe hurricane levys on vegetation and wildlife has its ecological compensation, because the storm action culls out weedy and interloping species and thus preserves the natural coastal mix of biota.

And finally, the awesome tempests add their own inimitable brand of wildness to an already wild landscape of which they are a natural part.

BIOTA

The natural assemblage of plants and animals which resides on the Aransas Refuge today is the current biotic response to the blend of components that makes up the physical environment.

If we accept the principles of organic evolution, then we admit that each kind of creature gradually diverged from its ancestors over a given span of time and in a given geographic locality. Since the Refuge is too young geologically and too small geographically to have served as the spawning ground for any of its resident species, it follows that all must have come here by their own random wanderings and according to their individual fortunes.

Once here, the pioneers of each species had to tolerate the averages and withstand the extremes of the coastal environment. And most important, they had to establish a thriving population of reproducing individuals that gradually adapted to and finally gained a firm foothold on Blackjack Peninsula and its environs.

In addition to becoming attuned to climate and terrain, each newly arrived species faced the difficult task of working its way among those species which were already established. Intense competition, predation or simply failure to adapt thwarted many wouldbe colonists. Those that managed are what you see on the Refuge today.

Since men have been on the land, beginning with the earliest prehistoric hunters, the biota has also had to contend with the human element and more recently with the host of domestic and feral plants and animals which have been introduced here by men.

Humans have had another significant impact upon the distribution of the local biota. By clearing enormous stretches of surrounding land for agriculture and sundry development, ancient routes of dispersal have been closed. The Refuge is a biological island isolated in a sterile sea of human activity. Nowadays when a resident population is reduced or extirpated, there is scant chance for natural restocking.

Origins

Where did the current biota on the Aransas Refuge come from? The best answer is simply from hither and yon, implying that lines of dispersal probably trace backward to all parts of the Western world. But we can be a bit more specific about a few of the larger creatures and some of the plants. For these, their immediate ancestors did not come from very far away and in many cases we know the direction of their homeland.

Many resident creatures on the Aransas have affinities with the moist southeastern Atlantic seaboard. Both the green treefrog and the squirrel treefrog find their limits of dehydration on the Refuge. So does the curious little eastern narrow-mouth toad. Among the lizards the ground skink hails from the humus-laden forests of the east and the slender glass lizard from the sandyland of the deep Southeast. Snakes with eastern ranges that do not progress westward much beyond the Aransas include the mud snake, eastern hognosed snake, prairie kingsnake and western cottonmouth. And of course, there is the alligator, a creature of the antediluvial swamplands if there ever was one.

Despite their high mobility, some eastern birds show up just often enough to put the Refuge on their western range limits: bluejays, eastern bluebirds, Carolina chickadees, tufted titmice, red-headed woodpeckers, red-shouldered hawks, common crows. Eastern mammals include the fox squirrel, least shrew, eastern mole, swamp rabbit and rice rat.

The wave of eastern immigrants is not limited to animals. Red bay, tree huckleberry, palmetto, poison ivy, Spanish moss, live oak and even the peninsula's namesake--blackjack oak--all hark from the east.

The biogeographic pursuit takes on added interest when one can find an eastern species and a complementary western species each reaching the limits of its range in the same area. Where one leaves off the other takes over. The Aransas Refuge is a meeting ground of many such pairs: Couch's and Hurter's spadefoot toads; checkered and Texas garter snakes; red-bellied and golden-fronted woodpeckers; pyrrhuloxia and cardinal; wild lime and prickly ash; cane bluestem and broomsedge bluestem.

The story is the same for the other cardinal directions: western diamondback rattlesnakes, western kingbirds and tanglewood from the west; prairie chickens, short-eared owls and grama grasses down from the plains to the north; pigmy mice, goldenweb spiders, groove-billed anis, cayenne ticks and spiny hackberries up from the south; diamondback terrapins, fiddler crabs and marsh hay cordgrass in from the Gulf. These plus the hundreds of thousands of migrating waterfowl, perching birds and monarch butterflies as well as seasonal movements of marine fishes and crustaceans.

To this wild bustle we must add the introduced species: feral hogs, starlings and house sparrows, domestic cattle, Bermuda and St. Augustine grass, Chinese tallow and eucalyptus trees. And people.

If your interest is piqued by the distributions of wild creatures, you might ponder some biogeographic puzzles associated with the Aransas Refuge. Why are there no kangaroo rats on the peninsula's extensive sandyland when these rodents abound on many of the adjacent barrier islands and the southern mainland? Why have badgers virtually disappeard despite the abundance of pocket gophers, their potential prey? Why no earless lizards or indigo snakes? Why did the bald eagles abandon their customary nest sites on the Refuge? Why have the jackrabbits virtually disappeared and the ground squirrels become locally extinct? Why are horned lizards common on the barrier islands but not on the mainland? Is the Refuge suffering an unsuspected ecological malaise, or are such turnovers a normal sequence of events? We can only speculate.

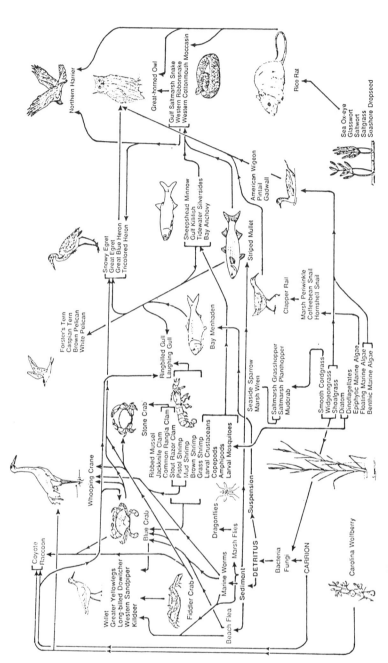

Figure 11 A small portion of the tangled winter food web at Mustang Lake. Arrowheads indicate the direction of consumption.

The Land: How it Works

Regardless of their specific interests, most visitors to the Aransas National Wildlife Refuge spend some time on the Observation Tower. The 40-foot high deck of the Tower is not only a good spot from which to view wildlife, especially birds; it also offers the best vantage for taking in the sweep of the marvelous ecosystem to which the Refuge is dedicated.

Climb the ramp, attain the deck and behold the grand coming-together of sky, wind, water and land. You can scan the length and breadth of Mustang Lake and work your binoculars along its fringing marshes and tidal flat. Elevate your view across the spoil islands to the southeast. Maybe you can make out one of the green channel markers which designate the busy Gulf Intracoastal Waterway. Turn due east and gaze across San Antonio Bay. With the help of an afternoon sun you should be able to discern the bright strip of sand on the lee side of Matagorda Island five miles distant.

If you turn to the west you will be looking across the interior of Blackjack Peninsula. Most of the dense tree canopy is composed of the crowns of live oaks. Here and there you might note a grassy opening or a clump of reeds. Can you detect the subtle ridge-and-swale undulation in the tiers of oaks? Certainly you cannot miss the beautiful wind sculpture so evident in the trees along the west bank of Mustang Lake and in those near the end of the Boardwalk on the edge of the bay. As you gaze out across the unmarred greenery, savor the splendid feeling of pristine isolation it affords.

Finally, turn to the north and look back up the paved access road. Just to the west of the road and only two hundred yards distant you should see a break in the trees and the tops of reeds, rattlepods and other bankside vegetation which border Hog and Jones lakes. Sometimes you can even catch a glimpse of the lakes themselves.

Check the sky, especially early and late in the day, to enjoy the shifting pastels and ever-changing shapes of the stupendous Gulf clouds.

Now reflect on your panoramic view. You have looked down on the three major ecological divisions of the Aransas Refuge: the marine (saltwater), the terrestrial and the freshwater. Doubtless you have observed some birds or other creatures as well as several different kinds of plants. How do they all fit together? meet their separate needs? know what to do? survive, day in and day out and through good seasons and bad? What vital interactions go on in the living fabric all around you that prevent it from unraveling? What makes this wonderful land *work*?

When you ponder rather difficult questions like these you are going beyond the realm of simple wildlife observation and embarking upon a quest for ecological understanding. The pursuit will give you a fresh appreciation for Nature as well as for the necessity of the several management tactics that are practiced to insure the perpetuation of the natural cycles on the Refuge.

The essence of ecology is in the interrelations between living things. Before deriving a few principles of ecology, let's take a closer look at how creatures interact.

About half way along the Big Tree Trail you will come to a stand of large, particularly impressive live oak trees with widespread branches. These trees are probably the oldest living organisms on the Aransas Refuge. The acorns which produced this magnificent grove of oaks sprouted just about the time that Cabeza de Vaca began his odyssey along the Texas coast over 400 years ago. Since then these iron trees have taken everything that Nature has thrown against them.

How do these fine old live oaks interweave into the lives of other creatures in this woods?

Look up. You cannot miss the hollows. Hollows are homes. Homes for raccoons, opossums and fox squirrels; for daddy longlegs, cobweb spiders and centipedes; even for an occasional hive of honeybees or a small colony of roosting pipistrelles (bats).

The deep cracks in the bark serve as homes, temporary shelters and feeding sites for a welter of tiny creatures: beetles, ants, barklice, springtails, millipedes, spiders, pseudoscorpions, mites. Some of the cracks retain enough moisture and debris to nourish clumps of ball moss and festoons of Spanish moss. Depending on their exposure to wind and sunshine, the intervening bark ridges may support a covering of gray lichen (How many different growth forms can you recognize?) or a green cushion of true moss.

Look among the leafy branches. Can you spot a spider's web? a paper wasp nest? a ragged wad of dead leaves where the fox squirrel takes his summer nap? a caterpillar-chewed leaf? You may have to use your mind's-eye to visualize the aphids, tree crickets, thrips, praying mantids, jumping spiders and whatnot that populate the higher foliage.

Sit awhile. Depending on the season, you may see an orange-crowned warbler, a blue-gray gnatcatcher or a Carolina wren flit through the branches beady-eyeing after tiny insect fare. If your visit coincides with the April spring migration, you may be treated to a warbler fallout, when these live oak branches are working alive with colorful, hungry passerines of a dozen fidgety species.

Be very still. Perhaps a sharp-shinned hawk or an American kestrel will alight briefly while it scans the surroundings for prey. The hawk can knock an unwary mourning dove from midair; the kestrel will be satisfied with a large grasshopper plucked from the grass. By night a great-horned owl will replace these daytime raptors, alert for a white-footed mouse or a cotton rat.

Look closely among the tips of the branches for two sorts of solid objects. One kind will be round and marble-sized. These are oak galls, swellings produced by the tree in response to the egg laying habits of tiny wasps. The fresh galls will contain wasp larvae; old ones serve as readymade domiciles for tiny spiders or colonies of highly specialized carpenter ants.

You can readily recognize the second kind of object among the branches as acorns. If there are none on the tree, you should be able to find remains of them on the ground.

It is through the medium of its nutritious acorn that the live oak tree works into the lives of a great array of creatures: feral hogs, javelinas and white-tailed deer; fox squirrels, raccoons and opossums; coyotes and gray foxes; mice and pocket gophers; whooping cranes, sandhill cranes, wild turkeys, and bobwhite quail; wood ducks and pintail ducks and Canada and snow geese; even small birds like Carolina chickadees and tufted titmice when they find acorns cracked open. It is little wonder that the live oak acorn is regarded as one of the principal wildlife food resources of the Refuge.

We are not done with acorns yet. Pick up a handful of old ones from the ground. Some of them are sure to have a neat round hole drilled in them. This is the exit portal of the acorn weevil which lived inside the acorn as a larva. If the hole is clogged with webbing, this means that the tiny caterpillar of the acorn moth has appropriated the acorn to feed on what the weevil missed and to snuggle there until winter is over.

Old, thin-shelled acorns have been partially consumed by fungi. Mites and springtails eat the fungi. In turn, pseudoscorpions stalk these tiny creatures. Finally, bacteria and fungi which produce cellulose-digesting enzymes cause the complete deterioration of the acorn and its contained fecal pellets. The released minerals may return to the live oak through its roots, and so begin another round of transformations.

While you have your thoughts on the ground beneath the live oak, visualize the enormous root system with its miles of tiny root hairs sucking up gallons of soil water and absorbing soil minerals. Look at the layers of decaying leaves, all leaking growth-inhibiting tannins which prevent many competing plants from growing directly beneath the oak. Note the patch of shade and its influence on the undergrowth. Move aside a fallen branch. Perhaps you will startle a ground skink or a least shrew from its daytime hiding place. Or maybe you will expose a field cricket, a roach or one end of an earthworm--all prime victuals for an armadillo or for an eastern mole.

As a final gesture, glance back up at the leaves again and think: photosynthesis, oxygen and carbon dioxide. Have *you* thanked a green plant today?

How many kinds of creatures are mentioned in this brief sketch of live oak ecology? What if we had gone into detail? Extrapolate these sorts of interconnections to every plant and animal that you have observed, and you will begin to grasp both the intricacy and the sheer wonderfulness that make up the ecology of the Aransas Refuge.

COMMUNITY ECOLOGY

When several or many living creatures occupy the same area and display such a close-knit set of interactions that they form a single, recognizable interdependent entity, the ecologist refers to that assemblage as a *biotic community.* The community is the natural base unit of ecology. Before describing the several communities which occur on the Refuge, we will briefly mention some of the properties common to them all. You may enjoy trying to discern these for yourself as you trek about.

Within the general confines of its community each member species will have its favored *habitat*--the particular setting where it spends most of its time. Sanderling habitat is open shoreline. Fulvous harvest mouse habitat is dense tall grass. Bulrush habitat is muddy freshwater or brackish shallows. Its habitat is the creature's ecological address.

Many individual animals occupy a *home range* within their species' habitat. The home range always includes the creature's nesting and resting sites, its main sources of food and water and all of the trails over which it routinely wanders. The sizes of home ranges vary with the needs and the mobility of the animal: a square foot for a fiddler crab; less than half an acre for a white-footed mouse; 180 acres for a flock of prairie chickens; eight square miles for a coyote.

Social animals frequently mark and defend their home ranges from trespass by members of their own kind. These guarded areas are called *territories.* Ever watch two mockingbirds in a flutter-fight over a territorial boundary? Or have you seen a bobcat spray urine on a shrub? What about a green anole vigorously pumping his pink dewlap at a rival male? The out-of-doors is laced with natural posted signs and fencelines of which we are seldom aware. Learning to recognize them is both instructive and fun.

If its habitat is a creature's ecological address, then its *niche* (rhymes with "hitch") is its ecological job. The niche describes what the animal does for a living. Since all animals spend most of their active lives searching for and consuming food, niches are usually defined by food habits. The niche of an eastern mole is succinctly expressed as a fossorial insectivore (a burrowing insect eater). A red-tailed hawk fills the soaring raptor niche; a snowy egret the wading-and-spearing niche.

The adult pipevine swallowtail butterfly is a nectar sipper while its larva is a leaf chewer. A female saltmarsh mosquito is a flying blood sucker. And so on.

It is a cardinal precept of ecology that no two species belonging to the same community have precisely the same niche. When niches overlap, competition for food results. The spontaneous attempt to avoid competition renders each kind of creature a specialist in some manner of food-getting. Evolution of unique anatomy and behaviour promote specialization and the amazing diversity of life results.

You can observe the segregation of niches within any group of similar species in a community. One of the most obvious is among the shorebirds and waterfowl that frequent Mustang Lake in the fall and wintertime. Use your binoculars from the Observation Tower and watch the birds at work. Especially note the shapes of their bills and the particular portion of the lake on which they choose to forage.

The wade-and-spear fishermen are easy to recognize: great-blue heron, great and snowy egrets, little blue heron, tricolored heron and reddish egret. Differences in length of neck, bill and legs bring in slightly different prey. Watch a bird stalk and strike. Exactly how does it go about it? Precisely what sort of fishing hole does it choose? How often does it succeed? What does it catch?

Whooping cranes occupy a slosh-and-scrounge niche, stalking the tidal flats snapping up a variety of crustaceans, molluscs and insects and also feeding on sundry greenery and fruits. Cranes use their heavy bills more as picker-uppers than as spears.

The lake shore supports a variety of probers (western sandpiper, common snipe, long-billed curlew, willet), pluckers (black-bellied plover, killdeer, greater yellowlegs), peckers (sora and clapper rails) and seedeaters (seaside and savannah sparrows). Other species of probers and pluckers prefer the open mudflats (long-billed dowitchers, dunlin, least and semipalmated sandpipers, sanderlings).

Again, watch these birds at work. Leg and toe length, shape of neck, coloration of plumage and feeding demeanor will mesh with bill type to fit each species to its niche. You will learn a lot of wildlife biology by working out the various adaptive combinations.

Most of the ducks in this shallow lake will be dabblers-- those which upend but do not dive (gadwall, pintail, northern shoveler), and the bill of each species allows it to exploit the bottom sediment and submerged vegetation in a different way.

Pied-billed grebes and double-crested cormorants surface-dive for fish; Caspian and Forster's terns dive-bomb for them; white pelicans scoop them up; ring-billed gulls get them any way they can. You take it from there.

The food connections are so important to the integrity of every biotic community that ecologists have given them special emphasis. Straightline eat-and-be-eaten sequences are called *food chains*.

yaupon fruit➡American robin➡Cooper's hawk

morning glory leaf➡broad-winged katydid➡green tree frog➡
western ribbon snake➡northern harrier

suspended organic detritus➡water flea➡dragonfly larva➡
hatchling alligator➡great blue heron

saline organic sediment➡fiddler crab➡raccoon

A *food web* results from the intermeshing of the several food chains in a biotic community. The accompanying diagram shows a small segment of the winter food web that succors your view of Mustang Lake from the Observation Tower.

Food webs are appropriately represented with the plants at the bottom and all food chains trending upward. Each species in the community can then be categorized according to the number of steps in its food chain that separates it from the basic plant level. The major groups recognizable in any community are:

Producers--the green plants (diatoms, Indian grass, yaupon).

Herbivores--the plant eaters (grasshoppers, white-tailed deer, mourning dove).

First-level carnivores--eat the herbivores (western diamond-back rattlesnake, bobcat, white-tailed hawk).

Second-level carnivores--eat the first-level carnivores (peregrine falcon, leopard frog, alligator).

Omnivores--opportunists that eat a variety of plant and animal matter (coyote, raccoon, whooping crane, laughing gull).

Detritivores--sift organic matter from substrate or water (mud shrimp, earthworm, fiddler crab).

Scavengers--specialize in carrion (turkey vulture, carrion beetle, blowfly).

Decomposers--microbes which transform organic material into simpler chemical components (bacteria, fungi).

Parasites--draw nourishment from living hosts (deer liver fluke, Gulf Coast tick, saltmarsh mosquito).

Saprophytes--bacteria and fungi which absorb organic matter from sediment and soil (soil bacteria, puffballs, earthstars, mushrooms).

Are you enough of an ecologist to place the creatures that you have seen on the Refuge into one of these feeding categories?

When an animal consumes its food it never obtains all of the potential calories. Some parts are inedible or unpalatable. Others are indigestible and are expelled as feces. A significant fraction is simply dropped and scattered. Most of the food calories which are absorbed are expended in routine metabolism. Relatively little of the food goes into actual growth.

Since this loss of calories occurs at each link in the food chain, it follows that there is a dwindling source of energy toward the top of the food web of any community. The geometrical analog is a pyramid, with most of the biomass at the bottom and progressively less toward the top. Reflect on the many pounds of mouse and gopher meat there must be on the Aransas Refuge compared to the few pounds of great-horned owl meat. Many blue crabs, far fewer whooping cranes; many grasshoppers, not so many American kestrels; lots of deer, perhaps only one cougar.

The relationship is inviolable: the top-level creatures are always the least abundant in any biotic community.

Every creature needs adequate food to survive, but all creatures have other vital needs: water, shelter, roaming ground, resting and nesting sites, access to members of the opposite sex. Clearly, any community has finite resources so that it can adequately support only a given number of individuals of a species at a time. If the number of individuals rises too high they must compete vigorously for the dwindling resources and they usually degrade the environment in their struggle to satisfy their needs.

So, every community has a *carrying capacity* for each of its component species, a population level that can be adequately and indefinitely supported. When a species exceeds its carrying capacity both the organism and the environment suffer.

In 1968-69, there was a tragic crash of the white-tail deer population after these animals soared beyond the carrying capacity of their Refuge habitat. There is even some worry that the Refuge population of whooping cranes is now beginning to feel growing pains. Lately some new birds are moving outside the limits of the Refuge to establish winter territories.

What about people? The Aransas Refuge has a definite carrying capacity for us too. There is a physical limit--how much touching, tromping, oggling, dust-raising, insect-spraying, and automobile exhaust the area can absorb without suffering lasting deterioration. There is also a social limit--how many people can simultaneously enjoy a quality experience in Nature without interfering with each other?
What do you think the human carrying capacity is for the Heron Flats Trail or the Tour Loop?   With an annual visitation rate of about 70,000 and with certain months outstandingly popular ones, you may be sure that Refuge personnel have given the question considerable thought.

Stratification refers to the layering in a community. When we mentioned the living things associated with various levels in the live oak trees on the Big Tree Trail we were discussing vertical stratification. You can experience the shift directly if you observe the changes in the surrounding branches, foliage, insects and birds as you climb the ramp to the Observation Tower. Even a grassland can exhibit vertical stratification on a small but vital scale. On a cold day with a biting north wind a slender glass lizard can be quite comfortable snuggled in the depths of a clump of broomsedge bluestem.
Horizontal stratification in a community is always correlated with a horizontal gradient in some important environmental factor. From the end of the pier overlooking Jones Lake notice the concentric rings of changing vegetation that border the waterline: Egyptian panic grass and cattails in and around the water; then a band of bushy bluestem grass; behind that a zone of rattlepod sprinkled with groundsel; finally live oak and yaupon.
Or try the Boardwalk from the Observation Tower to the edge of San Antonio Bay. Watch the vegetation change as you progress along the gradients of salinity and moisture: from large clumps of Gulf cordgrass on the inland edge through bushy sea-oxeye, glasswort and shoregrass zones to saltgrass and marshhay cordgrass near the end of the Boardwalk and finally to smooth cordgrass growing directly in the bay.
Although they are less clean cut, there are zones of animal life associated with the plant zones.

Biotic communities develop and mature over a period of time. The orderly sequence of changes through which a maturing community passes is called *succession*. Each stage of succession has a different constellation of species.

When a virgin area (a fresh sand dune, a newly graded roadside or a recently abandoned agricultural field) is first exploited by living things, only the hardiest species can survive there. Candidates for this pioneer stage must be able to withstand direct sunlight, soil with a low organic content and the brunt of whatever bad weather comes along.

Very gradually, as the pioneers gain a foothold, they begin to change the area. Shade, a veneer of top soil, more places to hide and things to eat, occur. The site becomes more favorable and less hardy species can successfully invade it. Slowly the pioneers are pushed out and a new complex of species reigns.

This second group continues to alter the environment: deeper soil, more diverse woody vegetation, more complex food web. A third and perhaps a fourth and fifth stage follow, all with the same progressive trend.

Finally the community achieves an equilibrium--a climax stage--in which it supports the maximum diversity and abundance of creatures possible at that time and place. Until the climate changes or some natural or man-induced catastrophe occurs, the climax community bears pretty witness to the "balance of Nature".

Certainly the best place to observe community succession on the Refuge is on the constantly shifting sands of Matagorda Island. There you can actually walk backward in time by treking from the beach inland across the progressively more vegetated dunes. We mentioned a much older example of the same phenomenon while discussing the Ingleside barrier and the ridge-and-swale topography on Blackjack Peninsula.

You can observe community succession on a recent time scale by observing the burned areas while you drive the Tour Loop. These deliberate burns are attempts by Refuge personnel to return the interior of Blackjack Peninsula to its pristine savannah-like condition. Compare not just the regrowth of greenery but the species composition between a burned and an unburned section. Can you age several burns by their degree of succession? Ask at the Visitors Center to confirm your judgement.

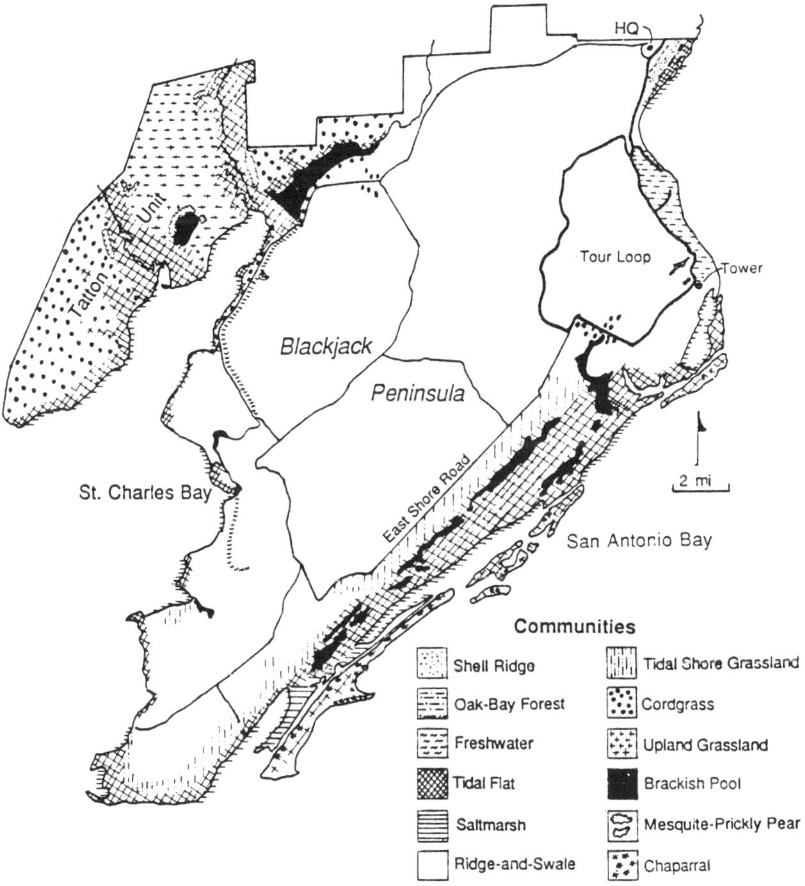
HQ
Tour Loop
Tower
Tatton Unit
Blackjack
Peninsula
St. Charles Bay
East Shore Road
2 mi
San Antonio Bay
Communities
Shell Ridge
Oak-Bay Forest
Freshwater
Tidal Flat
Saltmarsh
Ridge-and-Swale
Tidal Shore Grassland
Cordgrass
Upland Grassland
Brackish Pool
Mesquite-Prickly Pear
Chaparral

Figure 12 The major biotic communities on the mainland portion of the Aransas Refuge.

BIOTIC COMMUNITIES

Using round figures, we can begin the ecological organization of the mainland portion of the Aransas Refuge as follows.

7,800 acres wetland	➡freshwater	800 acres
	➡saltwater	7,000 acres
47,000 acres upland	➡grassland	23,000 acres
	➡brushland	24,000 acres

We have recognized twelve biotic communities and these are indicated on the accompanying map. Six of these communities are relatively minor and occur on portions of the Refuge that are not open to the routine visitor. The others are readily accessible and each represents a major component of the Aransas ecosystem, so we shall present them first and in greater detail.

The plants and animals mentioned in the brief descriptions are characterized in later chapters and described fully in appropriate field guides. Once you know your creatures, you should be able to attain a concept of the assemblage of living things that composes each community.

Shell ridge community

1. SHELL RIDGE

This is at once one of the smallest, most distinctive, most diverse and most commonly visited communities on the Refuge. To see it trek the Heron Flats Trail. Several brochures keyed to numbered posts along the trail are available at the Visitors Center.

The key to this community is the high lime content of the substrate, a result of its oystershell base. A unique assemblage of woody plants flourishes on the alkaline soil along the more mature inner ridge (the first half of the trail): Mexican persimmon, tanglewood, Mexican buckeye, anaqua, spiny and netleaf hackberry. The ubiquitous live oak dominates this stretch and yaupon is a common understory shrub.

This community supports the greatest diversity of vines on the Refuge: green briar, trumpet creeper, mustang grape, pepper-vine, Alamo vine, poison ivy, milkweed vine, pearl milkweed and more. Look for good growths of epiphytes (plants that grow on other plants): Spanish and ball moss, true mosses, fungi and lichens. Deep shade limits understory plants but watch for the shade-loving turk's cap and frostweed. The sunlit portions of the trail will yield a seasonal sampling of Refuge wildflowers.

Signs of animal life are mostly limited to cryptic rustles. Ground skinks, wolf spiders and white-footed mice skitter through the leaf litter. You might see eastern fence lizards on the ground and tree trunks and green anoles and rough green snakes in the branches. Passerine birds such as cardinals and white-eyed vireos flit through the dense growth, but these will be difficult to observe. Most nocturnal creatures will be curled up in their daytime retreats: raccoon, opossum, striped skunk. You may run across a foraging armadillo.

After crossing the bridge over Cattail Slough you get onto the less fertile, brushy middle ridge. Here the trail courses through a dense stand of lime prickly ash, brasil, torchwood and tanglewood punctuated with an occasional agarito, mesquite and prickly pear.

When you gain the more geologically recent outer shell ridge there is less woody vegetation. Gulf cordgrass and marshhay cordgrass creep up from the tidal flat community that borders the bay. Groundsel and mesquite trees are scattered through the diversity of grass species along the trail. Watch for the pretty lilac flowers of the snapdragon vine among the tangle of grasses and low branches. You cannot miss the impressive Spanish daggers that rise from the middle and outer ridges.

Over 150 species of plants have been identified in the shell ridge community and even this list is not exhaustive. (See Appendix C for a seasonal summary of the flowering plants along the Heron Flats Trail.)

2. OAK-BAY FOREST

Although no plant species is unique to this community, the assemblage of kinds reaches its finest growth on the deep sands that stretch along the bayshore between the Environmental Training Area and the Big Tree Trail. Both the Dagger Point Trail and the Big Tree Trail afford intimate access. The Wood Duck Pond Trail pushes into the dense midsection of this community. This forest can also be seen beyond all of the grassy clearings along the east side of the road between the Environmental Training Area and the Observation Tower.

Oak-Bay Forest community

The oak-bay forest is composed mainly of live oak, red bay and laurel oak. There are a few tall netleaf hackberries along the Big Tree Trail and widely scattered blackjack oaks in the trackless middle reaches of the community. These blackjacks are best observed in the fall when they take on purple and reddish hues against the green backdrop of evergreen oaks and bays.

Yaupon is the principal understory shrub, followed by beautyberry. Green briar is the most common vine. Along the Green Route on the Dagger Point Trail is the largest stand of tree huckleberry on the Refuge. (Because of this species, a high point on the trail is called Blueberry Ridge.) Look for the red flowers of turk's cap and coralbean along the trailsides in season. The occasional clumps of grass-like plants are nut rush. With the right combination of warmth and moisture the shaded leaf litter can spawn an amazing diversity of mushrooms.

No animals are restricted to this community, but it is the best place to observe fox squirrels. Raccoons and opossums den in hollows in the oaks. Armadillos and striped skunks account for most of the sandy burrows. Deer, javelina and feral hogs routinely forage through the undergrowth and you may notice their trails crossing your own. Watch for the little winding ridges of sand thrown up by the eastern mole. Although you are not likely to see them, white-footed mice and least shrews are common forest inhabitants.

Birds in the dense forest are mostly small passerines. It takes an experienced birder to identify these from the glimpses they afford, but anyone who is fortunate enough to be along the Big Tree Trail at warbler time (April-May) can enjoy the trees full of twitching colors. The evening gloom beneath the trees at the Environmental Training Area is the best place to hear the peculiar call of the parauque.

Keep your eyes open in this forest for everything from the huge web of the goldenweb spider to the harmless defensive antics of an eastern hog-nosed snake.

Freshwater community

3. FRESHWATER

Here we are concerned only with what you can see without actually entering or dipping into the water.

You can walk along the shoreline of freshwater sloughs on the Rail Trail and the Heron Flats Trail. Jones Lake has a pier overlook and Hog Lake has a wildlife observation blind as well as a perimeter trail. There is an ephemeral pond near the large live oaks on the Big Tree Trail. You will also encounter occasional temporary ponds along the Tour Loop.

The vegetation will depend on the permanence of the water. Thomas Slough (on the Rail Trail) almost always has water. Look there for submerged plants like hornwort and water nymph as well as floating ones like pondweed. Emergent plants along the shoreline include cattails, California and American bulrushes and common reed. The pretty little water-hyssop usually sprawls on the muddy margins. The main bankside tree is the black willow. Beneath and between the willows look for both rattlepods and coffebeans as well as dense stands of saltmarsh and spiny asters. The groundsel will also be there along with an occasional dwarf palmetto and buttonbush.

The edges of temporary pools are almost always marked by a thick stand of bushy bluestem grass and a variety of sedges, especially spikerushes. When the pools dry up other species rapidly invade the exposed mud.

The most spectacular denizen of this community is the alligator. The commonest snake is the western ribbonsnake, and cottonmouth moccasins are also abundant. If you spot a basking turtle it will most likely be the red-eared turtle. Leopard frogs leap into the water when startled on the bankside, and green tree frogs are frequently seen huddling on the cattails and bulrushes. The chug of bullfrogs often resounds from nearby.

The dense bankside vegetation is the special haunt of several species of secretive rails. All of the wading birds as well as roseate spoonbills and woodstorks occasionally use the ponds. Watch also for dabbling ducks, American coots, common moorhens, belted kingfishers, marsh and sedge wrens, swamp sparrows and occasional flocks of red-winged blackbirds and great-tailed grackles. Killdeers patrol the open shorelines. All of the small passerines visit the pools to drink and bathe.

You can hope to see any of the mammals at a poolside when they come to drink or wallow, but those most commonly seen are raccoon, deer and feral hog.

During droughts the drying waterholes take on added significance, and all types of wildlife concentrate nearby to take advantage of the water and of each other.

4. TIDAL FLAT

This is an extensive and important community on the Refuge, and it represents an intricate meeting ground of sea and land. A fine overview of the tidal flats can be gained from the Observation Tower. The Boardwalk between the Tower and the bay affords an excellent closeup look without sinking to your knees in the oozy saline mud. Heron Flats is the name for the extensive tidal flat between the outer shell ridge and the bay on the Heron Flats Trail, and this community continues along the bayside of the paved road as far as the picnic area.

Tidal Flat community

The most distinctive and widespread plant of the tidal flat is the knee-high, semiwoody bushy sea-oxeye. Other plants come in as the salinity and degree of tidal flooding allow: saltgrass and shoregrass; saltwort and glasswort; bulrush and common reed; Carolina wolfberry and marsh elder; goldenaster, saline aster, sea lavendar and saltmarsh morning-glory. The inland margin of the tidal flat is marked by a zone of marshhay cordgrass and a few clumps of Gulf cordgrass with scattered purple fleabane and seaside gerardia for color. The tallest woody plants in this community are chest-high groundsels.

Much of the animal life of the tidal flat is hidden from casual observation. Depending upon whether the mud is exposed or flooded, this is the abode of brown shimp, sheepshead minnows, razor clams, blue crabs, fiddler crabs, mud crabs, a variety of marine worms, saltmarsh snails, saltmarsh mosquitoes, saltmarsh grasshoppers, tiger beetles and wolfspiders. Crayfish burrow along the inland border of the tidal flat.

This community is too saline for amphibians, but the cottonmouth moccasin and Gulf saltmarsh snake are common here. All of the wading and mud-probing birds utilize the tidal flat, and clapper rails, eastern meadowlarks, seaside sparrows and sedge wrens are often flushed from the thickets of sea-oxeye. And the tidal flat is the special domain of the whooping crane.

Raccoon tracks are common throughout this community, and coyotes scrounge along its borders. Even bobcats deign to sog through it. The rice rat reaches its peak density here.

Saltmarsh community

5. SALTMARSH

The term "saltmarsh" should be used only sparingly in describing the lower Texas coast. A typical saltmarsh on the western shore of the Gulf of Mexico is composed of an extensive zone of smooth cordgrass backed by a broad belt of saltmarsh bulrush and black needlerush. Such saltmarshes occur along the upper Texas coast, but they dwindle rapidly southward. In the Coastal Bend "saltmarsh" usually means what we have described as the tidal flat community.

The mainland Refuge has a thin veneer of smooth cordgrass along the bayside margin of most tidal flats. You can most easily observe this narrow band of waist-high grass from the Observation Tower. It can be seen lining the immediate edge of Mustang Lake. From the end of the Boardwalk below the Tower you can closely scrutinize the patch of smooth cordgrass that grows on the edge of San Antonio Bay.

Smooth cordgrass is one of the few rooted plants that grows well in saltwater. It is not more common locally because the bays are usually more brackish than salty. Other brackish water species occasionally grow directly on the bayside: common reed, yellow cowpea, coastal dropseed, beach panic grass and various sedges.

Because the local saltmarsh is only a few feet to a few yards across, it does not support a community of animals distinct from that of the adjacent tidal flat. Where the smooth cordgrass forms occasional patches large enough to afford shelter amidst its dense growth, alligators lurk, clapper rails stalk, periwinkles graze, least bitterns nest and long-jawed orb weavers string their webs.

6. RIDGE-AND-SWALE

This is by far the most widespread community on Blackjack Peninsula. It is a community of the interior, and it owes its occurrence and appearance to both geological and human history.

We discussed the basis for the corrugated ridge-and-swale topography of the peninsula in Chapter 1. The sandy ridges provide the elevation (sometimes only several feet) necessary for woody perennial plants to keep their root systems from being flooded and asphyxiated after heavy downpours and storm induced tidal surges. So the ridges of sand support trees and shrubs.

The sandy swales are frequently flooded and some of these troughs may hold standing water for weeks on end. Annuals or water tolerant perennials grow in the swales. Most of the time these sunny openings are covered with a glorious sward of native grasses the like of which is seldom seen today elsewhere in the Coastal Bend.

In its pristine state the interior of Blackjack Peninsula was a park-like live oak savannah, with dense mottes of large live oaks on the uplands and tall grasses in the depressions. The widespread intermediate ground--the low upland flats--was also dominated by grasses. Apparently wildfires, mostly lightning-induced, gave the advantage to the quick growing perennial grasses in this middle terrain. The result was a sea of grass dotted with wind sculptured oak islands.

Then came men and livestock. Severe overgrazing and suppression of fires worked against the grasses. Probing lateral roots of the live oaks began to infiltrate the long-disputed upland flats. Soon a veritable thicket of waist-high oak sprouts overtopped the weakened grass sod. The consequence is what you see today--old mottes of large live oak trees, broad stretches of impenetrable chest-high "running live oak" and occasional low swales still valiantly held by tall grasses.

The vast areas of thicketized live oaks on the Refuge have received much attention. In a way they are natural and in a way they are man-induced. They benefit some forms of wildlife (jaguarundis and mockingbirds) and inhibit others (bobwhite quail and white-tailed deer). They provide a bountiful source of natural food (fresh-growth greenery and acorns), but they inhibit the growth of a diverse array of food-producing forbs and grasses. And they certainly interfere with human accessibility to wildlife for both enjoyment and management.

What to do, if anything? Over the years Refuge personnel have tried about everything, including nonaction and the current vogue of selective burning. To date the result is evident: a stalemate. Once entrenched, the running live oak is difficult to eradicate without destroying other elements of the community. In the long run it may be prudent to wage a low-key, periodic campaign based on carefully planned burns on a rotating schedule with the intent of checking rather than vanquishing the live oak thickets.

The ridge-and-swale community can conveniently be subdivided into three units: live oak motte, live oak thicket and grassland. These might be listed as three separate communities, but they are so fragmented and interdigitated that we have coalesced them for descriptive purposes.

The best way to observe the sweep and pattern of this community is from your automobile along the Tour Loop. You can sample it afoot on the Heritage Trail. Or you can simply gaze over its extensive canopy from atop the Tower.

Live oak motte, Ridge and Swale community

The live oak motte is dominated by large live oak trees with laurel oaks, red bays and prickly ashes along the edges. The shaded understory supports a dense growth of yaupon, a tangle of greenbriar and occasional clumps of beautyberry. The oaks are usually laced with mustang grape vines.

None of the larger animals is restricted to these picturesque live oak mottes, but many creatures rest, nest and feed in them. The mottes are especially valuable as wintertime windbreaks and summertime shade. Unfortunately for many creatures, they also offer sanctuary to mosquitoes and ticks. Drooping branches provide greenery for everything from insects to deer. And live oak acorns work into nearly every food chain on the Refuge.

Live oak thicket, Ridge and Swale community

The live oak thickets are incredibly dense (up to 50 sturdy stems per square foot, for acres and acres), waist-to-head-high stands of scrubby oak shoots that arise from a ramifying mass of pernicious rhizomes. Low-growing laurel oaks and occasional clumps of shrubby red bays contribute to this brushland. Blackjack oaks are sprinkled thinly through the drier areas, while clumps of wax myrtle occupy moist spots. The entire thicket is laced together with greenbriars to produce a barrier that is very nearly impregnable to all except the most low-slung and determined of the larger creatures. Deer and even the feral hogs generally wend their way through these thickets along game trails worn by generations of their kind.

Many of the most secretive wild creatures on the Refuge take advantage of the oak thickets for shelter and foraging grounds. (Despite their stunted size, the oak thickets usually produce an ample crop of acorns.) This is the place to anticipate a rare glimpse of one of the native cats--a bobcat, cougar or jaguarundi. Small packs of javelinas wander in and out of the fringes as do feral hogs, gray foxes, armadillos and cottontail rabbits. You may be lucky enough to see a long-tailed weasel shoot across the road from one thicket to another.

Then again, you may see none of these. Persistent, occasional sightings by Refuge personnel, oilfield workers and visitors confirm that all of these creatures reside on the Aransas. If you observe them, feel privileged; if not, feel satisfied in the knowledge that they are out there, secure in their natural bailiwicks and probably within earshot of your automobile. And always be alert around the next bend.

Look for mockingbirds, loggerhead shrikes, cardinals, mourning doves, brown thrashers, American kestrels and red-tailed hawks in the vicinity. If you have not noticed the sandy mounds of the plains pocket gopher elsewhere, they should be conspicuous along the margins of these oak thickets. But there will be scant evidence of the huge population of white-footed mice that resides in this portion of the community.

Grassland, Ridge and Swale community.

The interior grasslands are dominated by a wonderous array of mostly perennial, tall bunch grasses. This is the special domain of bluestems: big bluestem, seacoast bluestem, bushy bluestem, broomsedge bluestem, silver bluestem and others. Depending on the local topography the bluestems are joined by switch grass, dropseeds, paspalums, sprangletops, Indian grass and Gulf Coast muhly. About 85 species of grasses have been recorded on the Refuge and most of them occur somewhere in these open glades. Late fall is an excellent time to see these grasses when their foliage has turned a crisp brown and they sport full heads of silver seed fluff.

In areas where freshwater accumulates, stands of sawgrass, rattlepod, cattail and California bulrush along with occasional dwarf palmettoes replace the grasses. Where the swags are saline, marshhay and Gulf cordgrasses take over.

You are apt to see any of the large herbivores in the grassy swales, and these are also good spots to catch a glimpse of a coyote, a flock of wild turkeys, a soaring red-tailed hawk or a skimming northern harrier. Watch also for the explosion of a covey of bobwhite quail and for flocks of eastern meadowlarks and groups of savannah and vesper sparrows.

The dense grass is working alive with crackle-wing grasshoppers, vagabond spiders, slender glass lizards, fulvous harvest mice and pigmy mice.

7. TIDAL SHORE GRASSLAND

This is gently tilted, saline ground densely covered with marshhay cordgrass. Gulf cordgrass rims the community and several species of bluestem and an array of forbs capture the occasional sandy hillocks. Because of its heavy rodent population and its open aspect, this is good country for observing white-tailed hawks and black-shouldered kites. It is also prime habitat for fast moving snakes like the western coachwhip and the yellow-bellied racer.

8. CORDGRASS

This moist, slightly saline land is almost totally captured by Gulf cordgrass. It is good rattlesnake habitat and usually harbors high populations of hispid cotton rats, pigmy mice, sundry sparrows and sedge wrens and a prolific subterranean colony of crayfish.

9. UPLAND GRASSLAND

This is a prairie community developed on dark soil and composed primarily of seacoast and silver bluestems, fringed windmill grass, white tridens, Texas wintergrass and a variety of panic grasses. Both grazing by cattle and occasional mowing are necessary to counter invasion by shrubby groundsels. It is here that the Refuge's small population of Attwater's prairie chickens clings to existence. Eastern meadowlarks and bobwhite quail are at home in this community. Dickcissels nest here and upland sandpipers enjoy stopping in its spaciousness enroute to the ends of the Earth.

10. BRACKISH POOL

This is a community of shallow pools only a few inches deep and surrounded by barren tidal mud flats. Shorebirds frequent these sites to feed on crustaceans, killifishes, molluscs and mudworms. Because the oozy mud and open expanse provide security, many birds spend a significant portion of the day loafing around such sites. They frequently pass the night standing in the saline puddles.

11. MESQUITE-PRICKLY-PEAR

Mesquite trees, blackbrush, agarito, retama, spiny hackberry, Texas prickly pear, tasajillo and devil's head cacti have captured clay-loam uplands on the Tatton Unit around the western side of Goose Lake. Birds and mammals typical of the brush country of South Texas occasionally reach this isolated community. Cactus wrens, Bewick's wrens, road runners and wood rats are examples.

12. CHAPARRAL

Dry, somewhat saline clay-loam uplands and low shell ridges favor a dense, thorny vegetation: brasil, Carolina and Berlandier's wolfberries, lime prickly ash, mesquite, coma, spiny hackberry, Spanish dagger, Texas prickly pear and tasajillo. Tanglewood adds its maze of twisted branches to the nearly impenetrable growth. Because this community usually occurs in isolated fragments (sometimes only a few square yards in extent, wherever a favorable hillock of the proper substrate exists), it does not support a distinctive fauna. It is, however, prime diamondback rattler habitat, and many passerine birds seek shelter among the numerous branches.

By looking across Heron Flats from the outer shell ridge, you can see one of these brush covered mounds on the bayshore.

No one knows just when the first men laid eyes on the Coastal Bend. The earliest paleohunters were probably in the region at least 20,000 years ago. These people lived among, hunted and perhaps contributed to the demise of the late Pleistocene fauna which inhabited the Coastal Prairie. Although there is no direct evidence from the Aransas Refuge, archeological finds from elsewhere in Texas reveal that these primitive hunters routinely used both guile and gall to bring down mammoths and that they occasionally killed the large prehistoric bison wholesale. Doubtless they exploited a broad animal and plant food base.

By 10,000 years ago the local climate, terrain and biota were modernizing, and the resident people adapted their hunting-and-gathering lifestyle to the subtle shifts in natural resources. Eventually they acquired the geographic affinities and the cultural distinctions which we associate with historic North American Indians.

Three thousand years ago--about the time the barrier islands were taking shape--local Indians whom we call Karankawas inhabited the littoral margin of the Coastal Bend. A half-dozen major clans of these seaside natives haunted the offshore islands, bays, shoreline and a thin inland strip of the mainland from Galveston Bay to Corpus Christi Bay. The Karankawas were not a consolidated tribe. Each clan of forty or so people had its own territory and hegemony. Blackjack Peninsula was probably within the domain of the Copanes band.

Most of what we know about the lifestyle of the prehistoric Karankawas comes from inference. Theirs was not a culture of complex accouterments, and the erosive coastal environment has spared only their most durable traces. Shell middens--mounds of discarded oyster and whelk shells--and scattered burial grounds are occasionally uncovered by the wind. Fourteen such sites have been discovered along the margin of Blackjack Peninsula. Favored campsites have yielded a scant assortment of shell ornaments and tools, flint points and shards of a distinctive pottery. A small array of these items is on display in the Visitors Center.

By every indication the Karankawas had a lifestyle which was culturally unsophisticated but ecologically finely tuned. They were the aboriginal opportunistic exploiters of the coastline. Family groups ranged through the homeground of their respective bands according to the seasons, anticipating the natural fruiting times and animal movements, the turns of the tide, and taking immediate advantage of whatever windfalls came their way.

These Indians were habitually nomadic. Favored campsites were occupied periodically, not permanently. Generations of occasional use produced the middens which we discover today.

The Karankawas practiced no agriculture, had no domesticated animals and did not set aside many food stores. Theirs was a hand-to-mouth, search-and-glut existence. Their fare was varied and periodically bountiful: the fruits of prickly pear cactus, mustang grape, dewberry, agarito and mesquite; the roots of cattails, reeds, bulrushes and sedges; shallow water fishes, crustaceans, molluscs (especially whelks and oysters) and sea turtles; the myriad waterfowl and their eggs; alligators; every manner of fresh and spoiled wrack cast up by the sea; and from inland hunting sorties, everything from white-tailed deer and javelinas to prairie chickens, whooping cranes and beetle grubs.

Despite many exaggerated accounts to the contrary, the Karankawas were no more cannibalistic than the many other North American Indians who occasionally sampled the flesh of relatives or enemies for occult reasons.

The Karankawan men went naked. The women wore skirts fashioned from animal skins. Both sexes pierced their lips and nipples with cane splints and they painted and tatooed their bodies.

These Indians were adept at working flint, shell, bone and wood into weapons, tools and ornaments: flint points for their cane arrows; clamshell scrapers; whelk shell hammers; mesquite wood grubbing sticks; bois d'arc longbows strung with twisted deer sinew; shell-and-tooth tinkler beads. They made use of the natural asphaltum thrown up by the sea to affix flint to arrow shaft and to decorate their thin gray pottery ware. They fashioned fine cord from the tough fibers of Spanish dagger leaves. Although they wove cane wiers and poled heavy dugout canoes, they did not use a hook and line and so cannot be regarded as specialized fishermen.

For shelter these Indians relied on a flimsy leanto of tree branches sparsely covered with vegetation and animal hides. In wet, cold weather and during long nights rendered audible by the whine of mosquitoes the Karankawas substituted stoicism for comfort.

The men hunted, fished and occasionally bartered or skirmished with neighboring Karankawa bands or with the inland Coahuiltecans. The women and children beachcombed, gathered plant foods, chased down small animals and performed menial camp work. Everyone had ample time to loiter, gossip, swim and play. It was a primitive but by no means a bad life.

When the mood was upon them, these aborigines swilled great quantities of yaupon tea laced with the intoxicating mescal bean, and they chanted and gyrated to euphoric exhaustion. On most evenings they gathered around smoky fires, conversed briefly about the day's events and perhaps of events long past, and then they drifted into contented sleep as their kind had done in this wild land for 5,000 generations.

Red man first met white on the Texas coast on November 6, 1528, when Cabeza de Vaca and his destitute crewmates were shipwrecked near a Karankawa camp in the vicinity of Galveston Island.

The next significant contact came in 1685, when La Salle established Ft. St. Louis near the head of Lavaca Bay. Initially as innocent and curious as any aborigines, the Karankawas turned treacherous after exposure to the deceits of civilization. In 1688, they massacred the few remaining inhabitants of the French settlement and in so doing established a deserved reputation for haughty and hostile opposition toward all who entered their littoral domain.

During the Eighteenth century the Spanish tried to lure the Karankawas into mission life but with indifferent success. The Indians preferred their old haunts and old ways, spiced with persistent guerrilla warfare and nocturnal raids on livestock.

By the dawn of the Nineteenth Century the inevitable war of attrition was well under way.   At the time of the Texas Revolution in 1835, the despised "Kronks" had been hunted and harrassed to near extinction. A maurauding band of these Indians drew their last white blood when they killed John Kemper on the lower Guadalupe River in 1845. A group of Karankawas was annihilated in a final engagement near Austwell in 1851. After that the Coastal Bend was bereft of one of its most unique wild elements.

Probably because of a simple lack of documentation, there are few records of conflict between Karankawas and early settlers in the vicinity of the Aransas Refuge. Most serious Indian trouble came somewhat later from raiding parties of displaced Lipan Apache and Penateka Comanche who swept down along the frontier and then retreated to their interior strongholds. Like every pioneer community, the local stretch of the Coastal Bend has its own tense tales of Indian troubles, such as the Thomas kidnapping and the Gilliland massacre, but we must pass these by. By 1875, the local coastal country was secure from Indian attack.

Spanish and Mexican ranchers began moving into the Coastal Bend early in the Eighteenth Century, and at that time the padres began their missionary effort to save the souls and acculturate the minds of the Indians.

The closest Spanish mission to Blackjack Peninsula is *Nuestra Señora del Refugio*, which holds the distinction of being the last Spanish mission established in Texas. It was originally built of logs just north of the mouth of the Guadalupe River in 1793, and then it was moved to the site of presentday Refugio ("Rey-FURY-o", 25 miles west of the Refuge) in 1795. The site is on the grounds of Our Lady of Refuge Church on South Alamo Street. The old mission is amply commemorated on vicinity maps: Mission Bay, two Mission lakes, the Mission River and the city and county of Refugio.

Certainly the best nearby site where you can savor the architecture and aura of the Spanish mission era is the beautifully restored mission and presidio of *La Bahía* at Goliad, 45 miles northwest of the Aransas Refuge. Missionary work began there in 1749.

One slender thread connecting the Aransas Refuge with its Spanish sovereignty lies hidden in the name of the largest reservoir--Burgentine Lake. Long years ago, so the story goes, a fierce storm drove a Spanish brigantine into St. Charles Bay and on up the creek at its head. The ship finally went aground on the open prairie six miles from the bay. Old timers commemorated the event by christening the creek with a corruption of "brigantine".

And the very name "Aransas" is an anglicised version of the Spanish "Aranzazu", the name given to an early fort on Live Oak Peninsula which guarded the entrance to Copano Bay just south of Blackjack Peninsula.

While we are reminiscing, we should not ignore the buccaneer Jean La Fitte whose agile corsairs plundered the Spanish caravels and then ducked through Pass Cavallo and Cedar Bayou to the safety of the shallow uncharted bays. La Fitte becomes part of the legend of the Aransas Refuge through the tale of Grandma Frank, a venerable resident of False Live Oak Point and a legend in her own right.

In 1821, La Fitte was disbanding his crew prior to quitting the region. Ms. Frank tells of observing the pirate leader secrete his ample share of the booty nearby: "Many men went into the woods bearing heavy treasure-chests, but only one man came out." Whether actual fact or senile raving, the story lends a special charm to this already intriguing span of coastline.

When Mexico gained its independence in 1821, Blackjack Peninsula was removed from the dominion of New Spain to the Mexican state of Coahuila and Texas. Liberal colonization laws brought a flock of prospective Anglo colonists and speculators to the region.

In 1828, two Irish immigrants, James Power and James Hewetson, received permission to settle all coastal lands between the Guadalupe and the Nueces rivers. Before their land dealing was done the two men had gained personal possession of nearly 200,000 acres of local land, including

Live Oak, Lamar and Blackjack peninsulas as well as Matagorda and St. Joseph islands.

In 1836, the land became part of the Republic of Texas. Although the courts generally honored Mexican land statutes, the claims of Power and Hewetson were thrown into extended litigation which was not finally resolved until 1856. During the hiatus several squatters and quasilegal landholders lived on Blackjack Peninsula. All ran cattle freely on the unfenced range.

Through the days of the Republic and into statehood (1845) until the Civil War, the Coastal Bend saw steady growth and development. Houses and stores with foundations and walls of durable tabby (a product of pioneer ingenuity and marine resources: home-fired oyster shell lime mixed with sand and shell aggregate and cast in wooden molds into huge building blocks) appeared on every hillock and within every appealing grove of live oaks.

Towns, all associated with shipping interests, sprang up along the mainland: Copano, Aransas City, Lamar, Black Point, St. Mary's. Most of these soon succumbed to the vicissitudes of weather and fortune. Both Matagorda and St. Joseph islands were well populated. By 1851, there was even an overland stage route which began at Saluria on the north end of Matagorda Island, ferried across Cedar Bayou and continued to the southern tip of St. Joseph.

The Civil War brought a complete evacuation of the barrier islands, a blockade on shipping, destruction of many local wharves and warehouses and several indecisive skirmishes between blue and gray.

Local reconstruction succored on the teeming herds of longhorn cattle which had built up on the range. From 1865 to 1875, before there was a reliable northern market for beef, the longhorns were slaughtered for their hides, bones, horns and tallow. The grisly work went on 'round the clock at large packeries, and the products were shipped out from the local ports.

The bountiful wildlife of the region was also exploited commercially. Sea turtles were netted for their meat and plundered mercilessly for their eggs. Waterfowl and prairie chickens were shot by the hundreds of thousands and sold locally or salted down and shipped out by the barrel, or left to rot. The fabulous flocks of whistling swans were so harassed and gunned that they eventually gave up their traditional winter rendezvous in the Coastal Bend. Egrets and herons and roseate spoonbills were clubbed on their nests for their ornamental plumage. A great variety of marine fishes was caught, dried, salted and sent to market. Even the lowly horned lizards were collected and sent off by the crateload to be converted into mummified desktop trivia.

Salt works dotted the shores of St. Charles and Copano bays. At these sites native salt was scooped from evaporation ponds scraped in the tidal flats. Much of this salt was trundled to the interior by oxcart and wagon, where it was valued both as a condiment and even more so as a preservative.

With the Indians and Mexicans subdued, the war between the states over, the seaports booming, the economy on the upswing and good ranching land available for one dollar per acre, the countryside began to settle up with the optimistic and dedicated fervor so characteristic of the Anglo pioneer.

Much of Blackjack Peninsula had been declared public domain in 1856 when the courts ruled against the Power and Hewetson estates. By the late 1870's thirty landholders held legal claim to over 34,000 acres on the St. Charles Peninsula, as the promontory was then called. Many of these people had been displaced from the barrier islands during the Civil War, and they chose to resettle on the more accessible and fertile peninsula.

Although the last decades of the Nineteenth Century are not too distant, they are poorly documented on Blackjack Peninsula. Each resident landowner ranched and he also tilled small subsistence level fields. Most holdings were unfenced, so that the peninsula served as a commons for the free ranging livestock. Besides several thousand head of cattle, flocks of sheep and goats, loose groups of horses and mules and droves of domestic hogs roamed the country. Under such a system the abuse of overgrazing soon became manifest. The combined impact of the livestock and the landowner's habit of burning the winter range eventually reduced the peninsular terrain to one much more open and barren than we see today.

Toward the end of the period enough people inhabited the point of land to merit a community school, a post office and even a small village (Carlos City, located about halfway down the east shore of the peninsula). A few left their names on the land: William H. Jones (Jones Lake); Felix B. Webb (Webb's Point); B. L. Bludworth (Bludworth Island); Emile Dietrich (Melle Dietrich Point); Robert McHugh (McHugh Bayou). Most simply lived out their time and faded into oblivion.

You can sample this bygone era on the Refuge by walking the Heritage Trail and allowing your imagination to provide the bawl of the cattle from the old corral and the rhythmic squeal of the lift rods on the wooden windmill. Or you might pause in the Visitors Center and look deeply into the eyes of the photograph of George Brundrett who lived and ranched here in years long gone by. You cannot gaze upon his weathered countenance or at the adjacent picture of an early farmstead without gaining some appreciation and admiration for the sort of grit the land demanded of its early inhabitants. For instance, it took more than a little pluck to survive in the worst kind of mosquito country with only a dishpan of burning cowchips to serve as a poor substitute for window screens.

These were hard-working, self-sufficient people. The men farmed, ranched, hunted and fished. The women washed, churned, gardened and put up hundreds of jars of tediously home-canned produce. The children worked, played and ran hog-wild. An occasional risky sailboat trip across St. Charles Bay to Lamar brought back store-bought supplies. Mail came by horseback once a week around the head of the bay to the post office at Faulkner (on the northwestern side of the peninsula). Intrepid school marms were boated from Rockport to live-in for several months while they taught the children at communal school houses.

Life was simple, free, full and hazardous. Death came in mundane pioneer forms: childbirth fever, yellow fever, lockjaw, diphtheria, dysentery, being dragged by a horse, struck by a rattler, drowned at sea, engulfed in the flames of a kerosene stove explosion. But by and large, the redoubtable mettle paid off and the good times cancelled the bad.

If you would pursue the age, visit a public library and peruse a copy of *The History of Refugio County, Texas* or leaf through the definitive two volume work by Huson: *Refugio, A Comprehensive History of Refugio County from Aboriginal Times to 1953.*

During the early decades of the Twentieth Century the Coastal Bend settled into a pre-petroleum and pre-tourism economy based on beef, cotton and corn. Then as now, most acreage was given over to ranching. Among the many contemporary landowners was a wheeler-dealer named Cyrus B. Lucas who owned, leased, traded and sold thousands of acres of rangeland in the vicinity of the budding community of Austwell. By 1916, Lucas had managed to acquire nearly all of Blackjack Peninsula, and he ran several thousand head of Hereford and Durham cattle there. At that time the peninsula was referred to variously as the St. Charles Ranch, the Lucas Ranch or simply the Black Jacks. The original ranch headquarters was located near the center of the estate at a site now called Cow Camp, but it was soon moved to the northwestern part of the peninsula to a spot now occupied by the headquarters building of the Continental Oil Company. Cyrus Lucas himself never lived at either location.

Between 1919-1922, Cyrus B. Lucas negotiated mortgages totalling nearly $190,000 against his St. Charles Ranch. When he failed to pay his promissory notes, Lucas lost the ranch by foreclosure to the San Antonio Loan and Trust Company. In 1923, Leroy G. Denman took over the operation of the estate for S. A. Loan & Trust.

Although the property continued to be managed as a working ranch, Denman was also interested in both native and introduced wildlife. In 1924, he sealed off the head of the peninsula with an eight-foot tall game proof fence and proceeded to import an array of animals onto the ranch. The bloodlines of several native and alien species which inhabit the Refuge today trace to this early stocking program, and we consider these further in chapters 7 and 8

The half-century following the Civil War was a critical interval for wildlife in Texas. On the one hand, the destructive tendencies of unleashed market and sport hunting, avid predator eradication, persistent varment control, and the harvesting of wildlife for hides and plumage were aggravated by a burgeoning propulation, expanding settlement activities and a burdensome concentration of domestic livestock. The whole was bound together with the prevailing notions that wildlife resources were inexhaustible and that a man's right to exploit them as he saw fit was his inviolable privilege.

On the other hand, there were those who saw that without informed and energetic conservation, many kinds of native plants and animals could not long withstand the pressures being put upon them.   The crucial task for the conservationists was to turn the tide of public support in their favor.   Unfortunately, they did not succeed with frontier minded Texans until many wildlife populations were almost beyond recall.

Although commercial hunting was legally banned in Texas in 1903, the establishment of bag limits, the distinction between game/nongame species and an effective retinue of game wardens to enforce the state laws did not solidify until about 1930. One early glimmer of dawning enlightenment occurred in 1921, when Texas lawmakers agreed to grant a long-term free lease to the National Audubon Society for the custodianship of several small islands along the coast used as nesting sites by water birds. And the state soon began its system of wildlife management areas which now totals nearly 200,000 acres in eleven tracts.

Meanwhile the Federal government was also taking an active role in wildlife conservation.   The Migratory Bird Treaty Act of 1918, delegated to the Bureau of Biological Survey (ancestral to the U. S. Fish and Wildlife Service) the responsibility for the conservation of the nation's migratory bird species with an early emphasis on the beleaguered waterfowl.   As part of its obligation to preserve and manage waterfowl habitat along the Central Flyway the Survey recommended the purchase of the surface rights to the St. Charles Ranch from the San Antonio Loan and Trust Company.   When negotiations were completed on December 31, 1937, the Aransas Migratory Waterfowl Refuge was born, the first of its category in Texas.

Since its inception the Aransas Refuge has been under the administrations of 12 managers, seen continual upgrading of its physical facilities and roadways, more than doubled in size and survived five decades during which several profound changes in our philosophy of wildlife management have occurred.   This in an increasingly complex political environment and a steadily escalating public demand for wildlife-oriented education and recreation.

While the general goal of the Refuge has always been to enhance our local wildlife resource with emphasis on endangered and migratory species, specific policies have varied with the times.

In the formative years before World War II, the first Refuge manager, James O. Stevenson, was dedicated to his principal mission of raising the carrying capacity of the area for migratory ducks and geese. To this end an immense amount of ditching and diking work was carried out to increase the freshwater holding capacity on the Refuge. Four major dams, a diversion canal and many small ponds, scrapes and windmill outflows dot the peninsula. These generally benefit all forms of wildlife. The system of roadways, levees, culverts and firebreaks was also an early priority. Much of this work was achieved by CCC and WPA contract, and most of it was accomplished by back-breaking pick-and-shovel labor.

You might be interested to know that the waist-high cement pillar that stands near the martin house in the clearing beside the picnic area originally supported the flag pole that stood in the assembly ground for the CCC workers. Their barracks and work area were in the immediate vicinity. A superb photograph in the roadside display near the picnic site shows some of the men who contributed to this energetic era.

Although Manager Stevenson was well aware that the wintering whooping cranes were not common, neither he nor anyone else fully appreciated the dire plight of the species until about 1940. From that time, maintaining the critical winter habitat for the whoopers has been one of the foremost objectives of the Aransas Refuge.

In 1973, the U. S. Congress passed the Endangered Species Act, and the Aransas Refuge was immediately involved in the special custodianship due the several endangered/threatened species which live within or pass across its boundary. We consider these further in chapters 5 and 6.

Until well into the 1960's it was conventional wisdom to think of wildlife almost exclusively in terms of game species. An unfortunate concomitant of this thinking was that any resident nongame species on a wildlife refuge which might conceivably inhibit the growth of favored game populations was regarded as intolerable. This is the attitude that ushered in the dark era of predator control, and the Aransas was not exempt from its painful and misguided efforts. For over a quarter-century, bobcats, coyotes, red wolves, gray foxes, raccoons, opossums and striped skunks were systematically shot, trapped and baited with cyanide guns. Poisonous snakes--no matter what their role in the natural scheme of things--were destroyed at every opportunity.

With the grim lesson learned and the encompassing habitat approach accepted, predators now enjoy their place and perform their vital ecological role among the Refuge biota. However, for the red wolf the shift in attitude came too late.

The first public hunt was conducted on the Aransas National Wildlife Refuge in 1966, as a means of reducing the over-populous herd of white-tailed deer. That hunt was limited to the bow-and-arrow and only bucks could be taken. In 1968, the Refuge hosted its first combined deer hunt for both bow and rifle, and does were also fair game. Feral hogs were added to the huntable list in 1969, and in 1970 javelinas were included as well.

Depending upon the vagaries of the weather and the density of the game populations, public hunts are still routinely scheduled each autumn on the Aransas Refuge, but the purpose of the endeavour has changed. It quickly became evident that hunters were not able to make significant inroads on the deer and hog populations. (Javelinas were no longer hunted.) The kill rate was simply too low to matter. But the hunt itself rapidly became one of the most popular opportunities for public participation on the Refuge.

Recognizing controlled hunting as a legitimate (if suspect) form of wildlife-oriented recreation in concert with their goal of conserving wildlife for the people--and knowing a good public relations tactic when they see one--the Aransas staff expends a great deal of effort to insure that the annual hunt is conducted according to strict guidelines.

Yet, the idea of a public hunt on a wildlife refuge does not sit well with a growing proportion of people. Hunting, many contend, is exploitative, consumptive and contrary to the very spirit of a sanctuary for wild creatures. Even if sport killing is deemed a valid form of recreation, it still has no place on land deliberately set aside for the benefit of native biota.

They have a point, of course. The resolution lies precisely where it should lie--in the depths of our democratic system. When enough people raise enough political dust in the proper places at the right time, they will get what they want. If they are apathetic, then they will get what they deserve.

Public hunts for game animals have been conducted on Matagorda Island since 1978. These are monitored by the

Texas Parks and Wildlife Department personnel according to State hunting regulations.

Although there are continual worries about contamination from outside Refuge boundaries, it is satisfying to report that the Aransas weathered the decades of the flagrant use of chemical pesticides and herbicides without indulging in either of these indiscriminate types of toxins. Runoff from adjacent agricultural fields remains a worry.

A major current concern harks to the Gulf Intracoastal Waterway which slices through the tidal flats along the eastern edge of the peninsula. Boat traffic there is a source of harrassment to wildlife and a significant cause of shoreline erosion. Commercial cargo spills have already worked their way into marine sediments and may enter Refuge food chains. The tons of spoil dredged up during periodic maintenance of the Waterway foster another chronic problem. Disposal of this polluted liquid muck on the adjacent mainland and islets smothers the tidal flats and bird rookeries, thus reducing critical wildlife habitat. To date, no workable compromise for spoil disposal has been reached between the Corps of Engineers and the USFWS. Without question, the best solution for the Refuge would be to reroute the troublesome 15 mile segment of the Waterway further out into the bay.

The Federal government does not own the mineral rights on all Refuge property. Active drilling sites, storage tanks, roadways and a maze of underground pipes lace the area. Cooperative agreements between the petroleum companies and USFWS have kept spills, disfigurement of terrain and harrassment of wildlife to a minimum.

Second only after the well-being of the natural habitat and its biota, the Aransas Refuge is for people. Refuge personnel spend unending man-hours promoting the observation, interpretation, education and enjoyment of wildlife by routine visitors, special groups and professionals.

In addition to direct personal involvement at the information desk and in conducting tours and presenting lectures, there has been a continual upgrading of facilites to enhance the quality of the visitor's experience: 1970, the completion of the 16-mile paved auto Tour Loop; 1971, the opening of the Environmental Training Area for youth groups; 1972, the inauguration of the Heron Flats Trail; 1973, the dedication of the Observation Tower; 1981, the ribbon-cutting for the Wildlife Interpretataion Center (the Visitors

Center); 1984, completion of the Boardwalk across the tidal flat; 1985, construction of the photo-blind at Hog Lake; 1986, erection of six interpretive signs along the Tour Loop.

But we must beware of how we estimate progress on a wildlife refuge. The improvements mentioned above benefit people, not wild creatures. The Aransas is a Federal wildlife sanctuary, not a national park. When visitors occasionally ask for camping grounds, concession stands and additional tour roads they seldom realize the ecological cost of such facilities. It would seem that in the critical years to come the most enlightened measure of progress on the Aransas Refuge will not be in additional glitter or even in a larger roster of visitors but in the steadfast maintenance of the natural setting. Contrary as it is to the American tradition, progress in this case is best gauged not by how much we do but by how much we refrain from doing. The Aransas experience derives from what is already here. Every addition or subtraction puts that irreplaceable legacy at risk.

The Whooping Crane

The **whooping crane** not only symbolizes the Aransas National Wildlife Refuge, it has come to stand for Wild America in need of care and understanding.

In 1952, Robert Porter Allen extolled the wild spirit of the great white bird:

> For the Whooping Crane there is no freedom but that of unbounded wilderness, no life except its own. Without meekness, without a sign of humility, it has refused to accept our idea of what the World should be like. If we succeed in preserving the wild remnant that still survives, it will be no credit to us; the glory will rest on this bird whose stubborn vigor has kept it alive in the face of increasing and seemingly hopeless odds.

Allen was right to credit the whooper for its tenacity, but he was wrong to belittle our dedicated effort to give the species a boost. A more wholesome view is to regard our precious flock of wild whooping cranes as a triumph of both Nature and Man, a working compromise between the demands of wilderness and the demands of a high-tech civilization. Granted that it takes cranes to propagate cranes; but just as surely it takes visionary men to set aside crane refuges.

Seeing a wild whooper, or simply knowing that they still exist, should instill a feeling of pride in each of us. Every time one of the singular bugle-birds spreads his black-tipped wings and, after a half dozen leaping strides, pushes himself aloft with a powerful downstroke, we can justifiably let our own spirits rise with the majestic creature. The crane, as always, is doing its part and now we are doing ours. Together we have written a beautiful poem in the sky; prettier verse, perhaps, than either bird or man could have written alone.

Many of the traits of the whoopers confirm their inclusion in the Family Gruidae (the cranes) and distinguish them from other similar groups such as herons and storks. Cranes are large-bodied, long-legged and long-necked birds possessed of an aristocratic demeanor. During routine feeding cranes are prone to walk great distances. When airborne, the neck and legs are fully extended and the wings beat steadily.

Cranes are social creatures but they interact more as family groups than as clangorous flocks. They communicate with ritualized gesticulations, leaping dances and a variety of vocalizations. Adults usually mate for life, share duties on the nest, are very solicitous of the young and defend a familial territory against others of their kind.

Only two cranes are native to North America--the whoopers and the sandhills. Both visit the Refuge in the wintertime, but they seldom occur in the same habitat unless they simultaneously forage for food in a recently burned oak thicket. The whoopers seldom stray from the tidal flats. The sandhills prefer the open prairies and grain fields of the interior.

On the Aransas whooping cranes are generally seen only at great distance across the tidal flats. They can be recognized by their large size, rump bustle, gleaming white plumage and deliberate, long stride. When they take to the air the black wingtips become evident.

Any good bird guide will depict features which are usually not apparent in the field: the red skin on the crown and cheeks; the coarse black feathers at the corners of the mouth; the straight, rather heavy olive-gray bill and the fierce yellow eye; the dusky legs and huge feet.

Male and female can be distinguished only by subtle differences in size and behaviour. An adult male will stand just short of five feet tall, weigh about 16 pounds and spread his wings an impressive seven-and-a-half feet from tip to tip.

First-year cranes lack the red skin on the head and their body plumage is grayish-white heavily suffused with pinkish-cinnamon. By the time the juvenile birds are ready to make their first northbound journey their body feathers are nearly white but the neck and head are still patched with cinnamon. When they make their second trip south they will look like the adults.

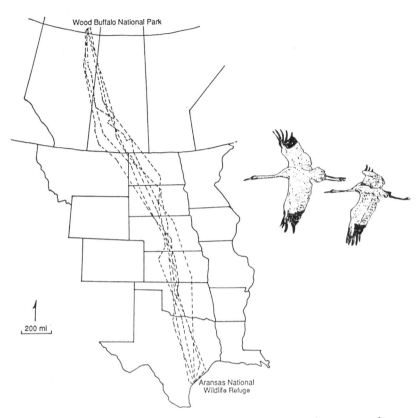

Figure 13 Migration routes of whooping cranes bearing radio transmitters, 1981-83.

Whooping cranes are ordinarily on the Aransas Refuge from mid-October through mid-April. At the end of this wintering interval they begin their northward journey, not simultaneously as one flock but over a period of several weeks as family groups, single birds and small aggregations.

Depending on the weather and with stops to rest and feed, the birds traverse the Great Plains of the United States and cross the international border into Saskatchewan, Canada. The paired adults push on with grim determination to a far corner of Wood Buffalo National Park, an 11-million acre wilderness of bogs and black spruce located in the Northwest Territories just south of Great Slave Lake and only 400 miles from the Arctic Circle. Nonbreeding whoopers usually leave the Refuge a bit later than the breeding birds, so they arrive tardily in Canada and scatter more irregularly across the wilderness. It generally takes the cranes three to four weeks to complete their 2600 mile trip from Texas.

By early May most pairs of adult whooping cranes will be brooding two large brown-flecked eggs atop bulky platforms of rotting marsh vegetation. Hatching occurs in early June. Although both eggs normally hatch, the older chick so dominates the younger one in the severe early competition for food and attention that usually only the dominant chick survives to leave the nest. Occasionally twins are raised.

Within a few days of hatching the downy, knobby-kneed chick is able to accompany its parents through the tangled muskeg environment. Although the adults carefully tend their charge, chickhood is a hazardous time. Dry years diminish the food supply and encourage predation by wolves. Severe weather is always a threat in far northern latitudes, especially to chicks that have hatched earlier or later than usual. Occasionally young birds are permanently disabled while learning to manipualte their long wings among the spruce and tamarack snags. But if all goes well, the rusty-colored juvenile will be nearly as large as its parents by late September, and it will be ready for its first flight to Texas.

During September and early October the whooping cranes gather to fatten on the grain fields and marshes in southern Saskatchewan. Then, when their hormones and weather sense tell them that the time is right, they lift off. They wing south, cruising at an altitude of 2,000 feet, occasionally soaring on rising thermals to 6,000 feet, and covering about 200 miles on a typical day that begins at midmorning and continues until dusk. Rarely, the birds push on into the night. They set down for food and rest, not at traditional sites but opportunistically--in remote and open wetlands, preferably within easy distance of grain fields. Strong headwinds can ground the birds for days on end, and they will hold up voluntarily if they discover a rich food source. Although the journey may take them more than two weeks, the cranes often complete the 1500 mile trip from Saskatchewan to Texas in about seven good flight days.

Not all make it. The fall migration coincides with the waterfowl hunting season and whoopers still occasionally fall to errant guns. (Happily, no Refuge crane has been shot since 1968.) Birds are routinely killed or maimed when they strike powerlines. Some weaken and simply disappear enroute. A few apparently get lost or are untracked by passing flights of sandhill cranes. The juveniles are especially prone to all of these hazards. In 1984, the cranes brooded 29 nests in Wood Buffalo; only 15 juveniles made it to the Aransas Refuge.

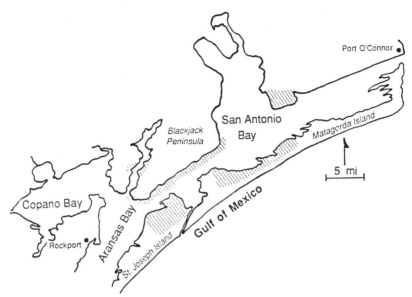

Figure 14 Whooping crane winter range on the Refuge and
   vicinity, 1984-85. (Data compiled by T.V. Stehn and E.F.
   Johnson.)

Except for their first weeks of life, it is the several weeks of
their semiannual migration that are most life-threatening
for the whooping cranes. Little wonder, then, that there are
anxious eyes watching the sky each October and on into
December on the Aransas Refuge, and sighs of relief or frowns
of concern according to how many of the great white birds
finally touch down.

While on the Aransas whooping cranes engage in three
primary activities: maintaining territories, feeding and,
finally, getting themselves emotionally prepared for their
spring migration.

The plot of ground staked out and defended by each pair of
adult birds is critical to the social organization of the cranes
on their wintering ground. It is customary for the same pair of
these long-lived birds to occupy the same territory year after
year, and when vacancies develop by attrition of one or both
members, other individuals move in to carry on the tradition.
When young birds form pairs at 3-5 years of age they are prone
to try to carve out a territory near that of their parents.

This tendency to cluster has led to progressive congestion
along the favored east shore tidal flats of the Refuge, where
some 15 adjacent whooper territores are currently strung out
between Mustang Lake and Dunham Point. Whoopers also

Figure 15 Whooping crane winter territories on Blackjack
   Peninsula, 1984-85. (Data compiled by T.V. Stehn and E. F.
   Johnson.)

routinely set up shop on the lee sides of St. Joseph and
Matagorda islands, and since 1971, pairs have established
themselves along the shores of St. Charles Bay and at Welder
Point on the north shore of San Antonio Bay.

Since their territory usually provides them with all of the
amenities of life--food, brackish water to drink, shallow
water to stand in at night, the security of an open vista by day-
-the resident cranes spend most of their time within its
confines. They seek the shelter of oak mottes only during
severe windy weather. After their Canadian upbringing
outright cold does not bother them.

Territorial sizes vary. On prime crane real estate along the
east shore, they average about 300 acres. On the less
frequented barrier islands a pair of birds may lay claim to
over 1000 acres. The pairs of cranes also defend nesting
territories of about 800 acres in Canada.

In a whooper's eyes the social boundary of its territory is
just as important as the physical resources within the
territory. There is considerable overlap between adjacent
territories and the cranes appear to rather enjoy engaging in

squabbles over their self-proclaimed fencelines. Indeed it seems that considerable suitable habitat goes unused simply because the cranes prefer to be where they can interact with others of their kind.

It is the adult male who most belligerently defends the territory, although the female joins in on occasion. Both birds are more defensive if they have a juvenile with them. The juvenile takes no part in the territorial business.

What defensive tactics do whooping cranes use? First, they watch members of adjacent groups constantly. (They haughtily ignore other species of birds and other forms of wildlife in general.) Invasion of the overlap zone often elicits a series of shrill warning bugles from the resident male. He may then fly toward the interlopers, followed by the rest of his family. The residents commonly settle near the invaders, and the latter may then retire thus ending the encounter.

Occasionally feeding cranes of adjacent groups wander close to each other along a boundary line. Then opposing males confront each other and stand bill-to-bill, glaring balefully. After this tense stare-down the two separate, each going into his own bailiwick, without ever actually trading blows.

So a whooper's territorial defense is all bark and no bite, but their bickering is nonetheless critical to the well-being of these very communal creatures. It is also of practical concern to Refuge personnel who now perceive that there is a social as well as a physical carrying capacity for the whoopers. They project that the Refuge and its immediate environs should be capable of supporting a wintering population of forty pairs of contented, quibbling whooping cranes.

From sunrise to sunset, with scant time out to preen, dawdle or territorialize, the whooping cranes stalk the tidal flats with giant strides in a never-ending search for food. The birds arrive ravenous in the fall and even in bountiful years they never seem sated. Both parents feed the young, but the female devotes much more time to the chore and she is also the youngster's tutor. Although they still beg and never turn down a handout, by mid-winter most juveniles are capable of catching their own fare.

Because whooping cranes are opportunistic feeders, their diet varies somewhat with the season, the tides and the productivity of each year. In general the Refuge provides more animal than vegetable food to their liking. Exceptionally dry or wet years are often lean ones for the whoopers because these conditions alter the salt content of their favorite tidal flat hunting grounds and thus reduce the abundance of their prey.

What do whooping cranes eat while they are on the Aransas Refuge? Answer: just about any creature they can grasp and swallow, from water moccasins and rice rats to sheepshead minnows and saltmarsh snails; along with a constant nibble at succulent greenery.

The more pertinent questions are: what do whoopers prefer to eat and what do they rely on as staples in their diet? In 1952, Robert Porter Allen published a list of 42 known food items for the Refuge cranes and he tabulated the results of an extensive fecal analysis.   More recent investigations have supplemented his results and corroborated his conclusions.

The food list of animal prey now includes 3 kinds of marine worms, 2 kinds of shrimp and 2 of crabs, 2 kinds of crayfish, an assortment of wetland adult and larval insects, 6 kinds of marine clams and 3 of marine snails, 3 kinds of marine fishes, one kind of frog and 2 kinds of snakes. The plant list is composed of a trace of manatee-grass (a shallowly submerged marine plant), the greenery of 3 upland grasses, the rootstocks of 2 shoreline grasses and of 2 sedges, the bulb of one kind of lily, the green sprouts of 2 tidal flat forbs, the fruits of one tidal flat shrub and the leaves of another, and the acorns of 3 kinds of oaks.

From this varied menu Allen drew some interesting conclusions. First, the cranes rely more on animal than on plant material. Second, among the animal prey, 7 kinds can be regarded as staples: one of the marine worms, the mud shrimp, the pistol shrimp, the blue crab, 2 kinds of razor clams and one of the crayfishes. All but the crayfish are denizens of the brackish tidal flats. Upshot: if you would save the crane, save the tidal flats.

From this list of prime animal prey the blue crab stands out as the creature taken with greatest frequency and in greatest bulk. Later investigators have shown that while the cranes

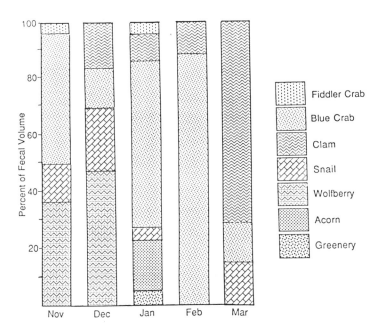

Figure 16 Winter diet of the whooping cranes based on the analysis of 171 fecal samples collected on the Refuge in 1984-85. (Data from Refuge files.)

take blue crabs throughout their stay on the Refuge, they rely on them most heavily during the winter months. During the low tides of springtime the birds shift their attention to the worms, mud shrimp and razor clams. When warmer weather brings out the fiddler crabs, the cranes, true to their opportunistic nature, begin to gobble up fiddlers. Dictum: to keep the cranes healthy, keep the marine crustacean food chains healthy.

It is of interest that although whooping cranes feed in and around the tidal flats, they are not notable fishermen. They can and do take shallow water fishes (mostly mullet and killifishes), but they are more adept at capturing crustaceans and molluscs. Apparently they are unable to routinely catch the delectable brown shrimp which commonly appear in their brackish water haunts.

The only native plant materials whoopers are reported to take in significant quantity are the bright red fruits of the wolfberry and acorns from any of the several species of oaks. The wolfberry grows on the tidal flats, and the birds pluck the fruits directly from the low branches, especially in the fall. Cranes invade the oak thickets after a prescribed burn has cleared the site of dense foliage. Then they avidly pick acorns off the ground. In addition, we have seen these birds graze for prolonged periods on the tidal flats, plucking the succulent leaves of saltwort.

Whooping cranes also readily feed on domestic grain, and this has been provided to them on the Refuge in lean years. They prefer corn. Captive whoopers thrive on a mixture of corn, chicken mash, shrimp, ground horsemeat, hard boiled egg and wheat germ oil.

By March the cranes' hormones have begun their springtime surge and one manifestation is the birds' dancing behaviour. The male is influenced first. The female becomes more enthusiastic as the weeks go by. Juveniles rarely take part, and in fact they seem totally disinterested in the goings-on.

Although frequently referred to as a courtship display, the dance of a pair of cranes has not been observed to culminate in copulation. On the Refuge at least, it seems to be an early release for the rising emotional tension leading up to the coming spring migration and nesting season. Certainly the mutual display serves to strengthen the lifetime bond between partners.

The brief dance generally begins with the male when he abruptly starts to pump his neck and crouch low to the ground. As he swings toward the female he engages in a variety of pirouettes and stiff-legged, flapping leaps. The while his pretty white bustle is unfurled and he may arch his neck and point his beak skyward. Sometimes he bugles. The female may appear to ignore her consort, but she is eventually enticed to complement his behaviour. For perhaps a minute or so the two large birds engage in their ancient and mystical *promenade a deux* on the tidal flat. Then they suddenly break off and return to their incessant search for food.

In March the staunch territoriality among the cranes weakens somewhat, and the birds are obviously restless. Then in late March, when the daylength is right, the southeast winds pick up and all of the environmental cues of springtime are strong, something clicks inside the whoopers and the first group hauls out. Few by few the rest follow. Soon they are all gone and in the evident vaccuum they leave behind we can only wish Godspeed to these great white birds-of-passage.

How are the whooping cranes faring? The best answer is: precariously, but with the same determination on the part of both man and beast that has seen them slowly increase over the past half-century.

As of January, 1985, there were 150 whooping cranes alive on earth. Of these, 115 were wild birds and 84 of them belonged to the Wood Buffalo flock which winters on the Aransas Refuge. (In December, 1986, the Aransas flock finally topped the 100 mark.) But we must put these numbers in perspective.

The whooping crane population probably enjoyed its heyday 10,000 years ago when the last of the Pleistocene glaciers were breaking up and creating vast expanses of open wetlands in North America. The birds then ranged from the high Canadian latitudes to central Mexico and from the Rocky Mountains to the Atlantic.

With the glaciers gone their favored habitat began to shrink and so did the population of birds. Early on, the whooping crane became a relict species--one not necessarily marked for immediate extinction, but certainly one destined to cling perilously to a withering habitat. By act of Nature, the cranes were already in ecological trouble.

In early historical times whooping cranes still numbered in the thousands. They mainly wintered along the Atlantic and Gulf coasts, especially in Louisiana. The principal nesting area spread from the pothole prairies of Iowa north through similar habitat in Canada. Each spring the birds streamed north along several traditional flyways. There also existed a nonmigratory resident population that nested in Louisiana.

From the beginning, wherever men and cranes met the cranes lost out. As Allen dryly observed, "As the human population curve goes up, the Whooping Crane curve goes down." Hunting for food and sport; shooting in the grain fields to save the crop; draining of wetlands; grazing and tilling of prairie lands; collection of eggs; plus every form of pioneer thoughtlessness and wantonness: all contributed to the rapid annihilation of the whoopers.

Allen reckoned that between 1850-1920, over 90% of the whooping crane population was unceremoniously wiped out. Certainly the statistics are grim:

1850-crane eggs going for $.50 each and skins for $2.

1877-cranes common winter migrants from Houston to Brownsville and inland onto the prairies and into the grasslands of the Texas Panhandle; popular winter game birds.

1894-wintering cranes reduced throughout their Texas range; entire population probably about 1,000; last migratory whooper nest recorded in the U.S., in Iowa.

1912-about 200 whooping cranes in the world.

1918-about 50 whoopers left; Louisiana migrants shot out; only wintering sites at King Ranch and Blackjack Peninsula; nonmigrant Louisiana population much reduced.

1922-about 35 migrant whooping cranes left; last known crane nest in Canada until the discovery of the Wood Buffalo site in 1954.

1924-Last whoopers seen in the Rio Grande Valley of Texas.

1936-Last whoopers seen on upper Texas coast.

1937-King Ranch migrants gone; Blackjack population down to 18; nonmigrant Louisiana group probably no more than a dozen--about 30 cranes in all.

We have already recounted the founding of the Aransas National Wildlife Refuge in 1937. It should now be evident that for the whooping cranes, the Refuge came during the waning minutes of their eleventh hour.

It is also worth noting that the Aransas is not really prime whooper habitat at all. The cranes prefer a wetter, more heavily vegetated searim terrain. But Blackjack Peninsula did have the one thing the cranes needed most--a respite from human harrassment. That coveted isolation gave them their chance.

Still the birds faded. A hurricane in 1940 was the beginning of the end for the small Louisiana flock. The Texas whoopers dipped to an all-time low of 15 migrants on the Refuge in the winter of 1941.

In 1945, the USFWS and the National Audubon Society began the concerted effort to save the whooping crane which continues today. The progress of the wintering flock on the Aransas is plotted in the accompanying graph.

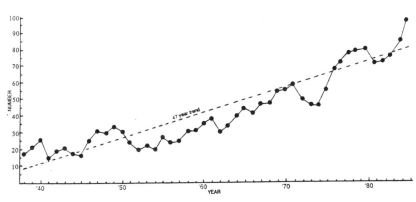

Figure 17 The number of whooping cranes wintering on the Refuge has increased steadily from 1937 to 1985.

We return to the guarded term "precarious" to describe the current whooper population. One hundred and fifty individuals is hardly a safe margin for a large, migratory social bird which reproduces relatively slowly. Yet, the wild Wood Buffalo flock seems healthy and able to hold its own. Many of these birds wear colored leg bands and a few have hauled radio transmitters along their flyway. Both devices have yielded valuable data which are being applied as management tools.

The USFWS maintains a small captive breeding colony of whooping cranes in Maryland, and in co-operation with the Canadian Wildlife service it has induced wild sandhill cranes to rear whooper chicks at the Grays Lake National Wildlife Refuge in Idaho. Thus, there is some insurance against a catstrophe eliminating the remaining whooping cranes at a single blow.

The keys to the continued survival of whooping cranes in the wild are precisely those which Robert Porter Allen stressed over thirty years ago: habitat and public education. As it always has been, the choice is ours.

Certainly you will want to see a whooping crane while you are on the Aransas Refuge. Everyone does, and many people come great distances for no other purpose. How can you promote your chance of success?

First, plan to be here when the cranes are here: November-March to be sure. Second, bring a good pair of binoculars.

After you register at the Visitors Center, observe the many whooper displays and get the birds' appearance and size firmly in mind. Next, ask at the desk about the current status of the whoopers. You will likely be directed to the Observation

Tower. Occasionally special guided tours are conducted to other observation points. Ask about arrangements.

Be highly suspicious of all white birds you see enroute to the Tower. Whooping cranes seldom use this portion of the shoreline. (In 1986-87, perhaps due to the mounting congestion in the wintering whooper population, a family of birds did spend several weeks on Heron Flats.) Check a bird book to rule out great and snowy egrets, white pelicans, white ibis and snow geese.

From atop the Tower scan the tidal flats with your binoculars or one of the public use telescopes. Remember, whoopers demand privacy so look afar. Search for anything white out in the vegetation. If you do not initially mistake one of the white signs that marks the Refuge boundary for a whooper, you are probably not looking far enough!

Then work by elimination: large (compare with something of known size to get proper perspective); all-white; rump bustle; long legs; neck straight or gently curved (never folded); deliberate movements; usually paired, occasionally accompanied by an orange-tinted juvenile (never in a flock). In flight (not often) check for the combination of extended neck and legs and black wing tips.

If everything concurs, you probably have your whooping crane.

Commercial tour boats which depart from Copano Bay offer a money-back guarantee of seeing a whooping crane. Although the four-hour cruises are not sponsored by the Aransas National Wildlife Refuge, you can get scheduling information and directions at the Visitors Center or from the Chamber of Commerce in Rockport.

The Endangered Ones

An endangered species is one which is so rare that it is judged to be in imminent danger of extinction. A threatened species is one which, although it may still be moderately abundant, is experiencing a rapid decline in numbers. An endangered species is in deep trouble; a threatened species is clearly headed that way. Both need help.

The national refuge system plays a clear and vital role in the sustaining effort. Although diminished species vary in their ability to recoup, the single best remedy is usually the provision of adequate suitable habitat and relative freedom from harrassment by people. A wildlife refuge provides sanctuary. Protective legislation coupled with sufficient public education can generate the atmosphere for quelling significant human disturbance of wildlife. Given such an even break, most beleaguered species begin to recover.

In all of the accounts which follow we shall necessarily be concerned with population numbers--always too few; occasionally perilously few; for some as far as the local area is concerned, a final extirpation to wistful memory.

Although its degree of involvement varies (in several cases being of historical significance only) the Aransas National Wildlife Refuge is implicated with 16 endangered and three threatened animal species on the current USFWS list.

The **whooping crane** has been dealt with in Chapter 5.

Brown Pelican

In the early decades of this century the Texas Coast supported a healthy population of about 5,000 brown pelicans. By the mid-'30's this number was reduced to 1,000. The decline was caused by wanton shooting and nest destruction by hunters and fishermen who were mistakenly convinced that the pelicans were serious competitors for game fish.

Then in the late 1950's the remnant Texas population of brown pelicans went into catastrophic decline until, by the mid-60's, only some 50 individuals remained. Most of these birds either did not try to nest or experienced nesting failure. The cause: poisoning by organochlorine pesticides washed into the bays from surrounding agricultural fields and concentrated in the bodies of the pelicans' favorite food fish, the Gulf menhaden. The toxin upset the birds' normal breeding cycle and caused them to lay thin-shelled eggs. When a brooding pelican lifted off the nest it inadvertently crushed its fragile clutch.

In 1972, only a single brown pelican was raised on the entire Texas Coast. The next year the species was placed on the endangered list.

Following legislation which curtailed pesticide abuse, the brown pelicans mounted a slow recovery on the Texas Coast. During the mid-70's birds moving up from Mexico managed to repopulate some of their old Texas haunts.

By 1983, two thriving nesting colonies of brown pelicans had been re-established. One of these was on an islet in San Antonio Bay just off the shoreline of the Aransas Refuge. The other was on an island 35 miles south of the Refuge in Corpus Christi Bay. A grand total of 96 nests produced 170 young in that year.

By 1984, all nesting birds had moved to the island in Corpus Christi Bay where they fledged 230 young. At the moment, the Texas population of brown pelicans is on the upswing.

One of the real delights of birding is watching a brown pelican feeding. The bird flaps along with a slow measured wingbeat while watching the shallow bay 50 feet below. When it spots a menhaden or mullet, the pelican goes into an abrupt half-roll, partly folds its wings and hurtles down like a banking divebomber. It smacks into the water bill-first and briefly disappears from view in a cascade of foam. The bird is buffered from the impact with the water by a special layer of air sacs beneath its skin, and these same air bags rapidly bob the pelican back to the surface when its brief dive is completed.

As soon as its head is submerged, the pelican opens its bill. Over two gallons of water pour into the gular pouch, and if the strike is successful the prey fish will be drawn in as well. While riding the surface like a cork, the bird presses its heavy pouch to its breast to drain the water out of its gaped bill.

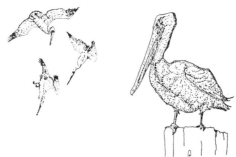

Then with an adroit backward toss of its head, it swallows the fish.

The pelican then wheels to face into the wind and labors to get airborne again. If it is finished hunting it may set out for a favorite bankside perch, skimming along with wingtips barely clearing the water.

Brown pelicans begin to congregate on their nesting islands in February. The nest is a large ragged basin of dead twigs and branches laid amid the shin-high vegetation of bushy sea-oxeye and clumps of prickly pear cacti. Nests are crowded to within pecking distance of each other.

The uncommonly ugly, leathery-skinned hatchlings appear in April and May. They grow rapidly on gullet loads of semidigested fish, and they fledge in July and August. As with all birds, nestlings lead a hazardous existence. Everything from tidal surges and an infestation of ticks to lethal encounters with cactus spines have plagued Texas fledgling brown pelicans.

Because both nests and young are defenseless, the pelicans are forced to use the offshore islets to escape predation by coyotes, raccoons and skunks; but they remain vulnerable to human disturbance, whether malicious or inadvertent. The National Audubon Society guards the islands against trespass during the breeding season, but few people realize that even a close pass in a boat can flush the tending adults and open the entire budding generation to one of the most dangerous elements in its environment--the direct rays of the broiling Texas sun.

You can reasonably anticipate seeing a brown pelican at any time of the year on the Aransas Refuge, though their numbers are usually highest in late summer. Many birds drift southward in the wintertime, but 65 were counted during the Christmas census in January, 1986.

From the vantage of the Observation Tower, work all pilings and channel markers with your binoculars in search of perching individuals. Also check any exposed oyster reefs in

San Antonio Bay. Stop at the picnic area and scan the broad expanse of sky over the bay for fishing birds.

Attwater's Greater Prairie Chicken

This southernmost grouse once ranged across the Gulf coastal prairie from southwestern Louisiana to the Nueces River in Texas. In a peak year a million birds occupied the prime mid- and tall grass habitat, with greatest concentrations on the upper and central Texas coast. Their troubles began with the arrival of the earliest white settlers. Prairie chickens were great sport to flush and shoot and they made delicious tablefare. During the latter half of the nineteenth century they were shot by the wagonload.

In 1937, a census showed the population of prairie chickens reduced to 8,700 birds in several widely scattered colonies. Hunting them was forbidden, but by that time a more formidable danger was stalking the birds. Habitat destruction in the form of row crops, grazing stock, brush invasion, indiscriminate burning, roadways and--most recently and most relentlessly, residential and industrial development-- uprooted and overlaid the grasses and shattered the isolation of the prairie habitat.

Hemmed in and harrassed at every turn, the Attwater population went into a tailspin until there were only about 1,000 left in 1967, when the species was placed on the endangered list.

For the past two decades the Attwater population has hovered around 1,500 birds scattered in woefully vulnerable colonies in eight coastal counties in Texas. Over half of these colonies reside on private ranchland near the Aransas Refuge in Aransas, Refugio and Goliad counties.

In 1972, the Attwater Prairie Chicken National Wildlife Refuge was established for the species in Colorado County. In 1986, a second Federal refuge, in Victoria County, was being considered.

In 1967, the Tatton Unit was donated to the Aransas National Wildlife Refuge, and with it came an endowment of about 30 resident prairie chickens. The Tatton is managed exclusively for the benefit of these birds. The rollercoaster fortunes of the Tatton colony can be traced on the accompanying graph.

It is in the courtship behaviour of the males that the Attwater displays its most grouse-like and most fascinating attribute. The ritual begins in the cold predawn in February when several cocks silently materialize in a fog-wrapped

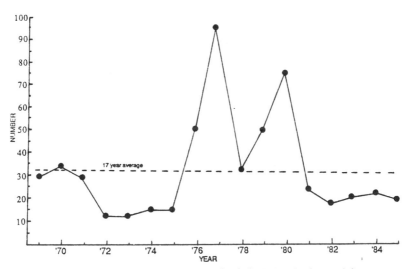

Figure 18 Population estimates of adult Attwater's prairie chickens on the Tatton Unit of the Refuge.

short grass clearing. This same hallowed spot may have been the stage for the coming drama for untold generations of these shy, tradition-bound social birds. If the courting site is destroyed, the demoralized colony may scatter and never regroup.

Each male selects his own small patch of ground. Then, when his mood begins to build, he stretches his neck out rigidly, erects the twin horns of stiff feathers behind his head and spreads his tail in a rich brown fan over his rump. He leans stiffly forward, extends his wings to the ground and suddenly sprints ahead several feet while maintaining his comical, humped posture.

He stops abruptly and commences to dance in place with his rapidly stamping feet creating an audible staccato and the primary feathers of his wings scraping the ground.

At the height of this brief shuffle the cock bows low until his chin brushes the grass stubble. With a few quick pumping motions he inflates his gular air sac into a pair of huge orange-yellow blisters on the sides of his neck. Then he brings his act to a rapid an eerie crescendo when he emits a melodious, somewhat melancholy and rather ventriloquil "whooo-LOO-wooo".

This is the so-called booming, a sound which has been aptly likened to that produced by blowing strongly across the top of a large jug. The gular sac serves as a resonating chamber which amplifies and modulates the call.

There are few more enthralling experiences than that of hearing the haunting moans from a group of fired-up Attwaters drifting through the mists of a dark and boundless prairie.

The entire display is over in 15 seconds, but it will be repeated many times before the rising sun drives the birds to cover. When the frenzy is full upon them adjacent cocks square off and flap and spar with each other; or they chase each other about while producing a variety of cackling sounds. This is all ritualized bluff. No blood is drawn, but a great deal of pent-up energy is released.

Eventually a hen or two appears on the edge of the arena. They seem totally disinterested in the goings-on, but finally they copulate with one or several of the more vigorous cocks. They then quit the field.

The booming peaks in March and tapers off in April. The hens hide their clutches of olive-colored eggs in grass clumps and brood them alone. Hatching occurs in April and May. The precocious chicks follow the hen almost immediately. In six weeks or so the survivors of the brood set out on their own.

For the remainder of the year prairie chickens lead cryptic lives and only occasionally burst above the grass clumps on whirring wings before they level off in a smooth glide and abruptly drop back into the safety of their grassy retreat.

You almost certainly will not see an Attwater's prairie chicken on the Aransas Wildlife Refuge. The few resident birds stay well concealed in their Tatton sanctuary.

At this low point in their history, it should be reward enough to simply gaze at good chicken habitat and know that there are still a few of the birds valiantly hanging on there. This you can do by driving along State 35 between its junction with FM774 and Salt Creek. The Tatton Unit borders the highway on the east. Simply look out your car window, muse about the way things used to be and the way they have become, and feel privileged to share in the secret that this is still Attwater country.

Bald Eagle

There are about 15,000 bald eagles in the United States today, only a fragment of the population of colonial times.

Despite being chosen as our national symbol, the eagle was not accorded either respect or protection in the field. It was commonly shot on sight, not to satisfy any particular grudge, but simply because it was a large and showy member of the generally maligned birds-of-prey. When favored nest trees were felled the tradition-bound eagles often quit an area rather than choose alternate sites. And the nesting birds demand isolation as well as security. If disturbed during incubation they abandon their eggs. Waterfront development, recreational boating and a tangle of high voltage power lines despoiled the eagles' hunting grounds. So, the big birds began to quietly fade away.

The DDT-decades were dark ones for all American wildlife, and their impact was heaviest at the top of the food web where the final consumers exist in relatively small natural populations and unwittingly feed upon prey loaded with concentrated quantities of toxic chemicals. Bald eagles belong in the highest trophic echelon, and they paid the price for their lofty status. Only the birds which nested in the unsullied wilderness in Alaska and Canada escaped the decimation.

Today the bald eagle is listed as endangered in 43 of the coterminous United States (including Texas) and threatened in the remaining five.

There are actually two races of bald eagles and Texas hosts both. The northern race nests in the far north and sporadically moves south to feed during the wintertime. The southern race scatters northward to feed during the summertime and returns south to nest in the fall. Therefore, from September through December several hundred bald eagles move into Texas, some as winter visitors and others as winter breeders. A few of the southern birds are resident all year.

In 1971, the Texas Parks and Wildlife Department began keeping a close watch on all nests of southern bald eagles in the state. For a decade they could find only 5-7 active nests each year. The number went up to 15 in 1981, and to 17 in 1985. Most nests were located in strips of dense forest along the lower reaches of rivers in the central coastal prairie. There are several active nests within a 50-mile radius of the Aransas Wildlife Refuge, all sequestered on private property.

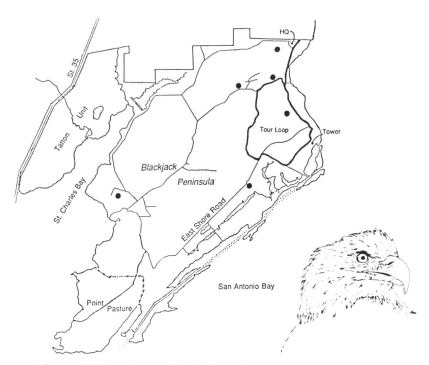

Figure 19 Nest sites of the bald eagle on the Refuge.

Between 1971-85, Texas bald eagles fledged 130 known young, so they are doing their part in a comeback effort.

Since the Aransas Refuge was established, bald eagles have attempted to nest within its confines on 26 recorded occasions: 13 times during the 1940's (including an annual record of 3 nests in 1944); 7 times during the 1950's; 5 times in the 1960's; and once in the 1970's. The last documented nesting was in 1971. The 26 nesting attempts occurred at six different sites on the Refuge.

Since bald eagles are long lived birds that mate for life and frequently reuse traditional nest sites, the Aransas records probably cover the activity of a small number of adults. When these died, there was no ready recruitment from the devastated local population. The persistent current nesting vacancy may be a consequence of increased human activity on and around the Refuge. Eagles have never tried to use the artificial nesting poles that were erected for them at three sites on the Aransas.

The annual narratives compiled by the Aransas staff contain scattered information of interest about bald eagles. Their huge platforms of sticks are routinely refurbished and lined with shredded grass in December. Favored sites have been atop tall live oaks. The eaglets are in the nest during the coldest months of January and February and they finally fledge in early April.

Food items found in the nests generally confirm the eagles' diet of fish and waterfowl: flounders, mullet, redfish; a white pelican, American coots, pintails, scaups and numerous grebes; swamp rabbits and cottontails. The remains of one armadillo may have come from carrion. One adult eagle was seen in flight carrying a struggling scaup duck in its talons. Another was observed over Dunham Bay dive bombing an osprey in an apparent attempt to make it drop its fish.

The records clearly reveal the hazards with which nesting eagles must contend. On two occasions tree limbs broke beneath the heavy accumulations of sticks, thus destroying the sites. In 1940, a pair of eagles abandoned their nest when an oil well blew up in flames nearby. There are several observations of eggs and no subsequent hatchlings, and many of hatchlings which never fledged. The causes of such failures could only be vaguely ascribed to predation. In one instance a half-eaten eaglet had apparently been attacked by its two nestmates.

In January, 1941, an unknown predator ate the eggs in an eagle nest and precipitated the only Refuge record of a renesting attempt. The same pair of adults had week-old eaglets in another nest at the end of March.

You can most reasonably aspire to see a bald eagle on the Aransas Refuge during fall migration. Although the birds are never common, if one is in residence it often has a favored perch and hunting ground. Ask at the Visitors Center.

Otherwise, simply keep an eye peeled throughout your visit. Even a glimpse of a fast-flying bald eagle is a thrill. And if you see a pair engaged in aerial courtship or an individual deftly pluck a mullet out of Mustang Lake, you have a lifetime memory to cherish.

The adults are easy to identify, but check your bird book so that you can distinguish young birds (which lack the white head and neck) from other raptors. Both northern and southern bald eagles may visit the Refuge. They cannot be distinguished in the field except by the nesting activity of the more common southern race.

Peregrine Falcon

Two races of peregrines occur in Texas. The American peregrine is a nonmigratory form which occupies a few mountain ranges in far West Texas. This is the bird which originally ranged the continent until it was extirpated east of the Mississippi River and severely reduced in the West during the DDT era. Its plight earned it endangered status and nationwide attention.

The Arctic peregrine is a migratory form that nests in the high North American tundra and in Greenland and winters in South America. The relative isolation of its nesting ground buffered the Arctic peregrine from the brunt of the pesticide onslaught, although migrating birds encountered contaminated prey. This race is currently listed as threatened.

It is the Arctic peregrine which passes across the Aransas Wildlife Refuge twice each year and occasionally drops off a wintering individual or two. Fall migrants generally appear from September through October and spring migrants from March through April. Because the peregrines prey heavily on shorebirds, they prefer to sweep along the open barrier islands, and most Refuge sightings have been on the Matagorda Unit.

Seeing a peregrine falcon stoop (dive on its prey) ranks as one of the most thrilling of wildlife observations. The drama may begin on Matagorda Island with a small flight of blue-winged teal batting steadily upwind against a brisk October norther. They are enroute to a freshwater depression on the central part of the island. The teal do not see the speck in the sky above them, but the speck sees the teal.

The peregrine begins its long slanting descent on folded wing. It picks up speed rapidly, pumping its wings now and then for added thrust. By the time the speck has transformed into a feathered divebomber it is moving at an incredible 150 miles per hour and accelerating.

Finally the teal spot it, and they immediately scatter and plunge for cover. But one of them is already marked for doom.

With feet balled into hard fists, the peregrine strikes the teal hard in the neck and back. The duck crumples in midair amid an explosion of feathers. The falcon pulls out of its dive in a graceful arc, wheels and lightly touches down beside its shattered prey.

Migrating peregrines are seen now and then along the margins of San Antonio and St. Charles bays, but most sightings occur on Matagorda Island. Prime time is October; for the past several years about 20 birds have been seen in a routine sunrise survey during the first three weeks of that month.

Aplomado Falcon

According to early accounts this trim, medium-sized falcon was rather common in the virgin grasslands of South and West Texas. However, by the 1930's its numbers had declined drastically, and it has not been known to nest in the state for 45 years. It is now a noteworthy event when a transient individual edges across the Rio Grande from Mexico.

No single factor stands out to account for the disappearance of the resident aplomado falcons from Texas. Deterioration of the prairies certainly contributed. Brush encroachment probably interfered with the falcons' swift pursuit and midair capture of passerine birds and grasshoppers. The reduced crop of grass seeds and loss of ground cover surely caused a change in the abundance and diversity of favored prey species. Because aplomado falcons prefer to rear their young in the abandoned nests of other raptors, available nesting sites became scarce as all birds of prey fell before the multifarious inroads of advancing civilization. For a change, we cannot incriminate DDT for the simple reason that the aplomado falcons were already virtually gone before the pesticide era began. Today they range through suitable habitat in Mexico and into South America.

The Aransas Refuge lies on the northern periphery of scattered recent sightings of this species. There were several sightings on the Tour Loop in the early '70's. The Tatton Unit is regarded as prime aplomado habitat, and it is currently being considered as a release site for captive-bred birds.

Piping Plover

These uncommon little shorebirds do not stand out from the several other species which run in stop-and-go fashion along the bay margin and the mudflats. Their one unfortunate distinction is that they are determined to nest nowhere except on isolated, clean sandy beaches--precisely the sort of places that lure sunbathers, beachcombers, fishermen and waterfront developers. Result: piping plovers have declined drastically in numbers in the past decade. In 1985, they were listed as endangered in their main nesting territory around the Great Lakes, and they were given threatened status throughout the remainder of their range.

Piping plovers are uncommon residents on the Aransas. Consult your bird guide and work out the proper combination of back, leg and bill colors (appropriately adjusted for the season) and the degree of breast banding. Then find a mudflat alive with tiny birds, most of them probably too far away to tell front from rear. And enter the delightfully frustrating world of the birder on the Texas Coast.

Eskimo Curlew

This species was once as abundant as any other common shorebird, but by 1900 it was almost extinct, and today it remains one of the rarest birds in the world.

Eskimo curlews bred in the Canadian tundra and wintered in South America. They aggregated in Newfoundland and Labrador before launching on a nonstop flight down the Atlantic seaboard. In the spring the birds followed a more leisurely inland route which took them over Texas and up the Central Flyway to Canada.

Because the gregarious, twittering flocks of curlews were easy to shoot and because their plump breasts were regarded as epicurean fare, the birds were forced to run a gauntlet of recreational and commercial guns throughout their migration route.

Immense flocks of Eskimo curlews were eagerly anticipated across Texas each April during the 1870's. But the numbers dropped so drastically that the species was hovering on extinction by the turn of the century.

Three birds were seen on the central coast in 1905. There were no more sightings for forty years. Then two individuals were spotted on Galveston Island in 1945. (Imagine the stir in the birding world!) During subsequent years just enough confirmed sightings have been made to justify the hope that the Eskimo curlew is hanging on.

Three recent observations have been made in the Coastal Bend in 1950, 1963 and 1968. On April 27, 1950, the only verified observation of an Eskimo curlew was made on the Aransas Refuge.

Clearly you cannot anticipate seeing an Eskimo curlew on the Aransas, but just as clearly you can hope. So, be prepared. Watch the shorebirds during March and April. Check your bird book carefully to distinguish the relatively common long-billed curlew and the less common whimbrel.

If you are convinced that you have spotted an Eskimo curlew, do not disturb it. Call nearby birders to confirm your suspicion, and get a photograph if you can. Highball to the Visitors Center and get a member of the staff to verify your observation.

Gray Wolf

As far as Texas is concerned, the designation of the gray wolf as an endangered species came much too late. Although an occasional animal still wanders across the Rio Grande into far West Texas, there has been no breeding population in the state since the early 1920's.

It is uncertain whether gray wolves ever traversed Blackjack Peninsula in recent historical times. Their original range was in West and Central Texas. Abundant pioneer references to wolves are notably untrustworthy, since these commonly confuse the state's two native species of wolves with coyotes.

Red Wolf

There are no more wild red wolves in Texas, and it is unlikely that the few in captivity can ever be manipulated to alter that situation. The fact is lamentable because with the gray wolf gone, Texas is now destitute of wolves. There can be no more telling testimony that the state is no longer as wild and open as we like to think it is.

Red wolves were exquisite, rangy beasts, smaller than a gray wolf but larger than a coyote. A large male went to 60 pounds. They were not red but tawny, heavily suffused with gray and darkening to blackish over the shoulders and back. Their heads were distinctively wolfish: broad pale muzzle; slanted, almond-shaped eyes rimmed with pale eyebrow spots; heavy jaws. Red wolves had triangular facial outlines because they held their long ears cocked out at an angle rather than vertically like gray wolves and coyotes.

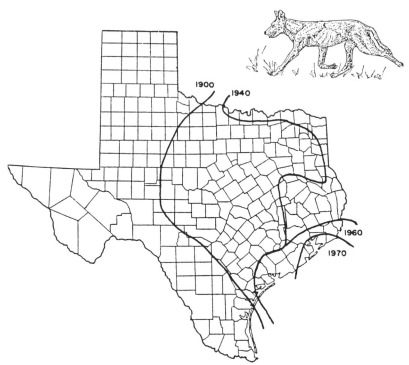

Figure 20 Historic range of the red wolf in Texas. Probably the state has no pure red wolves in the wild today.

These animals originally ranged in small packs of three to five individuals across the wooded eastern third of Texas and out onto the Coastal Prairie. They were primarily small game predators: swamp rabbits, cottontails, muskrats, rice rats, cotton rats, bobwhite quail, greater prairie chickens; and, after its introduction from South America, the nutria. They also took hogs, sheep and poultry when they had a chance.

But such petty stock pilferage was not the main reason that men turned against the red wolves. Rather, it was the simple fact that they were predators, meat-eaters, killers. Worse, they were *wolves* steeped in all of the venomous legend that Old World tales conveyed with that epithet.

Backed by such popular prejudice, men set themselves upon a relentless campaign of extermination which probably has no parallel for sheer determination and viciousness. Wolves were shot, trapped, poisoned, clubbed, maimed, trailed with dogs, spotted from airplanes, lured with chemicals and electronic devices, gassed in their dens, scalped for bounty money and skewered on barbed wire fences for show. Professional wolfers were respected members of society.

In 1915, the Federal government launched its predator control program with the intent of protecting livestock and game animals. Wolves were near the top of the want list and government trappers were the best in the grim trade. In the mid-1940's they began to use the potent poison called 1080 and the devilishly effective cyanide gun. By 1964, they had driven the red wolf into a small corner of its former range, and a new, more insidious menace was poised to finish the harried animal off.

Deforestation had for years been working against the red wolf and for the coyote. By the 1940's coyotes were moving eastward across the Blackland Prairie and into the cleared land. The more adaptable and elusive coyote was on the increase; the less adaptable and more gullible red wolf was on the decline. Wherever the two met in the zone of ecological disruption they tended to interbreed. Abundant coyote genes began to swamp rare wolf genes. By the 1970's there were only a few recognizably pure red wolves left in deep southeast Texas.

Finally, public sentiment did an about-face. In 1965, only a year after government trappers were taken off their trail, red wolves were finally recognized as being worth saving. They went on the endangered list in 1970.

For several years in the mid-1970's a concerted effort was made to save the wild remnant. The problem was more than one of scant numbers. It also involved protecting those precious few from a heavy infusion of coyote blood. It could not be done.

In desperation, captive stock was collected. Then, in 1980, everyone conceded that there was no point in going on. Sixty years of determined attack had won out. The red wolf in the wild was gone.

Red wolves were still moderately abundant on the central coast when the Aransas Refuge was established in 1937. But the Refuge was born during the heyday of the notion that predator control (=predator eradication) was an important means of conserving wild game species.

The first red wolf of record was trapped on Blackjack Peninsula in 1939. The onslaught was waged with customary zeal for the next quarter-century. During that time the resident trapper often drove over 40 miles to check his 50 steel traps and 70 cyanide "getters".

These trappers were skillful and meticulous men who worked long hours in the field, who grunted their satisfaction when they caught a pregnant wolf or a nursing female, who did their paperwork, weighed their catch and dutifully sent off skulls, hides and stomach contents to Washington. They had no reason whatsoever for not sleeping well after a good day's work. In hindsight, they did their job too well.

By 1960, there was a growing awareness of the vital role predators play in maintaining prey species--including game species--in harmony with their resource base. Mercifully and astutely, the predator control program was halted on the Aransas Refuge in 1963. Unfortunately, this was too late to save the red wolf.

In 1956, the skulls of six canids trapped on the Refuge were sent to Washington. Five were confirmed to be red wolves. The sixth was a large coyote. Between 1956-63, eighty-six more canids were taken. All looked more like coyotes than wolves. In 1971, seventeen canids were tranquilized, checked and released. All were large coyotes. The narrative report for 1972 provides the epitaph for the red wolf on the Refuge: "...a dismal fact looms larger than ever...the red wolf is gone from the Aransas."

So, the red wolf, along with its phantom voice and its long tireless stride, is gone forever from the Coastal Bend. We can only redeem ourselves if we have learned a lesson by its passing.

Jaguar
El tigre, largest cat of the Americas, is known from the Texas Gulf Coast both as Pleistocene fossils and from scattered early historical records. There is no documentation of this species from the Aransas Refuge, although one late Nineteenth Century reference mentions its occurrence in Aransas County.

Jaguars definitely used to thread their way through the dense brush of the Rio Grande Valley and the thick woods along water courses up the coast and on into the tangled vegetation of southeast Texas; but they were always scarce. Even in earliest times, every encounter with one of the great blotched cats was worthy of mention, so the pioneers' tales of jaguars reflect the animal's occurrence rather than its abundance.

It is doubtful if there has been a breeding population of jaguars in Texas in historical times. Displaced or restless old males set to wandering afar from their normal haunts in Mexico probably account for most sightings in the state.

There have been only two verified kills in Texas since 1900, the last in 1946.

Jaguars have everything going against them: large predators; stock killers; isolationists; thrilling adversaries; and the possessors of beautiful spotted coats. They well deserved the endangered status conferred upon them in 1972. They are in trouble even in the depths of their tropical strongholds.

Ocelot

Many people regard *el tigre chiquito* as the most appealing and beautiful of the native cats of Texas. It is about the size of a bobcat but with a better proportioned, lithe feline body and long tail. Its coat is tawny yellow overlaid with a soft pearl-gray opalescence and it is profusely ornamented with black spots, streaks, bars and blotches. The tail is marked with broken black rings. No two ocelots bear the same pattern. Unfortunately, men covet the pretty pelts.

Ocelots are creatures of the densest undergrowth and the dead of night. Because of their secretive habits and rarity, their presence is seldom suspicioned and sightings are few.

These little tiger cats were once moderately common in the dense brush of South Texas and the rugged portions of the southern Edwards Plateau, and they ranged up the coast into East Texas and beyond. Always, they drew back from civilization. The last time they were listed as "occasional" over most of their Texas range was about 1900.

Today ocelots are considered to be very rare in the vanishing South Texas brushlands. One was trapped on the Santa Ana Wildlife Refuge in 1967. Another was shot near Falcon Dam in 1971. A small population was discovered on and near the Laguna Atascosa National Wildlife Refuge in the 1970's. Two dozen sightings were made in deep South Texas between 1978-80. How many of these animals are residents and how many are immigrants from Mexico is not known.

Although ocelots live south through Central America to Paraguay, in 1972, the species was listed as endangered throughout its range.

One thing is certain about ocelots: they require the seclusion of thick undergrowth with its attendant prey fauna of rodents, cottontails and low-flying birds. The progressive disappearance of such habitat is the single most threatening aspect of ocelot ecology. When their cover goes the ocelots go.

Are there ocelots on the Aransas? No one knows for sure. There is no question that ocelots occurred in Aransas County in historical times.   In its original savannah aspect Blackjack Peninsula would not have been attractive to these spotted cats, but today the dense live oak thickets should be prime ocelot habitat.   However, the Refuge is not extensive enough to harbor more than a few pairs of these territorial creatures.

The interesting questions are whether ocelots can reside permanently and breed here, and whether occasional individuals can run the gauntlet of civilization which surrounds this island refugium and so bring fresh blood into a confined resident population.   The situation is tenuous at best.

Despite countless man-hours in the field and a recent live-trapping effort, Refuge personnel have never confirmed the presence of an ocelot on the Aransas.   However, in March of 1979, a pair of visitors gave a good description of such an animal which they saw while driving the Tour Loop.

So we can all hope.   It is part of the mystique of the Aransas Refuge that any time we clear a bend in a trail we just might find ourselves--for a fleeting instant--face to face with a shy spotted cat with huge brown eyes. Then it will vanish, and we will never be the same again.

Jaguarundi

This is surely the most enigmatic of the native cats of Texas. Indeed, it does not even look much like a cat.

A jaguarundi is a slab-sided, short-legged, long-tailed creature with a body a little larger than that of a large tom cat. It has an unusually small head with a flattened forehead, small rounded ears and a snub nose bordered by inconspicuous whiskers.   The yellow eyes are rather small and their uncatlike round pupils give the animal a somewhat treacherous expression.   The sinister aura is enhanced by the beast's nervous, slinking demeanor.

Both of the color phases, salt-and-pepper gray and a grizzled rusty-brown, may occur in the same litter.   In another departure from the feline mold, young jaguarundis develop the adult coloration directly without passing through the juvenile spotted pattern usual in young felines.

The low-slung, weasel-like body of *el leoncillo* is well adapted to threading its favored habitat of thick thornbrush. Here the animal creeps and glides with ease, moving by day and night in the perpetual gloom, stalking everything from packrats to chachalacas. The creature is so secretive that it is only seen by chance.   It is uncommonly difficult to trap and

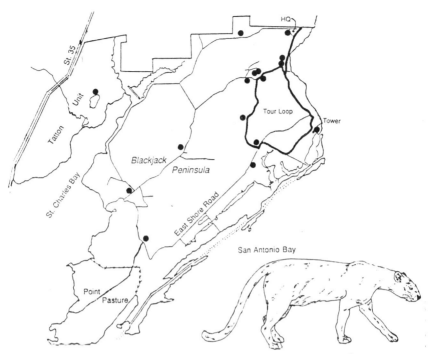

Figure 21 Reported sightings of jaguarundi on the Refuge
through 1985.

can only be flushed from its impenetrable haunts by specially
trained dogs.

The jaguarundi ranges from the proximity of the Rio Grande
in Texas southward to Argentina. Except for a thin coastal
extension, it apparently never occurred more widely in the
state. (There is now some evidence that the jaguarundi is
moving into the forests of East Texas.)

In both Texas and Mexico this retiring little cat is in trouble
for one main reason--the opening up of its brushy habitat for
agriculture. When fields and pastures replace natural
chaparral the entire native community disintegrates, and the
shy jaguarundi is among the first members to vanish. Then
we lose something unique that we were hardly ever even aware
we possessed.

Such wholesale environmental disruption has transformed
all but small isolated patches of the original brushland in
South Texas, so the jaguarundi well deserved the endangered
status conferred upon it in 1975.

Do jaguarundis occur on the Aransas Refuge? Happily, they
certainly do. How many individuals are present and whether
they constitute a viable resident population is not known.

Efforts to live-trap them have failed, as have trip wires attached to flash cameras. But every year since 1978, jaguarundis have been glimpsed by both visitors and staff.

So keep your eyes open, especially at dusk, for a slinking, long-tailed phantom darting from one live oak thicket to the next.

American Alligator

On any balmy afternoon two hundred years ago, hundreds of thousands of alligators of all sizes would have been lying criss-crossed and in heaps like so much driftwood along the rivers, sloughs and estuaries from South Carolina to South Texas. As they basked contentedly in the sunshine these great reptiles were carrying on a lethargic tradition that had been handed down unchanged among their stolid kind for over 200 million years. That insouciant habit was to change abruptly over the span of a few decades when the slaughter of these vulnerable beasts began.

Alligators were shot for idle sport, for meat and for the domestic use of their belly skins from the days of the earliest white explorers and settlers. Then in the 1850's, alligator leather became fashionable and the pace of the killing stepped up. By the 1870's commercial buyers and tanneries made the market hunting of alligators a profitable business and the era of the professional 'gator hunter was ushered in.

By the 1960's continued unregulated hunting had woefully reduced the American alligator in all portions of its range, and the creatures were further suffering a loss of habitat to waterfront development and the drainage of wetlands. In 1967, the reptile went onto the Federal endangered species list.

Relieved of harrassment, the alligator made a spectacular recovery, and by the mid-1970's the wild population had rebounded so well that it was reclassified as threatened. Within a few years 'gators had become so numerous that limited and carefully regulated hunting was allowed. Texas held its first alligator hunt in selected counties in September, 1984.

The alligator is one of the most popular species on the Aransas Refuge. It is a rare time when there are not at least a few visitors observing and photographing the several large 'gators which enjoy loafing at the edge of Thomas Slough beside the Visitors Center. Indeed, a fence had to be erected there to keep reptile and admirer safely separated. Another favorite observation spot is the pier overlooking Jones Lake.

What is the fascination of an alligator? It is a survivor from an alien, antediluvian era, and it exudes an aura of awesome power even when it lies unmoving on a sunlit mud bank. Somehow, alligators always manage to generate a thrill in "children of all ages".

Questions about alligators are endless.

How big do alligators get? About 19 feet, from tip of snout to tip of tail, but this is exceptional. Any alligator over 12 feet long is regarded as unusually large. One of the individuals which haunts Thomas Slough has been estimated to be a 13-footer, and another in Jones Lake must be at least that large. Most wild ones are in the 4-10 foot range. Hatchlings are eight inches long. They grow about a foot per year for the first five years. Then their growth rate slows, but these reptiles continue to grow throughout life. An alligator matures when it is six feet long. A 12-foot bull alligator may be 20 years old and weigh 400 pounds.

For idle amusement try this. Estimate the distance in inches between a 'gator's nostril and eye. This will be approximately equivalent to the animal's total length in feet. By using this handy ratio you can judge an alligator's size even when you can only see its head above the surface of the water.

How many alligators are there on the Refuge? Counts during the annual June census yield an estimate of 250.

How do alligators reproduce? They lay eggs. Mating on the Refuge occurs from April to June, nesting in June and July and hatching in August and September. The female alligator spends several days dragging bankside vegetation into a flat-topped mound about six feet across and two feet high in the center. She digs into the mound with her hind legs and deposits several dozen three-inch long leathery eggs in the cavity. When she covers these with rotting vegetation and mud the mound becomes a natural incubator.

Although the female attempts to guard her nest, raccoons and feral hogs manage to filch many alligator eggs. Hatchling alligators face a world of predators, ranging from raccoons and great blue herons to alligator gars and larger alligators.

What do alligators do in the wintertime? Very little. Being cold-blooded creatures, they become quite torpid, although they do not actually hibernate on the Aransas. They cease to feed. They enjoy soaking up the sunshine even on quite cool days. In really cold weather alligators remain submerged except to surface at infrequent intervals for a breath of air. Alligators can survive being frozen in ice for brief periods, but the resultant stress often causes them to succumb to respiratory disease weeks later.

Do alligators make any sounds? They certainly do. During the mating season the bull 'gator produces a loud guttural roar. It is thought that this sound challenges other males and also attracts females. The female utters a less intimidating groaning call in response to the male, and she also emits grunt-like sounds to her hatchlings. Baby alligators produce appealing low burping and chirruping sounds. All 'gators can produce a wicked hiss when provoked.

What do alligators do if the water dries up? Actually, this happens rather frequently on the Aransas Refuge, and the alligators usually react in one of three ways. They may simply lie up in the surrounding vegetation and passively await a rain. Alternatively, they may retreat to a familiar depression or den which they have excavated and which still retains some stagnant water. Again, they simply wait for better times.

Finally, alligators are quite capable of lumbering overland for a mile or so in search of water. Although the animals on the Refuge are not marked for positive identification, it is felt that individuals do move from pond to pond according to the vagaries of the weather and the dictates of their own social fraternity.

Can alligators live in saltwater? They can for awhile at least, but they seem to prefer brackish or freshwater. Certainly these animals occasionally cruise along the bayshore, and in 1965 a 'gator became entangled in a shrimper's trawl well out in San Antonio Bay.

What do alligators eat? Any live animal they can catch and swallow. They also eat carrion.

Their diet varies with the season and the size of the alligator. Individuals up to about five feet long consume a smorgasboard of invertebrate fare: crayfish, blue crabs, fiddler crabs, adult and larval aquatic insects, surface-walking spiders, errant grasshoppers. They also eat frogs and whatever fishes they can catch. Larger alligators take a greater proportion of vertebrate prey. They eat a considerable number of fish, and when they discover fishes trapped in drying pools they will gorge on them. When Jones Lake was reduced to a muddy puddle in the summer of 1984, fifty-six alligators were congregated there feasting on alligator gar and carp.

Reptiles also loom large on the adult's menu: nonvenomous watersnakes, water moccasins, all kinds of turtles and small alligators. Birds are taken opportunistically. Alligators wait beneath rookeries to snap up fallen nestlings. They also snatch occasional adults of most waterfowl, but during the heavy winter concentrations of ducks and geese the alligators are usually in their dormant, nonfeeding mode. Any mammal which comes within range may be taken by an alligator: nutria, swamp rabbit, raccoon, rice rat, feral hogs and white-tailed deer.

In the Refuge files there is a record of a 150 pound feral hog being killed and totally consumed by an alligator. In another entry, an adult great-blue heron was removed from the stomach of a six-foot 'gator. And then there was the contented alligator found in the duck trap along with the remains of at least nine ducks.

Sea Turtles

Five species of sea turtles are native to the Gulf of Mexico. All five are widely distributed in the warmer portions of the Atlantic Ocean and most of them range throughout the warm seas of the world. However, all of these marine reptiles are so continually harrassed and so reduced in numbers that each is currently listed as either threatened or endangered.

Although the pelagic or littoral adults are routinely harpooned and netted in various parts of their range, it is the vulnerability of their beachside nesting grounds that has brought the sea turtles to dire straits. Persistent over-exploitation of the nesting females for meat, shell, skin and oil and the wholesale collection of their eggs for food and a presumed aphrodisiac quality account for most human depredation. Seaside resort development and recreational activity have usurped or disrupted many of the favored nesting sites of these tradition-bound reptiles. Natural predation on the eggs by raccoons, coyotes and crabs has been augmented by the activities of domestic and feral dogs and hogs.

Conservation plans have been hampered by the lack of a unified effort among the many maritime countries which are implicated in the life histories and welfare of the wide-ranging sea turtles.

Both the **leatherback** and the **Atlantic hawksbill sea turtles** are very rare vagrants along the Texas coast. There is no record of either of these species ever nesting on the local barrier islands.

The **green sea turtle** is the most economically important reptile in the world, and it is the species which briefly supported a local industry in the last decades of the Nineteenth Century.

When the cattle drives and the railroads began to move live longhorns northward, the dockside beef canneries were put out of business. They turned to green turtles. One of the busiest of these new enterprises was located at Fulton, on Live Oak Peninsula half a dozen miles south of Blackjack Peninsula.

Men began actively netting green turtles in Aransas Bay in 1881. In 1890, they hauled in nearly a quarter million pounds (over 900 turtles). Some of these animals were trussed up and sold alive in the local markets. The bulk was processed into canned meat and soup at the bustling Fulton plant.

By 1895, the local green sea turtle industry had practically exhausted its resource base. Hunted and harried throughout its range, the Gulf population has continued to decline.

It is quite likely that green turtles once nested on the surfside of the Texas barrier islands, but there are no recent records. Individuals still appear in Texas waters, where they account for about four per cent of the annual sightings of sea turtles.

The **Atlantic loggerhead** is a rather hardy sea turtle which ranges from tropical into temperate seas around the world. Because its flesh is less esteemed than that of the green turtle, the loggerhead has suffered less devastating commercial exploitation. Yet, these turtles are hunted and their nests are robbed in a multitude of small scale operations, so they well deserve their current threatened status.

Loggerheads make up about 80% of the annual sea turtle sightings in Texas. This species probably nested on the local barrier beaches in early historical times, but the only recent documentation occurred in 1977 and in 1979 on South Padre Island.

Although individuals are frequently swept into the North Atlantic by the Gulf Stream, the **Atlantic ridley** is more narrowly restricted to the Gulf of Mexico than any other sea turtle. The ridley is also the most critically endangered species. Its precarious status is the result of gross over-exploitation of its egg clutches on the single known eight-mile stretch of nesting beach on the coast of Tamaulipas between Tampico, Mexico and Brownsville, Texas.

In 1966, the Mexican government began protecting the nesting site. In 1978, a consortium of U.S. governmental agencies started an effort to establish a nesting colony of Atlantic ridleys on South Padre Island. Eggs collected in Tamaulipas were exposed to Padre sand and the hatchlings were given a dip in Padre surf in an attempt to imprint the little turtles to their foster locale. Then the young turtles were nurtured in facilities at Galveston until they were a year old and had grown to the diameter of a salad plate.

The first batch of manipulated ridleys was released off Padre Island in 1979. About 2,000 have been released there in each subsequent year. If they return to nest as sexually mature adults, 1986 will be the earliest the ridleys can be expected.

Atlantic ridleys once nested from the vicinity of Corpus Christi south to Vera Cruz. A few nested on South Padre Island in the late 1970's. Their principal feeding grounds are located off the Mississippi delta and in the Bay of Campeche, where the turtles forage for crabs. Only time will tell whether the rehabilitation effort will reinstate this sea turtle on a portion of its ancestral range.

None of the five species of Gulf sea turtles is known to have nested on the Matagorda Island Unit of the Aransas Wildlife Refuge in recent historical times.

Intensive beach patrols on the surfside of Matagorda have yielded only sightings of sea turtle carcasses washed up on the beach. During the five year period between 1978-82, 108 dead turtles were discovered: 94 loggerheads, 13 Atlantic ridleys and 1 green sea turtle. It is suspected that many of these turtles were killed or maimed when they became entangled in shrimp trawls. (It is currently planned to make turtle excluder devices mandatory equipment for commercial shrimpers by 1987.)

Your chances of seeing a live sea turtle on the Aransas are slim. You might try walking the beach on the Matagorda Unit during the spring or fall. If you see a beached turtle--live or dead--do not disturb it, but report your observation to the resident personnel.

The Texas Parks and Wildlife Department maintains its own list of threatened/endangered species. Criteria generally follow Federal guidelines but the scope is limited to the confines of the state. All species on the Federal list which occur in Texas are also on the state list. There are some creatures which are rare and declining in Texas even while they maintain healthy populations elsewhere. These appear on the State list but not on the Federal list.

As of January, 1987, the following animals appeared exclusively on the threatened/endangered list of the State of Texas and have been recorded from the Aransas National Wildlife Refuge.

Endangered

MAMMALS	BIRDS
coati	**least tern**

Threatened

BIRDS	REPTILES
reddish egret	**Texas horned lizard**
white-faced ibis	**Texas scarlet snake**
wood stork	
sooty tern	
American swallow-tailed kite	
white-tailed hawk	
zone-tailed hawk	

None of the native plants which are on either the Federal or State threatened/endangered lists is known to occur on the Aransas Wildlife Refuge.

Game Animals

In this chapter we include all those forms of wildlife which occur on the Aransas Wildlife Refuge that are regarded as game animals by the State of Texas.

White-tailed Deer

Without question, this animal provides more enjoyment to more visitors than any other resident species on the Aransas Refuge. The half-tame deer which wander around the lawns at the Headquarters allow close observation and photography, while the more nervous individuals that frequent the roadsides provide a genuine opportunity to observe white-tails in their native habitat. The sight of magnificent, thick-necked bucks or of large groups of feeding deer is routine Aransas fare. And wherever seen, there can be few wild creatures more appealing than an innocent eyed, wobbly legged fawn.

You can appreciate the deer better if you are familiar with their annual life cycle.

In early spring (late March-early April), the bucks have nubbin antlers covered with soft fuzzy skin. All of the adult does and most of the female yearlings will be heavy with young.

By late springtime (late April-May) the bucks' antlers have grown remarkably and branched into rounded tines. Because the antlers are still covered with skin and hair, the deer are said to be "in velvet".

From mid-April through the first half of May most fawns are born. (Late fawns may appear throughout the summer. On June 9, 1983, Ginger, a friendly doe, had twins in the Refuge manager's backyard. The following year, on May 9, she bore a single fawn in the same place.) Although the young are relatively inactive and remain hidden at first, they are soon seen following their mothers.

During the early summer (June-July) the bucks are in the final stages of antler growth and still in velvet. The successful does are accompanied by their single or twin offspring. Although the youngsters can forage for themselves by this time, they nurse as long as the does will put up with them.

By late summer (August) the bucks have rubbed the dried skin from their antlers and each now carries a fully developed and polished rack. The rapidly growing offspring are still at their mothers' sides, but by this time nearly three-quarters of the year's progeny may have succumbed in various natural tragedies.

It is in the autumn (late September-early December) that the deer are most active. This is the season of rut when the bucks clash with each other, pursue the does endlessly and finally mate with as many of them as they can. This vigorous interval peaks from late October to mid-November. Also, all of the deer begin to shed their cinnamon-brown summer coats and acquire a darker, shaggier winter pelage. By this time the young of the year have lost their spots.

At the onset of winter (late December) the exhausted bucks finally begin to wind down and they start to shed their antlers. You may see a lopsided individual with only one antler still clinging to the knob on its skull, but usually by the end of February all antlers have been dropped. Now the deer settle in to feed and survive the brief winter months. The bucks may roam singly or in two's and three's. Several does and their young cluster in feeding groups under the influence of a dominant matriarch.

A deer which makes it through its first summer stands a good chance of living several years, and it may reach the relatively ripe old age of 10-12 years. Death of aged adults usually results from poor nutrition and reduced resistance to parasites and disease which are brought on by severely worn teeth.

As with so many forms of wildlife, the brunt of the mortality among white-tail deer falls upon the very young animals. Three-quarters of all the deaths in the Aransas herd each year occur among the fawns. Only six out of ten live for two weeks. By the end of their first summer another three will have succumbed, leaving just three fawns out of the original ten for recruitment into the population.

What strikes the fawns down? A dry summer, which saps the does, will leave the fawns undernourished and weak. Parasites can further wear the young animals down: ticks, deer flies, mosquitoes, liver flukes, round worms. In unusually wet years the fawns are prone to contract salmonellosis, a fatal bacterial disease of the lower intestine.

When deer occur at high densities, as they sometimes do on the Aransas, social stress can interfere with the mother-young bond. Does seek out a secluded spot to give birth and for the first week the fawn moves about very little. If other deer wander past, or if favored protected sites are already occupied, then the doe may get upset and abandon or lose her offspring. Or the fawn may be frightened into the open or try to follow the wrong doe. What appear to be mere annoyances may easily prove fatal for the delicate fawns.

Of course, there are also predators ready to take advantage of a succulent fawn whose main defense is its camouflaged coat and an absence of body odor.

Predation in the wild is difficult to study, but some relevant data were recently gathered on the Welder Wildlife Refuge 25 miles southwest of the Aransas. There newborn fawns were fitted with radio transmitters so that they could be closely monitored. Predators eventually got half of these free-ranging animals. In all but one case coyotes were implicated. The exception involved a bobcat. It is quite likely that the same two species are the principal predators on Aransas deer.

Threat display of a white-tail buck

How does a deer herd stand such heavy annual attrition? Actually, it could not make ecological and adaptive ends meet without it. Behind the grim deaths of the fawns lies the natural mechanism for keeping the deer population genetically tuned up and in balance with the resources in its habitat. Since the Aransas Refuge was established its deer herd has had one outstanding experience with a temporary breach in the universal dictum called carrying capacity.

In 1938, there were about 3,000 deer on Blackjack Peninsula. An intensive 25-year predator control program allowed an exceptionally high fawn survival rate. In the early 1960's the predator control effort was phased out, but by that time deer numbers were spiralling out of control.

By 1965, the Aransas herd had doubled to some 6,000 animals and browse lines (leaves and twigs snipped off as high as a hungry deer can reach) began to appear on the mustang grape vines and the prickly ash trees. Favored sedges disappeared from the moist banks of the ponds. The range looked bad. So did the deer. Still the herd rocketed on.

Driven to desperate measures, the USFWS arranged the first public hunt ever held on the Aransas. For the entire month of October, 1966, archers were given access to the big bucks. Over 3,000 hunters tried their luck and skill. They got 185 bucks, far too few to alter the population trend.

In 1968, a survey indicated that there was an all-time high of over 13,000 deer on Blackjack Peninsula, a staggering ratio of one animal for every three acres of deer range.

At last, Nature stepped in to right things. Two hurricanes in as many years turned the Refuge into a vast lake. Deer habitat was reduced by 80%, boosting the crowded animals into an impossible density of nearly two per acre. Apparently many deer migrated to the mainland. Salmonellosis and hoof rot ran through the congested population. Hunters sloshed about in the first combined archery/rifle hunt and managed to bag 908 of the starved and overcrowded animals. Adult deer began to die from malnutrition and fawn production and survival was almost nil.

Finally, neatly and subtly, without even telltale carcasses lying about (Dense oak brush teeming with scavengers and a climate that fosters rapid decomposition do not leave lingering evidence of death.), the size of the deer herd began to drop. It plunged to 5,400 in 1969 and to 1,800 by 1970. The population has since stabilized at about 2,000 healthy animals.

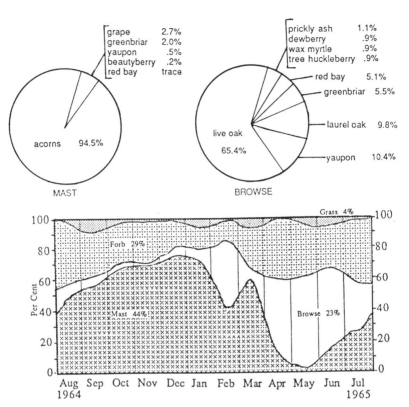

Figure 22 Annual diet of the white tailed deer on the Refuge.
Mast is the fruits of woody plants; browse is foliage;forbs
are non-woody plants other than grasses. (Modified from
White, M. 1973. Tex Journ. Sci. 30(4):457-89.)

What do the deer on the Aransas Refuge eat? Over half their
annual food mass comes from the commonest tree on the
Refuge--the live oak. Deer browse its growing leaves and twig
tips and they eat its pendulous flower clusters. They consume
live oak acorns (as well as acorns from the other oak species)
in great quantity whenever these are available. Acorns are
considered the hands-down staple for Aransas deer,
especially during fall and winter.

Deer also consume the fruits of greenbriar, beautyberry,
yaupon, red bay and mustang grape. They browse the greenery
of these plants as well as that of prickly ash, wax myrtle and
tree huckleberry and a wide variety of herbs. Although deer
avidly graze the tender grasses which emerge after burns,
grass does not make up a significant part of their yearly
intake.

You can enjoy the Aransas deer by simply observing them from your car window. Early or late in the day are the best times. If you can read their body language you can even watch them communicate with each other.

Watch for male interactions during the rut. If one buck shakes his head slightly and drops the angle of his ears, he is telling a second buck to move on. If his gesture is ignored he will flatten his ears, stretch out his neck and glare fiercely at the other deer. If he simply gets a mean look in return, the first buck may tuck his chin on his chest, raise the hair on his neck and take several prancing side-steps toward his adversary.

If this display does not send the object of his threats into retreat, then the angered buck will drop his head and make several wicked mock thrusts with his antlers in the direction of the other deer. Finally, if all these attempts at intimidation are met by similar behaviour from the opposing white-tail, then the two will usually close on each other with a loud crackle of antlers. A bone-rattling shoving match may go on for a quarter-hour, until one of the combatants has had enough and breaks for the nearest oak thicket.

The does scuffle with each other over social rank. Their body gestures are like those of the bucks until it comes to the antlers. Lacking these, the does substitute their sharp forehooves, sometimes rearing up on their hindlegs and flailing at their opponent.

You can see rudimentary versions of most of these body movements by watching young deer at play.

A startled deer may let out a whistling snort as it wheels and takes off, and it always shows the white underside of the tail for which it is named.

Javelina

If you see a family group of these unique little native pigs snuffling along the roadside, by all means stop and enjoy them from your car.

Javelinas ("hava-LEEN-ahs"; Do not confuse your Spanish, as some visitors do, and refer to these animals as "jalapeños"!) are moderately common on the Refuge, but they are notoriously erratic. When they deign to make an abrupt appearance from the oak thickets, you cannot miss them. If they choose to remain hidden there is no way to find or follow them in their impenetrable domain.

Be sure to distinguish these native animals from the introduced feral hogs. The best field mark is the tail. If you see a tail you are looking at a feral hog. (Javelinas have tails but they are very short and kept tucked against the body.) From the side javelinas have a more humped and smoothly rounded profile than a hog; their snouts are relatively shorter and their ears never flop down. When seen from fore or aft it is obvious that javelinas are very slab-sided, which allows them to thread their way through dense brush with ease. Adult javelinas are much smaller than adult hogs: about 22 inches at the shoulder and weighing about 60 pounds.

While feral hogs come in a variety of colors, javelinas are always a grizzled gray-black with a silver-gray band across the shoulders and around the neck. (This characteristic mark is the basis for another name--collared peccary.) The pelage is very bristly, especially along the neck and back, and the animals raise these stiff hairs when they are suspicious or disturbed.

If you can get a rear view of an individual with its hackles up, you may notice a hairless area high on its rump where the scent gland is located. When agitated these pigs release a musky, pungent odor from the gland. At close range the smell is like that of a skunk.

It is thought that group members maintain contact in dense brush by their scent. They also mark their herd territories by rubbing the gland against tree trunks and shrubs. Such odorous signposts may be stained brown from the repeated applications.

If you are lucky, you may see two javelinas confirming social relations by exchanging chemical signals. The pigs stand parallel, each with its chin on the other's rump; then by vigorously throwing its head sideways in rapid succession, each pig rubs its jowls across the partner's scent gland. This brief interchange is usually accompanied by soft grunts and snuffles of satisfaction.

Peccaries usually move about in small groups; each group maintaining a territory several hundred acres in extent. In the summertime they are mostly nocturnal, but they may be seen abroad any time during the winter or on overcast or rainy days. Most young are born in spring or fall, but they have been recorded at all times of the year on the Aransas. If you see one of these darling little brownish piglets, marvel at how adeptly it stays at its mother's ankle. Not even a shadow could stick closer.

Although javelinas will chomp up what insects they come across, they are basically herbivores. Like so much of the local wildlife, they stuff themselves on all the acorns they can find. They also feed on the fallen fruits of persimmon, mesquite, yaupon and greenbriar. Though they do not root deeply like the feral hogs, javelinas do nose along the top of the soil for tender greenery, rhizomes, tubers and fungi. Cacti are a staple for these animals in Southwest Texas, but the widely scattered prickly pears on the Refuge are not heavily used. Acorns very likely take their place.

These relatively innocuous creatures have an unjustified reputation for being aggressive and dangerous toward man. Actually, they beat a hasty retreat on contact. But they are near-sighted and when a group scatters one or more may inadvertently blunder toward rather than away from an intruder. Members of a dispersed group usually mill about in the brush, fouling the air with their scent glands, uttering alarming woofing sounds and popping their teeth ominously. This is all bluff, however, and if you stand quietly the entire group will melt away until only their peculiar redolence lingers in your nostrils.

Javelinas are less disturbed by automobiles than by people afoot. Watch for them along all the Refuge roads, and observe them with binoculars from your car window. If a troop shows up while you are picnicking, resist the temptation to feed them.

Fox Squirrel

Most of the larger mottes of live oaks on the Refuge form a part of the home range of one or more fox squirrels, but in their dense twiggy environment they are not readily visible. You can expect to see squirrels hurrying through the branches along the Big Tree and the Dagger Point trails, and they are occasionally seen scampering across the roads. Those living at the picnic area and around the Headquarters are less shy than others.

One of the most obvious signs of squirrels is their bulky summer nests. These are unkempt globular masses of dead leaves and twigs lodged high in the trees. The squirrels use them during the warmer months. Each animal also maintains a permanent den site in a hollow tree limb. The young are born in the dens in February and in September.

Fox squirrels are most active at sunrise, when they are busy feeding. Acorns are their staple on the Aransas Refuge. These are gleaned from the trees and picked up off the ground. Squirrels bury many acorns for emergency use. They also consume a variety of leaf and flower buds, hackberries, beautyberries and yaupon fruits. They spend considerable time foraging on the ground for mushrooms as well as any insects they can catch.

If you startle a fox squirrel in a tree it will probably flip to the opposite side of the limb. Sit or stand quietly. Squirrels are curious and they are one of the few forms of wildlife with less patience than humans. Soon an ear, then an eye will appear over the edge of the limb. Eventually the squirrel will be in full view. If it is sufficiently piqued by your presence it may switch its tail and utter a scolding chatter.

Wild Turkey

Like the white-tailed deer, the wild turkey seems to captivate every observer with its streamlined beauty, its air of resourcefulness and its genuinely wild, alert demeanor. The sight of a flock of these vigilant, high-stepping birds provides an extra thrill because they are not as commonly encountered as deer and they do not ordinarily stay in view for prolonged periods. So, if you are fortunate enough to see wild turkeys get your binoculars and telephoto lenses up in a hurry and enjoy the privilege.

On the Aransas Refuge you are most likely to find turkeys near the picnic area and along the roadside enroute to the Observation Tower. They also frequent the live oak mottes in the vicinity of the Tower itself. These birds belong to the variety called the Rio Grande turkey.

Male and female turkeys spend the winter months foraging in separate flocks. About February, the toms' hormones begin to bubble and they separate and seek out open areas for their courtship displays.

A twenty pound dominant gobbler in peak performance is a regal spectacle. He puffs up to his fullest, and fluffs his breast and back feathers until they shimmer like molten copper and emit iridescent flashes of purple and greenish-bronze. His huge black-barred, brown tail with its chestnut-cream trim is fanned vertically above his back. The skin of his naked head is a gleaming turquoise, and his briliant carmine wattles spill out over his breast just above his unique beard of bristly black, feathers.

The gobbler thrums the ground with the tips of his stiffened wings as he slowly pivots to take best advantage of the early morning light. Periodically he stretches out his neck and puts every ounce of vigor into a proclamation of his own elegance: "obble-obble, gobble-gobble-gobble".

The call is both a challenge and a lure. Rival males gobble back and forth. Sometimes they close on each other flapping, spurring and pecking. Upstart young toms brash enough to get in the way are quickly put in their place. The hens are drawn in at the height of display in late February and early March. The several dominant gobblers lay claim to almost all of the available hens.

By April the toms will have toned down and the hens will be brooding their 10-14 eggs in nests concealed in the tall grass. Predators usually destroy at least half the nests. The hatchlings are ready to follow the hen and begin feeding on insects almost as soon as their down feathers are dry.

Throughout the summer the young turkey poults lead a hazardous existence. Predators, accident, disease, a dry year with few insects and scant ground cover, a wet year with chilling nights and saturated feeding grounds--all take a toll. If they make it to their first autumn, when they will be eating a variety of plant material and relying heavily on acorns, the poults may survive as adults for another half dozen years.

Wild turkeys are ground-living birds. They walk continually as they forage, pausing occasionally to scratch at the leaf litter. (They eagerly flap up into the trees in the summertime to feast on the high-climbing mustang grapes.) Their sharp eyes and ears miss little. When alarmed they attempt to walk or run for cover, but if pressed they readily crouch a moment and explode into the air like enormous pheasants. They quickly level off and flap-glide over the tree tops for several hundred yards before setting down and slinking into the undergrowth.

Turkeys need a secure roost to pass the night. They prefer to roost in tall streamside trees. On the Aransas they settle for the larger live oak trees near a reliable outflow of water from a windmill.

Because the hatch and survival of the young of ground-nesting birds like turkeys is heavily influenced by weather and range conditions, the population size varies greatly from year to year. The Aransas flock oscillates between a low of less than 100 and a high of over 400 adults. For the past several years only a dozen or so birds have been routinely seen on the Refuge.

These turkeys range in small groups across the more open portions of Blackjack Peninsula, and a few individuals occasionally show up on Matagorda Island.

If you have the opportunity, try eavesdropping on a little turkey talk. You are most apt to hear the choppy "pit-pit" of suspicuous discovery followed by a liquid "putt-putt" of alarm. But these social birds have quite a vocabulary. If a startled group of birds has gotten separated, listen for the plaintive, sing-song "yip-yip, yarp-yarp-yarp" as they regroup.

Bob-white Quail

Of the four species of quail native to Texas, the bobwhite is by far the most widespread, and it is the only one found on the Aransas Refuge. Although Blackjack Peninsula supports a moderate population of bobwhites, these birds are not often seen along the public access routes. The quail prefer relatively open ground free of dense stands of tall grass and extensive live oak thickets. They are more common on the Tatton and Matagorda units.

Along the Tour Loop in April you may hear the unmated males repeatedly pouring out their distinctive "bob-bob-WHITE". During autumn and winter the quail are silent, and if you encounter them at all it may be in a startling explosion of whirring wings as a covey of a dozen birds takes off from the grass at your feet. Stand your ground, let your nerves settle and listen for their pretty little aggregation whistles.

Bobwhite chicks depend on insects and the adults snap up an assortment of invertebrates as they forage, but these birds are mainly herbivorous. The seeds of sundry forbs are among their staples: doveweed, partridge pea, broomweed, ragweed, sunflower. Quail eat grass seeds, but they do not push into dense growths of tall grass where they are vulnerable to predators. Fruits of greenbriar, yaupon, mustang grape, prickly ash, hackberry, bumelia, brasil and mesquite are readily consumed.

Would you believe that a bobwhite can swallow an acorn whole? They can and will, although they prefer smaller morsels. In the spring bobwhites pluck much tender greenery and to do so they readily enter the fresh regrowth in prescribed burns.

Doves and Pigeons

Texas boasts five native species of doves. Four of them have been recorded from the Aransas Refuge, and two of these are regarded as game birds.

The **mourning dove** is a common year-round resident and very nearly a year-round nester. The soft cooing of the males can be expected at any season. The mourning dove population increases perceptibly in the autumn and winter as a weak progression of northern birds arrives in the Coastal Bend.

From March through November **white-winged doves** inhabit the brush country of South Texas. Individuals appear sporadically on the Refuge, but the species is not known to nest here.

On December 18, 1971, a solitary **band-tailed pigeon** was seen near the Observation Tower. This bird, which is at home in the mountains of far West Texas, was evidently lost. Although the species is accorded game status, it has been protected with a closed season for decades.

Sandhill Crane

Sandhills begin arriving in the Coastal Bend on the early northers of mid-October. Their numbers increase erratically and by mid-December of a good year the Refuge population may peak at several thousand birds.

How long the cranes stay depends upon the availability of waste grain and stubble in the local fields and the birds' success at foraging on open ranchland. In any case, the sandhills begin to get restless by early springtime. By mid-March they have usually spiralled up into mere specks in the sky and caught a brisk southeasterly airstream which pushes them north to that great sandhill rendezous on the mudflats of the Platte River in Nebraska. From there it is off to Alaska and the Canadian Arctic to nest.

Sandhill cranes use the Aransas primarily as a roosting and resting site. At night the birds stand in the shallows of Goose Lake and Burgentine Lake or on the boggy tidal flats near Sundown Bay. Occasionally they settle on the tidal flat opposite the Heron Flats Trail.

At first light the birds begin to move out in groups, flying low in lines and ragged V's and trumpeting their distinctive, throaty rolling trill. The powerful yodel can be heard for a mile and it is a quickly recognizable element of the avian clamor that enlivens wintertime on the Texas coast. (Do not mistake the trill of the sandhills for the sharper bugle of the whoopers.)

The morning flights of cranes are off to feeding grounds which by late in the winter may be as much as 40 miles away. Cranes may feed in a winter field that appears barren but harbors waste grain, scattered greenery, sundry rhizomes, earthworms and insect larvae that can be easily extracted from the loose soil.

On the unplowed prairie the birds search for equivalent fare. Although they frequently probe in moist areas, the sandhills mostly stride across the grassy uplands and do not ordinarily feed in or around water. On the Aransas small flocks of these cranes readily forage across recently burned tracts, pulling at fresh greenery, gobbling up parched acorns and waylaying careless crayfish at the entrances to their burrows. They also probe the ground for bulbs of false garlic, purple pleatleaf and alophia.

Late in the day the sky again resounds with the rattling calls of the sandhills as the feeding flocks come home to roost.

You are likely to hear sandhills and to see the graceful birds in flight during a fall or winter visit to the Refuge, but your best chance to observe them will be in the extensive tilled fields and open pasturelands on the surrounding Coastal Prairie.

Watch for flocks of several dozen typically crane-like birds standing alertly on open ground a hundred yards or more from the roadway. Pull over and use your binoculars from the car window. Do not confuse sandhills with whooping cranes as many anxious observers do. Note the soft gray body. The white whoopers do not ordinarily occur in flocks and they are virtually never seen in such inland terrain.

WATERFOWL

Whooping cranes were not even mentioned in the presidential proclamation which established the Aransas Migratory Waterfowl Refuge in 1937. The area was set aside specifically as a sanctuary for the multitude of geese and ducks which paused in or passed through the region during their annual passage along the Central and Mississippi flyways. This remains one of the preeminent roles of the Refuge, now rendered even more critical in an age of disappearing natural habitat. Each year thousands of waterbirds of some twenty-five species descend upon the Aransas to rest, roost and feed.

The arrival and departure of migratory waterbirds on the Aransas follows a fairly predictable schedule, but actual numbers and species composition vary from year to year. Winter numbers are basically influenced by the degree of success on the northern nesting grounds. Severe cold may push migrating birds south of the Coastal Bend, while mild weather may persuade them to hold up further north. Many flocks of waterfowl await favorable northwesterly tailwinds

BIRD	1976	1977	1978	1979	1980	1981	1982	1983	1984	1985	TOTAL SEEN	10 YR AVG	TIMES SEEN
Common Loon	2	3	0	0	3	3	2	0	4	2	19	2	9
Pied-billed Grebe	33	18	25	51	11	17	17	51	10	75	308	31	10
Horned Grebe	0	0	0	0	2	1	0	0	2	2	7	1	4
Eared Grebe	39	17	5	23	5	3	58	15	162	15	342	34	10
White Pelican	254	133	137	210	186	427	294	96	326	435	2498	250	10
Brown Pelican	0	7	9	19	13	79	84	25	21	65	322	32	9
Dbl-crested Cormorant	75	46	1045	905	298	976	2277	611	103	808	7144	714	10
Olivaceous Cormorant	0	0	0	0	0	1	0	0	0	0	1	0	1
Anhinga	1	0	0	5	13	1	0	0	1	0	21	2	5
Canada Goose	155	1135	5200	3635	1450	447	368	439	1185	800	14814	1481	10
White-fronted Goose	30	4	22	15	163	0	70	0	12	36	384	35	8
Snow Goose	790	2000	1033	2346	1467	487	604	1226	4444	1268	15665	1567	10
Blue Goose	50	0	49	180	40	213	2	53	521	138	1246	125	9
White-winged Scoter	0	0	1	1	0	0	0	0	0	2	4	0	2
Blk-bellied Whistling Duck	0	0	4	4	0	2	6	0	0	0	16	2	4
Fulvous Whistling Duck	0	0	0	0	0	1	0	7	1	0	9	1	3
Mallard	24	37	29	30	32	28	1	4	0	3	188	19	9
Black Duck	0	0	0	0	0	0	1	0	0	0	1	0	1
Mottled Duck	41	26	90	133	83	99	31	41	16	81	641	64	10
Gadwall	589	319	386	820	841	426	831	493	77	33	4665	467	10
Pintail	1053	390	860	1456	769	3090	956	1086	841	712	11213	1121	10
Green-winged Teal	339	191	1072	212	102	62	178	471	43	60	2730	273	10
Blue-Winged Teal	174	1	19	96	21	30	0	19	13	104	477	48	3
Cinnamon Teal	0	2	0	0	0	0	2	8	0	0	12	1	3
American Wigeon	293	261	251	2025	57	1119	113	426	22	383	4950	495	10
Shoveler	66	13	55	92	184	169	105	52	60	146	942	94	10
Wood Duck	41	0	0	6	1	2	0	5	0	0	55	6	5
Redhead	0	157	0	40	318	574	906	28	385	73	2481	248	8
Ring-necked Duck	28	0	39	115	2	80	0	48	31	0	343	34	7
Canvasback	2	10	9	11	150	3	6	16	19	86	312	31	10
Greater Scaup	0	0	0	0	0	0	0	0	1	0	1	0	1
Lesser Scaup	150	85	43	120	12	763	22	100	982	714	2991	299	10
Common Goldeneye	3	27	0	7	19	30	2	8	40	2	138	14	10
Bufflehead	76	47	62	203	79	33	68	115	220	81	984	98	10
Ruddy Duck	12	3	6	2	1232	6	109	183	17	6	1576	158	10
Hooded Merganser	6	1	4	3	5	6	4	7	2	14	52	5	10
Red-breasted Merganser	3	7	2	4	8	32	74	6	84	13	233	23	10
	4329	4936	10457	12769	7566	9210	6741	5639	9645	6457			

Table 1 Waterbirds seen in 10 years of Audubon Christmas Counts.

before moving south. A wet winter fills more inland waterways, allowing the birds to scatter more widely so fewer of them are seen. Drought makes the bays hypersaline and freshwater for drinking becomes scarce. Waterbirds forced to congregate in drying ponds may be decimated by fowl cholera or avian botulism.

Goose numbers are quite dependent on the status of the local grain fields. If weather conditions have permitted complete tillage, there will be less available scattered grain and stubble and the geese may move on. Both geese and ducks quickly detect the sudden cessation of shotgun pressure in January, and their numbers dwindle on the Refuge as they move into the relatively secure adjacent bays and prairie watercourses.

All this aside, there is a discernable pattern in waterfowl use of the Aransas. Geese begin arriving during the last half of October. Two species, the **Canada goose** and the **snow goose** make up most of the winter goose population. Several thousand **white-fronted geese** may be among the early arrivals, but most of these birds soon move on south. Any **Ross's geese** which appear will be rare individuals displaced from their usual route along the Pacific Flyway.

The numbers of Canadas and snows increase through November and peak in December or January. During these months most of the geese roost in the shallows of Goose Lake and Burgentine Lake, with lesser concentrations in the protected bay shallows bordering the peninsula.

By day the birds fly off to feed in grain fields and grassy pasturelands across the local coastal prairie. Flights of both species can usually be heard or spotted early and late in the day from any vantage on the Refuge. Canadas frequently feed and rest in San Antonio Bay opposite the picnic area and at the Observation Tower. Snows often settle on Heron Flats.

If you get the chance to observe these geese feeding on terrestrial greenery, see if you can detect why Canada geese are referred to as grazers while snow geese are called grubbers. Their mannerisms and food preferences are quite distinctive.

Although goose numbers may remain high through February, in early March the birds abruptly begin to haul out, and the last ones will have deserted the Refuge by the end of the month.

Duck season makes an unlikely beginning in the crackling heat of midAugust when the first **blue-winged teal** splash down on the Aransas. Considerable numbers of these small ducks will be on the area throughout the winter, but most move on southward.

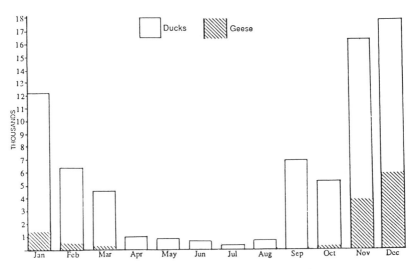

Figure 23 Peak numbers of waterfowl on the Refuge in 1982.

The first **pintails** usually arrive in early September. After that the other migratory species of ducks begin to appear according to the frequency and severity of the northers. By the end of October at least a few representatives of all the commoner kinds will be on the Refuge: **gadwall, American wigeon, green-winged teal**, and **northern shoveler**.

The number and diversity of ducks continues to rise in November and December. Depending on the year, a sudden influx of **redheads, lesser scaups**, or **ruddy ducks** may dramatically increase the count. The species composition will be augmented by variable numbers of **canvasbacks, buffleheads**, and **ring-necked ducks**.

By the end of the year participants in the Audubon Christmas Count usually spot over 15 species of ducks in their one-day survey on the Aransas. This census generally includes some of the less common species: **mallard, black duck, cinnamon teal, wood duck, greater scaup, common goldeneye**, and **hooded, common** and **red-breasted mergansers**.

Refuge personnel are justifiably proud of their lone sighting in 1980, of the rare and erratic little **masked duck** in a drainage canal near McHugh Bayou.

From November through January ducks can be expected in all aquatic habitats on the Refuge. Some of the best spots for viewing birds in San Antonio Bay are at the picnic area and the Bay Overlook, the end of the Boardwalk at the Observation

Tower and from the Tower itself. Take advantage of an afternoon sun to watch for a variety of species at close range on Heron Flats. Ducks can sometimes be found on Jones and Hog lakes.

There is a difference between dabbling ducks and diving ducks. Dabblers frequent the bay margins and freshwater ponds. They upend when they feed and spring directly off the water when they take to the air. Gadwall and pintail are dabblers. Divers, on the other hand, prefer the deeper waters of the open bay. They briefly disappear from view while they search for submerged vegetation, and typically patter across the surface before getting airborne. Redheads and scaups are divers.

All of these ducks are primarily herbivorous. In the freshwater ponds they feed on a variety of bankside, floating and submerged plants. The most important food plants in the bays are algae, shoalgrass and widgeongrass. Only the mergansers have distinctively different food habits. They feed mainly on fish and crustaceans.

There are usually several thousand ducks still on the Aransas through February, but the numbers decline rapidly in March despite the influx of northbound blue-winged teal. By the first of April the only migratory ducks left are a few lingering gadwall, wigeon, shovelers and teal. Most of these are gone by early May.

After serving as duck heaven for the five winter months, it may seem strange that the Aransas can boast only one resident nesting species. The **mottled duck** is a common year-round dabbler that prefers the freshwater pond habitat. The first ducklings appear in April and nesting continues through the summer. Mottled duck hens must contend with everything from predatory raccoons to drying waterholes in order to bring a few of their brood to full term.

The two species of whistling ducks that visit the Aransas in small numbers do not fit the pattern set by the northern migratory species. Both the **fulvous whistling duck** and the **black-bellied whistling duck** are Mexican species which have migratory components that move northward to nest along the

Gulf Coast in the springtime. The fulvous whistling ducks mostly bypass the Aransas Refuge and continue to the rice belt along the upper central coast.

The Aransas is near the northern limit for routine nesting by black-bellied whistling ducks. The species was added to the Refuge checklist in 1972, when a pair of adults and a brood of 11 young were observed near Patrol Station Pond. The ducks have been seen around freshwater ponds on the west side of Blackjack Peninsula in most subsequent years. They arrive in April and are accompanied by ducklings in July and August. They leave for South Texas and Mexico in the last half of October, although a few laggards are still seen during the Christmas counts on the Aransas.

These ducks routinely nest in hollow trees and they will utilize nest boxes. In 1981, a brood was hatched from a nest box on the Refuge, but efforts to entice further box use have been unsuccessful.

You can greatly enhance your enjoyment of the waterfowl if you learn the fieldmarks which distinguish the various species of ducks. Although many of these birds will be observed only at great distance and in unfavorable light, a good bird book, a pair of binoculars and determination can usually resolve them. Recognizing the glitter of male buffleheads amid the whitecaps, the startlingly white bellies of tippling gadwall or the resplendent colors of a male green-winged teal caught in full sunlight are delights worth working for.

Rails

All nine American species of rail have been recorded from the Aransas. The **American coot** is by far the commonest and most visible of these. Most visitors regard this bird as one more kind of duck. Coots do have duck-like habits. However, notice their white, chicken-like bill, relatively small head and the pumping motion of their neck when they swim. These traits mark them as rails. Coots dabble, dive and surface feed, and they patter extensively on takeoff.

Rafts of coots are almost always evident somewhere in the shallows of San Antonio Bay during the winter months, and scattered individuals can often be seen at close range in Thomas Slough.

Watch also in Thomas Slough for both the **common moorhen** and the **purple gallinule**. The gallinule provides a stunning display in purple and bronze. A winter visit to the Refuge is not complete without the maniacal cackling and eerie hooting of the coots and gallinules issuing mysteriously from the vegetation across the road from the Visitors Center.

Clapper rails are common enough in the tidal flat community, but they are secretive birds. Look for them from the Tower. If you are lucky, you may spot one slinking along the fringe of cordgrass bordering Mustang Lake.

There are rails along the Rail Trail--**king**, **sora**, **black** and **yellow**--but your chance of flushing one is slim. If you know their weird calls you will do better by ear than by eye.

Shorebirds

Although all species of shorebirds are accorded game status by the state of Texas, the hunting season is closed semipermanently for all but two of them: the **common snipe** and **American woodcock**. You might spot a snipe moving mouse-like along the edge of any slough or pond, but you are most likely to experience it as an explosive burst of wings when it erupts from an unseen frozen crouch. The Aransas Refuge does not have the mesic woodland favored by the woodcock, but this spicies is seen rarely along Burgentine Creek on the western side of the peninsula.

Introduced Species

In this chapter we consider those animals and plants which have been deliberately introduced onto Blackjack Peninsula.

In 1924, the last private owner of Blackjack Peninsula, Leroy G. Denman Sr. of the San Antonio Loan and Trust Company, had a game-proof fence built across the neck of the peninsula. He prohibited public hunting and commenced to introduce native and exotic wildlife onto the area. Although the records are not complete, it appears that between 1925-36, some 1,200 individual animals of seven species were released. Five of these species were exotic; three have persisted, two native and one exotic.

Ringnecked Pheasant

A total of about 400 adult and cage-hatched fledglings of this adaptable Asian pheasant was released between 1933-34. Some of these birds nested but no young were raised. The last individual that might reasonably be traced to these introductions was collected in January, 1939.

No more pheasants were seen on on the Refuge for over 40 years. Then, in 1981, a pair was observed in Point Pasture. Solitary cocks were seen in 1982 and 1983. These recent sightings are probably of escapees from nearby private landholders.

In 1963, the Texas Parks and Wildlife Department began an intensive effort to establish ring-necked pheasants on the Gulf Coast. By 1977, carefully selected hybrid stock had achieved huntable proportions. To date these birds have spread from the central coast eastward. The closest feral population to the Aransas is just across the Lavaca River, 45 miles up the coast.

The Refuge can well do without hybrid exotic ground-living birds which can only compete with the native species, including the endangered Attwater's prairie chicken.

California Quail

Records show the release of 252 adults between 1933-35, and there is an indication that cage-hatched fledglings were also liberated during this interval. Most of the birds probably fell to predators. None was seen during extensive surveys when the Refuge was established.

Wild Turkey

This is, of course, a bird native to the area, but it was apparently extirpated from Blackjack Peninsula by the time Leroy Denman took over the St. Charles Ranch.

From 1933-35, approximately 600 turkeys were released on the ranch. About half of these birds turned out to be indistinguishable from the domestic variety. They did not disperse into the wild and were finally destroyed to prevent hybridization with wild stock.

The remaining 300 turkeys all derived from a wild population in Kenedy County, 100 miles south of Blackjack Peninsula. These were, therefore, native Rio Grande wild turkeys, and they are presumably ancestral to the current Refuge population.

Fallow Deer

From 1930-36, the San Antonio Loan and Trust Company spent $2,639 for 73 of these European deer and released them on Blackjack Peninsula. Twenty-two animals were on the area when it became a Federal Refuge. Fourteen individuals were live-trapped and removed. A group of three fallow deer was seen occasionally through the 1940's. The last sighting was of a solitary animal near the site of the current picnic area in December, 1949.

Fallow deer are popular with novelty-minded landowners. The species is known to compete with the native white-tails. It certainly has no place on a national refuge.

Mule Deer

The records on this species are incomplete. Apparently about 50 individuals were liberated on the St. Charles Ranch from 1931-35. These animals were purchased from a dealer in Salt Lake City, Utah, so they were presumably not even the variety which is native to West Texas. Little wonder, then, that these deer failed to adapt to the Texas Gulf coast. None was alive at the time of a survey in 1939.

White-tailed Deer

Native white-tails were very scarce and seldom seen on Blackjack Peninsula when the game fence was built in 1924. The relatively open, overgrazed condition of the area as well as heavy hunting pressure probably accounted for the rarity of the animals.

Once the fence was in place this native remnant began to proliferate. In addition, between 1925-36, approximately 50 imported white-tails were released on the peninsula. Almost all of these were of Texas origin.

By 1937, there was a healthy and growing herd of about 4,000 white-tail deer on the Refuge. The bloodline was almost purely native and it gave rise to the deer which occupy the Aransas today.

Feral Hog

This is the only exotic animal that has established a viable breeding population on the Aransas National Wildlife Refuge. Feral hogs are at once stirring creatures to observe and the most destructive animals in residence. Whatever statement is made regarding them, their presence cannot be ignored.

Domestic hogs came into the Coastal Bend with the earliest settlers. These animals were mostly allowed to roam freely and to forage off the land. Hogs were shot, trapped or penned as needed. Many went wild. This loose sort of pioneer swine management was practiced on Blackjack Peninsula into the early decades of the twentieth century. Consequently, there was a population of these semi-wild hogs on the area when Leroy Denman closed it off with his game fence in 1924.

Between 1930-33, Mr. Denman purchased and released 11 adult and yearling European boar on the St. Charles Ranch. All of these animals were procured from zoos. Although their ancestry is uncertain, it is likely that all derived from wild stock direct from Europe or Asia.

The domestic hog is merely a selected variety of the European boar, so it is not surprising that the two readily interbreed. Such hybridization probably began immediately on the Aransas. Despite being far outnumbered, the several boar managed to influence the appearance of the swine herd on the peninsula. A study of skull characteristics conducted in 1978, revealed that about half the hogs show intermediate traits, a quarter favors the boar and the remaining quarter is nearly indentical with domestic hogs.

Although there is much variation, most individuals do exhibit external evidence of the more distinctive traits of the

European boar: long guard hairs with grizzled tips; a mane of long coarse black hairs extending down the spine from neck to tail; a straight tail with a tuft of hairs on the tip (this is one of the best field traits to distinguish hogs from the native javelinas); ears covered with long hairs; a long narrow muzzle. In addition, these animals are invariably rather long-legged and rangy in build.

Traditional boar coloration is brown or black, and the piglets are light brown with distinctive dark brown longitudinal stripes. Aransas hogs come in a variety of colors, and many show the white shoulder stripe characteristic of the domestic Hampshire breed. Among a sample of 64 fetuses, half had the longitudinal color pattern.

Regardless of their appearance, the mixed stock of feral hogs adapted well to Blackjack Peninsula. They bred all year long, ate almost anything, were not prone to debilitating disease, had few predators and were neither hunted nor harvested by man. So they multiplied in hogs' heaven.

When the Refuge was established the feral hogs were recognized as both a nuisance and a competitive threat to native wildlife. In an intensive campaign waged from October, 1936, through July, 1939, an astounding total of 3,301 hogs was removed from Blackjack Peninsula. With the population diminished, control efforts were reduced to incidental trapping and the practice of shooting the animals on sight. The Narrative Report for 1945 anticipates the imminent eradication of feral hogs from the Aransas.

However, the hogs were far from finished, and the casual control efforts had only served to make them more elusive. Beginning in 1955, Refuge personnel began a more determined program of attrition still based on trapping and especially on nighttime baiting and shooting. This has continued to date. The annual removal rate is about 250 animals, which translates into approximately 7,500 hogs over the past 30 years. That this approach does nothing more than crop the surplus is evidenced by the fact that the current population of feral hogs on the Aransas Refuge is conservatively estimated to total over 500 animals.

An important reason that there has not been a more determined effort to rid the Refuge of feral hogs is that they confer a definite political advantage. There is no question that most visitors are genuinely thrilled at the sight of one of these bristle-backed beasts with the ominous aura of power and viciousness. Indeed, the "big old Federal hogs" have become somewhat of a legend on the Aransas. They are not only exciting to see, they offer a big game experience to stalk and shoot. The taking of several hundred hogs a year definitely breaks the tedium of routine Refuge duty.

In 1969, the general public got its first opportunity to hunt hogs on the Aransas when a special archery season was allowed. The public hunt was eventually extended to include firearms and it is now conducted concurrently with the Texas white-tail deer hunting season. Although the number of hogs taken is insignificant for control purposes (an annual kill rate of about 30), the public hunt has become the single most popular event on the Aransas, and the feral hogs are an important part of it.

Finally, it has long been the policy of the Aransas Refuge to make freshly butchered pork available free to selected local charitable organizations and sundry VIP's. On many occasions outdoor bar-b-ques are conducted for such gatherings at special group sites on the Refuge itself. Needless to say, the tradition has proven of immense public relations value. As one Narrative Report comments, "After chomping down on a juicy bit of hog, everyone agrees that Aransas and wild hog is a winning combination." There are, however, some serious attendant losses.

Consider a lanky feral hog weighing 125 pounds. Day in and day out such an animal puts a heavy drain on the resources of a natural community: food; water; cover; deposition of body wastes; dispersion of parasites; alteration of the soil along routine trails, at foraging sites and in favored resting places; wallowing in waterholes; the outright disturbance generated by the passage of a large body.

Multiply the individual impact by 500 or more. Exacerbate the result to account for sows with piglets. Aggravate the situation with a drought or a hurricane. You can begin to

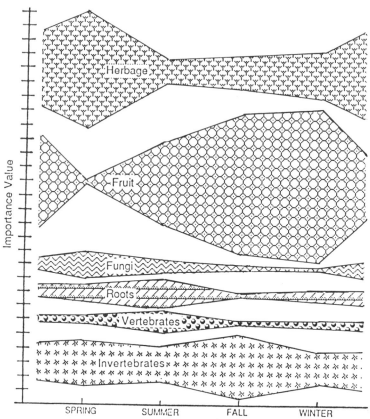

Figure 24 Annual diet of feral hogs. Importance value
incorporates both volume and frequency of occurence of
food items in hog stomachs. (From Springer, M.D. 1975 MS
Thesis, Texas A&M Univ.)

appreciate the unremitting burden that feral hogs place on the
delicate natural cycles which oscillate on Blackjack
Peninsula.

It is easiest to grasp the competitive nature of feral hogs by
considering their food. They disrupt the natural food web in
three important ways: by eating foodstuffs that might
otherwise succor native animals; by disrupting soil and
vegetation while foraging; and by acting as outright predators.

Hogs are not only arch omnivores, they are alert
opportunists. When the acorns drop the hogs consume them
by the peck for as long as they last. When the mustang grapes
ripen, the hogs feast on this choice wildlife food almost
exclusively, often rearing up to drag the fruit-laden vines to
the ground. When the yaupon and greenbriar fruits fall, the
hogs are there to nuzzle them up.

All bankside and shallowly submerged freshwater vegetation is hog fodder--both the greenery and the rhizomes. The animals are also inveterate beachcombers, consuming everything from crabs to masses of marine algae. Many upland sprouts, forbs and bulbs are hog delicacies. All fungi go into their maws. Earthworms, insect larvae, stranded fishes, meadow frogs, ribbonsnakes, rice rats, carrion--all are chomped up with equal gusto.

There is no more relentless and destructive predator on ground-nesting birds than the feral hog. The nests of lizards, turtles and alligators are in equal jeopardy. The predatory nature of the hogs takes on a particularly savage twist when it is learned that they occasionally kill and consume white-tail fawns.

The activities of feral hogs touch virtually all other lifeforms on the Refuge. They are in direct and total competition with javelinas all year long. In the early spring they beat the geese to the fresh Bermuda grass sprouts. No attempt to rehabilitate the Attwater prairie chicken population can succeed with hogs on the Tatton. There will never be an undisturbed freshwater community so long as there are hogs on the peninsula. No tidal flat is free of hog rooting and trampling. When times are hard, they will always be harder with the aggressive hogs on the scene.

What to do? Perhaps hog-proof crossfencing with traps set at critical gaps would be effective. It is likely that the introduction of a swine-specific disease could achieve in a few years what half a century of cropping has failed to do. There are other options.

If you desire to see a feral hog be alert early and late in the day. Foraging animals may be glimpsed in grassy clearings and groups are frequently seen hustling across the road anywhere along the Tour Loop. Individuals are commonly spotted on the tidal flat at the Observation Tower. Look carefully as you approach the end of the pier at Jones Lake and enter the blind at Hog Lake. Hogs are often seen at the water's edge.

As you drive and walk around the Refuge you cannot fail to notice the extensive areas of plowed up soil. This is all hog work. Ponder its ecological ramifications.

Domestic Cattle
Cattle have been on Blackjack Peninsula in significant numbers since the 1880's. The small holdings were gradually

consolidated and by 1919, the entire peninsula was essentially ranched as a unit. From that date to the establishment of the Aransas Refuge an annual average of 6,000 head of cattle plus sundry horses, mules, goats and hogs roamed the area. The cumulative impact was far beyond carrying capacity.

The San Antonio Loan and Trust Company maintained grazing rights on the newly-formed Refuge. Through the 1940's, the severe drought of the 1950's and until 1964, from 3,500 to 4,000 head of cattle foraged virtually unfettered across the peninsula.

Because of severe overgrazing, the stocking rate was mercifully reduced to 2,500 head in 1965. In 1967, cattle were finally fenced away from the bayshore between Headquarters and Mustang Lake. In that same year the Tatton Unit was acquired and a grazing permit was granted to a second livestock owner.

A grazing rotation program was begun in 1971, and cattle were taken off the tidal flats used by the whooping cranes. The overall stocking rate was reduced to less than 1,000 head.

From 1973-1982--for the first time in well over a century-- there were no cattle on Blackjack Peninsula. Everyone professed amazement at the phenomenal growth of the native grasses.

In 1978, the Aransas inherited the negligently liberal grazing policy on the Matagorda Unit.

Going into 1986, cattle were grazing in three sections of the Refuge, each under a carefully scrutinized rotation schedule. The 7,500 acre Tatton Unit supported 350 head. Point Pasture (the southern tip of Blackjack Peninsula) contains 6,000 acres and had 300 cattle. The 17,700 acre Matagorda Unit was grazed by 1,100 head of stock. The cattle definitely help keep the Tatton open for the prairie chickens. The animals in Point Pasture are a dubious part of an attempt to entice whooping cranes to inland forage. The presence of livestock on Matagorda is an ecological blunder.

Regardless of the stocking rate, cattle have many negative influences on sandy coastal terrain subject to frequent summer stress. Grazing manifestly changes the composition of native vegetation. Overgrazing degrades the range, and on the Aransas it promotes sand erosion and the spead of running liveoak. Cattle feed on acorns and browse on greenery in direct competition with wildlife. Cow hooves cut deep eroding trails across the land, muck the waterholes and severely degrade the tidal flats. Wherever cattle roam they spread several species of ticks and attract numerous kinds of flies. Cow droppings alter the chemical composition of the soil and succor unnatural communities of insects.

The presence of cattle also demands other sorts of attendant interference in what should be an undisturbed environment: fencing, corrals, roadways, salt blocks, water troughs, plants escaped from imported feed, rats and mice at outbuildings, blackbirds and cowbirds at feed lots, prescribed burning to remove native woody plants, the periodic rattle of vehicles and intrusion of men.

In a region which has always been cattle country, it is difficult to break entirely with a hallowed tradition.

EXOTIC PLANTS

Although it is more buffered from intrusion than most areas, the Aransas Refuge harbors many species of herbs, weeds and grasses which have been imported incidental to human activities. (You might reflect upon what seeds dropped from your tire treads, radiator grill and the undersides of the fenders and bumper of your vehicle while you visited the Refuge.) Here we only consider those species which were deliberately introduced.

Over the years plantings have been attempted on the Refuge for a variety of reasons. Some were meant to supplement native wildlife food resources. Others were intended to lure wildlife into public view. Plants are also used for ornamental landscaping around Headquarters and for windbreaks and control of soil erosion. In a few cases, especially in the early years, sundry seeds and cuttings were broadcast randomly without any clear objective other than to add variety to the monotonous coastal vegetation.

Fortunately, most of these endeavors were self-limiting. Either the introduced plants failed to survive or they remained highly localized. Yet, anyone with an eye for native vegetation will notice some alien plants.

Thousands of tubers and hundreds of pounds of seeds have been sown in the freshwater lakes, ponds and scrapes to make these more attractive to waterfowl and to entice the birds into view for visitors. These include **wild celery, duck potato, sago pondweed, coontail, American lotus, smartweed, wild millet, spike rush, southern naiad, muskgrass, chufa, giant bristlegrass** and the **California, American** and **three-square bulrushes**.

Bahia grass was sown along rights-of-way. **Bermuda grass** has been extensively spread for erosion control, lawn cover and as springtime goose fodder. **Blue panic, rye grass, King Ranch bluestem, sand lovegrass** and **weeping lovegrass** were broadcast across the interior uplands. **St. Augustine grass** is planted at Headquarters and patches of this species can be found near old house sites all over the Refuge.

Indiscriminate introductions include the hauling of three cubic yards of mud from a fish hatchery in Uvalde and heaving this into ponds on the Aransas in hope that some sort of duck food might result. In an attempt to start **phlox** and **bluebonnets,** several pickup loads of soil were brought in from outside the Refuge and spread along the roadside. In one instance over 200 pounds of assorted grass seeds were broadcast over the interior of the peninsula from an airplane.

Many trees still linger to mark the vicinity of the St. Charles Ranch headquarters and the Patrol Station on the west side of the Refuge: **Chinese arbor vitae, Chinese tallow, Russian olive, chinaberry, cottonwood, athel, petticoat palm**. Some of these are entwined with **Japanese honeysuckle** and **bougainvillea**. There is one small patch of **oleander**.

Various ornamentals have been planted at Headquarters and around public use sites. A large **slash pine** struggles to survive near one residence. Three small **sago palms** grow on the slope at the Visitors Center and **red gums** back up the parking lot. A pair of **hairy palms** guards the entrance to the ramp at the Observation Tower and another grows at the alligator observation site across the road from the Visitors Center. There is a fine large **sycamore** in the clearing between the picnic area and the Bay Overlook and a young one in the parking lot at the Visitors Center.

None of the above can eclipse the ambitions of the Refuge's first manager. Taking advantage of CCC and WPA labor in 1938-39, he directed the planting of 30,250 **white mulberry** and 7,350 **American plum** seedlings all over the peninsula and of 125 **cenizos** around the parking lots. At Headquarters he started 500 **Arizona cypress** and 300 **Kentucky coffee trees** for later transplantation. He had his men scatter 50 pounds of Russian olive seed and another 50 of elderberry seed at Jones and Big Tree lakes.

For better or worse, only an occasional white mulberry exists today to testify to this spirited enterprise.

Mammals

Thirty-nine species of native mammals have been recorded from the Aransas National Wildlife Refuge. If you are unfamiliar with the mammals of the state you might get a copy of *The Mammals of Texas* by W. B. Davis. If you know your mammals but want to learn more about them, we recommend *Texas Mammals East of the Balcones Escarpment* by D. J. Schmidly.

OPOSSUM

Because opossums are almost exclusively nocturnal, visitors seldom observe them unless an early-rising 'possum decides to visit the garbage cans at the picnic area. Yet, these creatures are one of the commonest medium-sized mammals on the Refuge. One night in April, 1981, six live traps set in the vicinity of the Youth Environmental Training Area caught five 'possums, two of them carrying young in their pouches.

These marsupials may actually be more common around the public access area than in the interior of the Refuge, because near man they find more varied fare and more nooks for their daytime retreats.

Even if you have never seen an opossum, you will recognize one at first glance. Watch for the a long naked, semi-prehensile tail; soft tangled gray fur with long white guard hairs; bulging black button eyes; papery black ears; a drooling, toothy pink 'possum grin; and a comical, shambling gait. Put it all together and you can have nothing but an opossum.

Opossums are consummate omnivores and scavengers. Because they are adept raiders of birds' nests, they are generally relegated to the varment category by Refuge personnel. Opossums were much persecuted during the predator control days. However, today they are allowed their

place in the natural food web and both 'possums and birds seem to have struck a tolerable balance with each other.

Short on gumption but long on perserverance, the opossum has been content to let the higher-strung world pass it by for 50 million years. To call it a living fossil is to pay it life's highest compliment.

INSECTIVORES

These mammals feed primarily on insects. The Aransas has three species--two shrews and a mole.

Shrews are small, secretive, quick moving, mouse-like predators with long snouts, tiny eyes and ears that are hidden in the fur. They live in shallow subterranean tunnels and surface runways amid dense grass and leaf litter. There they stalk and consume all manner of insect larvae, grasshoppers, crickets, spiders and pillbugs. Shrews are in turn preyed upon by hawks, owls, skunks, gray foxes and rat snakes. They are important links in the food web.

You are very unlikely to see a shrew, but it is satisfying to appreciate that the little creatures must be all around you as you tour the Refuge. The **least shrew** is the more common of the two resident species, and it is also the tiniest mammal on the Aransas. From snout to tail tip, an adult will span three inches, and it will weigh about as much as a dozen aspirin tablets. So the least shrew merits its name.

The **southwestern short-tailed shrew** is only slightly larger than the least shrew. When it was discovered on the Refuge in 1941, it was described as an unique variety. Its closest relatives occur in deep East Texas.

How and when did the southwestern short-tail make the 250 mile leap to its isolated location on the Aransas? Answer: it never did. Fossils document that two million years ago, when the Coastal Plain was more moist and forested, short-tailed shrews ranged completely across it. When the region dried out the shrews followed the retreating forests eastward--except for Aransas' own variety, which got left behind in the dense oak-bay thickets that cap the Pleistocene sand dunes.

Although you are also unlikely to see an **eastern mole**, you might notice occasional evidence of its presence--a low meandering ridge of earth snaking across one of the nature trails through the oak mottes. (Do not confuse this ripple with the much more common sandy mounds made by pocket gophers.) This is the roof of a shallow feeding tunnel.

The rat-sized mole literally swims through the sandy soil with breast-strokes of its powerful forelegs, searching for insect larvae, wolf spiders and earthworms. Their feeding ridges have also been seen in moist sand on the tidal flats where the moles may be in search of fiddler crabs.

Moles are moderately common on the Refuge but they are restricted to sand with enough moisture to support their tunnel walls. During the dry months these animals burrow more deeply. After rain showers they are particularly active in their subsurface passageways. Despite their subterranean life style, moles routinely fall prey to owls, foxes and skunks.

BATS

Only four species of bats have been documented on the Refuge, but a total of at least eight kinds is likely to roost and feed here, especially during the spring and fall migratory seasons.

The **Mexican free-tailed bat** stops over on the Aransas enroute between its wintering ground in Mexico and its summer haunts on the Edwards Plateau in Central Texas. In April, 1983, approximately one hundred free-tails were found roosting on the ceiling of a shop building at Headquarters. You are most likely to see these relatively large bats at dusk during March-April and October-November. They typically fly high and fast with frequent changes of direction but little alteration in altitude. Their favorite prey is moths.

The **big free-tailed bat** is very similar to the Mexican free-tailed, but it is considerably larger and has relatively longer ears. This bat is usually encountered in West Texas. Yet, one was found roosting in a shop building at Refuge Headquarters in November, 1974. Very likely it was enroute to its South American wintering ground.

The narrative reports mention one **red bat** found roosting on a window screen and another discovered dangling from a grapevine in a live oak tree. This is also a migratory species, but individuals are doubtless on the Refuge throughout the summer. Bats are not noted for their beauty, but this one is an exception. Males have bright brick-red fur. The red hairs on the female are tipped with white, giving her an appealing frosted appearance. Red bats are habitually solitary animals. Watch for them at dusk near live oak mottes. They usually fly close to the ground, and they frequently flutter along beneath the tree canopy.

In September, 1978, the Refuge's only recorded **silver-haired bat** was found roosting in a building at Headquarters. This species certainly stops over on the Aransas routinely during its spring and fall migration flights which apparently take it directly across a portion of the Gulf of Mexico.

Judging from known distributions, at least four other species of bats should migrate across and perhaps spend the summer months on the Aransas Refuge: the eastern pipistrelle, hoary bat, northern yellow bat and the evening bat.

RODENTS

These animals are for the most part small, fidgety, secretive, nonmigratory and numerous. At any given moment there are certainly more individual rodents on the Aransas Refuge than individuals of all other mammal species combined. This is partly because tiny creatures demand fewer resources and so can live at higher densities. It is also a consequence of living in the fast lane. In the Coastal Bend rodents are not only active the year around, they breed all year. Litters are large and lifespan is short. Populations wax and wane with the times.

Rodents play an immensely important ecological role in all of the terrestrial communities on the Refuge. Most kinds are primarily herbivorous. Rats and mice, along with the insects and crustaceans, are the principal means by which plant material is converted into tempting packets of meat of sufficient size and abundance to support the first-level carnivores. Indeed, rodents are the staple item in the diets of many raptors (hawks and owls) and snakes, and they are an important supplement for most carnivorous mammals.

Without rodents, the diversity and abundance of other wildlife on the Aransas would be greatly reduced.

Of course, rodents are also interesting in their own right. They are quite diversified. Most live on the ground, but some live underground. Others live in trees. A few live near the water and voluntarily swim. Many eat seeds and all take some greenery. Most even eat a bit of meat now and then. Rodents have their own social arrangements, territories, homeranges, competitive struggles and courtship patterns.

Although you may not see a single rodent during your visit to the Aransas, you certainly should appreciate the pivotal contribution of this often-maligned group to the natural cycles which so delight the eye.

Since the establishment of the Aransas National Widlife Refuge, 13 resident species of rodents have been documented. One of these is probably now extirpated. Three are introduced species. There is a likelihood that at least one and perhaps as many as four more kinds may occur on the Aransas and have so far escaped verification.

Mice and Rats

Every grassy acre of the Aransas Refuge supports members of the principal triumverate of rodent species: **pigmy mice, hispid cotton rats**, and **fulvous harvest mice**. These reach their peak densities in the luxuriant stands of grasses in the ridge-and-swale, tidal shore grassland, cordgrass and upland grass communities. Collectively these three rodents are staples in the diets of all hawks and owls on the Refuge, and they are heavily utilized by rat snakes, kingsnakes, racers and rattlesnakes. Coyotes, gray foxes, bobcats and striped skunks also routinely prey on them.

The pigmy mouse is at once the tiniest and the cutest rodent on the Refuge. These gray mites hustle along appropriately miniscule runways amidst the jungle of grass stems. The fulvous harvest mouse is one of the prettiest species, with a golden-brown back and a soft wash of orange on its sides. This long-tailed mouse sometimes constructs globular aerial nests of shredded grass in low shrubs.

The hispid cotton rat is a plump, fist-sized rodent with coarse brown pelage. Its presence is revealed by its maze of trailways ramifying beneath the canopy of the grass. Even for rodents, cotton rats have an exceptionally high reproductive rate, and in favorable years their populations increase dramatically. Because they are aggressive competitors, the density of neighboring kinds of rodents drops when the cotton rats are riding a high. Several narrative reports mention cotton rat plagues. At such times the predators feast, rendering service to man and nature alike.

The **white-footed mouse** occurs throughout the Refuge. It lives in any grassy habitat but prefers access to woody plants, logs and a diversity of herbs. This big-eared, beady-eyed species is the commonest rodent in the oak-bay forest community, and all Refuge personnel will testify that it frequently invades buildings.

The **rice rat** is most at home in the moist grassy swales, cordgrass and tidal flats. It readily moves over boggy ground and through shallow water in search of grass and sedge greenery, and if pressed can swim rapidly underwater for short distances. As you scan the tidal flats and the saltmarsh communities from the Observation Tower, you are looking down on prime rice rat habitat.

The Aransas Refuge lies on the northern edge of the range of the **south plains woodrat**. This very large, slate-gray rat is at home in the dry, mesquite and prickly pear country of South Texas. It was apparently once common on Blackjack Peninsula when the area was open and overgrazed. Although old woodrat middens (den sites composed of mounds of sticks, cow chips and oyster shells) can still be found, these rodents are apparently rare on the peninsula today. One was trapped beneath the mesquites on the Heron Flats Trail in 1981. Woodrats are currently common only in the mesquite and prickly pear community on the Tatton. They do not occur on Matagorda Island.

The **hispid pocket mouse** is a medium-sized, rather slow-moving rodent that prefers open, weedy habitat. After plugging the entrance to its burrow with sand, the hispid pocket mouse sleeps the day away. By night it moves about on the surface, stuffing its fur-lined cheek pouches with the seeds of Indian blanket, primrose, winecup and grassbur. Its underground food store sometimes contains a pint of assorted seeds. This mouse is probably more abundant on Matagorda Island than on Blackjack Peninsula.

Pocket Gopher

Another rodent with cheek pouches is seldom seen, but it leaves evidence of its subterranean existence all over Blackjack Peninsula and Matagorda Island. This is the **Attwater's pocket gopher,** and you cannot help noticing the many mounds of sand which these animals leave piled up while excavating their extensive system of underground tunnels. The bright sandy piles are especially noticeable in recently burned tracts.

The Aransas Refuge, with its sandy substrate and dense herbaceous cover, is a regular pocket gopher heaven; but since the gophers' sandy mounds persist for months, their abundance probably exaggerates the standing population of these rodents.

Each individual gopher turns over more than five tons of soil annually, so these animals significantly influence the soil texture and vegetation of many sections of the Refuge. Drummond's phlox, for instance, grows especially well on old gopher diggings, as do several species of grasses.

Scattered through the ridge-and-swale community there occur large rounded hillocks of sand called pimple mounds. (An interpretive sign on the Tour Loop points out a pimple mound.) Because these sand piles lie several feet above the shallow water table they are rapidly colonized by live oaks, yaupon, Gulf Coast toads, ground skinks, hog-nosed snakes and Attwater's pocket gophers. It has been suggested that the localized digging activity of generations of gophers actually created the pimple mounds, but it is at least as likely that wind blown sand was captured by the oaks and the gophers then invaded the   readymade sand piles. Regardless of the sequence of events leading to their formation, pimple mounds harbor a diverse and rather distinctive array of life.

The pocket gopher is about the size of a rat, but it is not at all rat-shaped. Its body is compact and cylindrical. The blunt head joins the heavy forequarters without a noticeable neck. The muscular forelegs are armed with stout curved claws. The foreclaws and large incisors are the gopher's digging tools.

The animal has tiny eyes and ears and a stubby naked tail. It is covered with a pelage of short brown hair.

Pocket gophers are solitary creatures that spend most of their time underground, either hustling along their passageways or energetically digging fresh ones. Most tunneling is done in search of food: roots, tubers and succulent greenery. Gophers will venture onto the surface of the ground to harvest acorns.

Even though they keep their burrow systems plugged, pocket gophers are frequently exposed at the surface when they begin to construct a fresh mound of sand. Many predators are alert to the slight movements and the odor of the fresh moist sand at the new mound. Coyotes, bobcats, foxes, hawks and owls routinely snatch up working gophers. Snakes and weasels can enter the burrow system, while badgers and striped skunks are equipped to dig into them.

Other Rodents

The **fox squirrel** is considered in Chapter 7. Although the **Mexican ground squirrel** has been reported from the Aransas, since these diurnal and readily observed animals have not been seen in recent years, they are probably extirpated on the Refuge. The soil on portions of the Tatton Unit is the sort they prefer, but they like more open ground than is now available.

The spotted ground squirrel occurs on Padre and Mustang islands, but it is curiously absent from Matagorda Island.

Three introduced rodents are known to occur on the Aransas. The **black rat** is confined to the residential area. **House mice** are likewise limited, but small groups of individuals occasionally move into adjacent weedy and grassy habitats.

The **nutria** is a large muskrat-like South American rodent which has been feral on the Gulf Coast for over 40 years. The first one was sighted on the Refuge in 1962. Nutria were moderately common during the wet years following Hurricane Beulah, but it is likely that in routine years the Aransas' alligators snap them up about as fast as they arrive. The few recent sightings have been in Thomas Slough.

The Aransas Refuge is situated on the extreme eastern edge of the distributions of three more mice: the silky pocket mouse, the deer mouse and the Northern grasshopper mouse. All of these prefer more open and sparse vegetation than now exists on the area. None has been documented since the Refuge was established. If anywhere, they might be expected on the Tatton Unit.

Finally, though there is no specific record for the Norway rat on the Refuge, it is hard to believe that this universal immigrant does not occasionally appear in the residential area.

RABBITS

Like the rodents, rabbits are herbivores and are therefore ecologically important because they transform vegetation into meat. Although rabbits may reach high densities, they are larger than rodents and so are never as numerous as the smaller mammals. Rabbits are preyed upon by coyotes, foxes, bobcats, owls, hawks, rat snakes and rattlesnakes.

Historically the Aransas has supported populations of three species of rabbits: the **black-tailed jackrabbit**, the **eastern cottontail** and the **swamp rabbit**.

The jackrabbit and the cottontail have been the common rabbits, but their fortunes have varied with the times. For the first two decades after the Refuge was established, both jackrabbits and cottontails were abundant. Usually the jackrabbits were more numerous than the cottontails by about 5:1. This was in the days of heavy grazing pressure, the drought of the '50's and less thicketized live oak. Blackjack Peninsula was much more open than it is today.

Then, in 1961, Hurricane Carla wracked the area and according to the narrative report for that year, the jackrabbits and cottontails "vanished". The populations of both species were still low when Hurricane Beulah put all but the highest ground under water in 1967. Not until 1972 were a few jackrabbits and an occasional cottontail seen on night surveys.

From 1973-82 cattle were removed from Blackjack Peninsula and the grasses resurged phenomenally. Jackrabbits demand sparsely vegetated, open ground. Cottontails prefer brambles and short grass studded with herbs. The lush grass and barren islands of running live oak suited neither kind of rabbit.

Going into the '80's both jackrabbits and cottontails were at a low ebb on the Aransas. Although the reasons have never been worked out, the numbers of jackrabbits in the entire Coastal Bend have recently plummeted. Without outside recruitment and with the maintenance of dense herbaceous cover, it is not surprising that jackrabbits have not been seen at all on the Aransas for the past several years.

Cottontails are currently present in low numbers. Being creatures of community edges, they live along the border between ridge and swale, and at night they feed on the roadsides. Cottontails also utilize the greenery in freshly burned tracts. You might see one at dawn or dusk on any of the Refuge drives.

The case of the swamp rabbit is different. This dark and robust close relative of the cottontail is at home in the wetlands of East Texas. The Aransas lies at the southwestern edge of its range. Here it ekes out a living among the common reeds and sedges at the edge of the tidal flat and freshwater communities.

Probably because of frequent droughts and the population of hungry alligators, swamp rabbits have never been common on the Refuge. Look for these secretive creatures while you walk around Thomas Slough and Hog Lake. Individuals have recently been seen on the roadside at the Bay Overlook.

Swamp rabbits are larger and stockier than cottontails and they tend to skulk along under the protection of bankside vegetation. If you startle one you may hear it thump the ground with a hindfoot before it bounds away.

ARMADILLO

Though most native Texans and other residents of the Gulf Coast will take this animal for granted, for many visitors the armadillo may be the most curious denizen of the Aransas National Wildlife Refuge.

The armadillo was probably the last mammal to establish itself on the Aransas without the direct intervention of man. These creatures originated in South America and only one species has extended its range into the United States. As it moved north, the armadillo pushed through the Coastal Bend about 1880. (It may have now reached its northern limit in Kansas and Missouri.) So the earliest pioneers on Blackjack Peninsula never saw armadillos.

Armadillos are unmistakable. They are the only native mammals with bony plates fused into their skin. A little larger than a football, adults weigh 12-15 pounds. They have a solid shield over the shoulders and rump and an accordian-like set of nine segments in between. The forehead is likewise heavily armored, and the long tapering tail is encased in bony rings. The legs are less heavily sheathed and the belly is merely clothed with a tangle of long hairs. The muzzle is tapered to a naked pig-like snout. All four of the stocky limbs are armed with stout claws.

Armadillos have exceptionally poor eyesight. They navigate and forage primarily by smell and count on their keen sense of hearing both to help locate prey and to detect the approach of potential predators.

These animals feed mostly upon small creatures which they uncover in the ground litter and the top several inches of soil: insect larvae, earthworms, crickets, millipedes, pillbugs, ground spiders, small lizards and snakes. On occasion they dig into fire ant nests and lap up both adults and larvae with their sticky tongues. Armadillos also relish the pulpy fruits of persimmon, dewberry and yaupon, but they are one of the few resident creatures that do not eat acorns.

Home for an armadillo is a series of burrows among which it rotates when the mood strikes it. Each burrow has an entrance about eight inches wide, and in the easily dug sandy soil of the Aransas the sloping unbranched tunnel may be over 10 feet long. In addition to serving their makers, armadillo holes are used as dodge-in escape sites by everything from fence lizards to cottontails. Rattlesnakes commonly pass the day in them. A large array of insects and arachnids retreats into the cool, dank interiors. Abandoned armadillo dens are soon taken over by raccoons, opossums or skunks. Even coyotes sometimes enlarge them for their own use at whelping time.

Young armadillos, which are tender miniaturized versions of the adults, fall prey to coyotes, bobcats, raccoons, feral hogs and horned owls. The adults are more immune to attack, but any coyote, if he catches one in the open, can flip and kill an armadillo.

Regardless of popular myth and even photographs in reputable fieldbooks, when startled or attacked the one thing no live armadillo ever does is roll into a ball. Instead, it sets off at a hopping gallop directly for the nearest burrow. The armored body pays for itself when the racing animal barges through the thickest undergrowth on its way to safety. No man and few other mammals can close on a wheezing, fear-struck armadillo running hellbent through the brush.

Armadillos are common enough on Blackjack Peninsula, but it is usually difficult to purposely locate one. They are active the year round. In the summertime they are mainly nocturnal, but they generally emerge from their burrows before sunset. On cloudy days they are abroad earlier. There is nothing like a shower of rain to bring the armadillos out in force to forage in the moist soil. In very cold weather armadillos remain in their dens, but on most cool sunny days they move out to feed.

The best way to see an armadillo is to scan the roadsides and clearings as you tour the Refuge in your vehicle. If you spot one snuffling along watch it from your window or quietly approach it from downwind for a photograph. Sometimes you can locate an armadillo by the heedless commotion it makes while searching for food.

CLOVEN-HOOFED MAMMALS

The two native species, the **javelina** and the **white-tailed deer**, have been considered in Chapter 7. The several deliberately introduced species are included in Chapter 8. A few **axis deer** occasionally wander onto the Refuge from adjacent ranches, but none of these Asian deer has taken up residence.

RACCOONS AND THEIR KIN

It is a tribute to the adaptability of **raccoons** that they are abundant on the Aransas to the point of being pestiferous. They raid camp stores at the Youth Environmental Training Area, scavenge in the Refuge dump ground, rummage through the garbage cans at the picnic area and skulk around the residences. An occasional individual will even beg at the picnic area. They prefer to forage along the margins of freshwater ponds, tidal pools and the edges of the bays, but the omnivorous raccoons range through all of the local biotic communities.

Because they are such adept and perservering predators of birds' nests, there has never been any love lost between raccoons and the Refuge personnel. During the predator control days the conflict took on a particularly grim aspect.

In the late 1940's a big concern was to build up the wild turkey population. To that end over 500 raccoons were live trapped and removed in 1948. The turkeys did not increase and the resident raccoon population appeared undiminished.

In 1950, the only whooping crane chick ever hatched on the Aransas Refuge was housed in a special enclosure on the tidal flats opposite Headquarters. When the precious chick was only three days old it was killed by a predator. A raccoon was suspected. So, when another whooper egg was laid in 1951, the raccoons paid the price for their nefarious reputation. Dog food mixed with warfarin was set out in hoppers. Shrimp and prunes laced with strychnine were scattered up and down the East Shore. Several hundred raccoons--and no telling what else--died. And the whooper egg never even hatched.

Raccoon control continued in high gear until such tactics were finally abolished in 1963. It is conservatively estimated that nearly 4,000 of the animals were dealt with before the modern notion of refuge management took hold.

Raccoons are mainly nocturnal, but you might well see one abroad in the daytime. Watch for them grabbling in the shallows of any roadside ditch or pond as you drive the roadways. In the early summertime you might even see a mama accompanied by several cute little 'coons busily learning their versatile trade. Sometimes you can spot a raccoon poking around on the tidal flats below the Observation Tower. Any place you find a muddy spot you should be able to locate a set of the raccoon's distinctive handprints.

The **ringtail** is an agile, rather cat-like relative of the raccoon. These secretive and strictly nocturnal animals prefer more broken terrain than the Aransas affords. Only one individual has been seen on the Refuge. It was flushed from a lumber pile at Headquarters in 1954.

The **coati** is also related to the raccoon. It is a larger animal with a more elongate body and a tapered snout. It holds its long indistinctly banded tail in an erect curve over its back. Coatis range from northern South America through Mexico, and a few individuals occasionally cross the Rio Grande into

Texas. It is doubtful if a breeding population occurs anywhere in the state.

A coati was seen several times near Mustang Lake in 1938. Another was seen near the Big Tree Trail in April, 1974. No more were observed until 1984, when a maintenance worker managed to coax a semi-tame coati into his pickup truck and a second animal was reported from the west side of Blackjack Peninsula. At least the first of these two recent sightings surely involved an escaped or released animal.

SKUNKS AND THEIR KIN

Three species of skunks have been recorded on the Aransas. Because they are all nocturnal, they are seldom observed by visitors.

The **striped skunk** is the commonest of the three. It spends the day curled up in a den of its own making or in a remodeled armadillo burrow. Early in the evening this omnivore emerges to forage along the ground and around poolsides for insects, spiders, birds and their eggs, unwary rodents and whatever pulpy fruits it happens across.

The **spotted skunk** is less common and it is much more secretive. It is also more prone to climb into trees and shrubs in search of prey, although it is known to occur on the nearly treeless Tatton and Matagorda units. **Gulf Coast hog-nosed skunk** is the rarest of the three. It has exceptionally long foreclaws and an enlarged snout to go along with its habit of rooting and digging through the topsoil in search of insect larvae and earthworms.

These skunks can be distinguished by the pattern of white markings on their black backs. The striped skunk has two white stripes which join at the neck and continue together atop the head. The spotted skunk has six thin white stripes that break into a series of dashes and spots on its rump. The Gulf Coast hog-nosed skunk has a single broad white band from head to rump. All three species can emit the well-known odorous defensive spray.

The broad backed, low slung **badger** uses its long foreclaws and muscular shoulders to rake the sandy coastal soil aside in search of pocket gophers and cotton rats. It supplements these staples with any other small animals it encounters: insects, arachnids, lizards and snakes, ground nesting birds and their eggs, nests of cottontail rabbits.

Badgers lead solitary lives and they are not abundant anywhere in their extensive range across the western three-quarters of Texas. Although they may have been somewhat more common when the local area was more open and supported ground squirrels (a favorite prey species), badgers have been very rare on Blackjack Peninsula since the establishment of the Refuge. Two were seen in the early 1940's, one in 1958 and another in 1970. On Matagorda Island, however, badgers are occasionally spotted by night patrols.

The virtual disappearance of the badger from Blackjack Peninsula is puzzling since the abundance of pocket gophers should provide an ample food source and the deep sand should be to the badgers' liking. Badgers were probably inhibited by the progressive overgrowth of woody and herbaceous plants, and the few animals originally present may have been incidentally wiped out during early predator control campaigns. (Both of the individuals seen in the 1940's were "collected".) Once they were gone from the peninsula, recruitment by natural immigration across the surrounding blackland fields was unlikely. The reintroduction of badgers into their native haunts on Blackjack Peninsula might have ecological merit.

Only two **long-tailed weasels** have been seen on Blackjack Peninsula, the latest in 1985. They seem to be uncommon throughout their range, but these slender, quick moving little carnivores may be routine residents and simply avoid detection. They prey almost exclusively on rodents, and pocket gophers are among their favorites. They should find good hunting on the Aransas.

The **mink** is at the southern border of its range on the Aransas Refuge. This semiaquatic weasel tolerates either fresh or brackish water, and it prefers waterways choked with debris and vegetation. The only two mink ever observed on the Refuge were both seen at the one site best suited for them-- Thomas Slough.

CARNIVORES

The status of the **gray wolf** and the extirpation of the **red wolf** are recounted in Chapter 6. Two more wild dogs occur on the Aransas: the coyote and the gray fox.

The reputation of the **coyote** ("kye-YO-tee", or in many parts of Texas, "KYE-yoat") is well established in art, literature and legend. It is the archetypical wild dog: slender, dog-like build trimmed for endurance running; long legs; erect ears; narrow muzzle; bushy tail; sharp, clear yellow eyes; acute hearing; keen nose; rather intricate social behaviour including distinctive mannerisms as well as chemical and vocal cues; an overall alertness which is often better referred to as cunning or even as downright cleverness.

Coyotes can adapt to almost any habitat, so they occur statewide, but they definitely prefer open terrain. Although the animals are common on Blackjack Peninsula, they are not abundant. The dense inland vegetation and the coyotes' own social interactions probably limit the population to about 40 adults. There are surely many vagrant animals, since coyotes can easily move back and forth from the adjacent Coastal Prairie. A thriving population of coyotes also exists on Matagorda Island.

One of the coyote's most adaptive features is its opportunistic feeding behaviour. It will consume anything from carrion to feathers to keep going. On Blackjack Peninsula coyotes probably subsist largely on cotton rats and pocket gophers. If the cottontail rabbit population rises, the coyotes turn to them as a major prey species. On Matagorda Island, jackrabbits are an important food item.

In the springtime coyotes eat a surprising amount of fresh grass. In the summertime they consume large numbers of grasshoppers and beetles. In season they enjoy persimmons, mustang grapes, yaupon fruits, acorns, mesquite beans, dewberries, prickly pears and wolfberries, and they even eat a variety of mushrooms. They snap up any frog, crayfish or small snake they run across, and they routinely patrol the beaches and tidal flats for marine offal.

Coyotes can be devastating predators on birds, and they surely find many nesting bobwhite quail, wild turkey and some of the few Attwater's prairie chicken nests on the Refuge.

Defense from coyotes is the main reason that the winter waterfowl spend their nights standing or floating in the water or roosting on islets and oyster reefs. The same threat forces resident shorebirds to nest on isolated islands and spoil banks.

The coyote is justifiably regarded as the principal predator on white-tailed deer, and virtually all of its impact is levied in the springtime on the freshly dropped fawns.

Your best chance to see a coyote is to keep a sharp eye out as you drive the Refuge roads. Watch for animals crossing the road or hustling across clearings on their way to cover. The creatures are wary, so expect no more than a glimpse. You can find their very dog-like tracks in the moist sand along the edge of San Antonio Bay and beside the Boardwalk.

If you are very lucky, you may be treated to the haunting, mournful howl which coyotes produce on occasion. Midwinter at sundown is a good time to listen. Usually one animal will be answered by others, and these may eventually build into a brief and ecstatic chorus which trails off into a series of feisty yip-yaps. Listen to the full repertory. You will not hear a more sincere expression of wildness on the Refuge.

The **gray fox** is not much larger than a house cat and it glides along the game trails on dainty ghost feet. These are pretty animals--a grizzled steel gray with a bright chestnut trim. The ample tail is gray with a black stripe along the upper margin and it is tipped in black.

Gray foxes are at home in the dense interior of Blackjack Peninsula. They also hunt the grassy swales and of all of the wild dogs they most readily take to the trees while foraging. Foxes mainly eat rodents, shrews, moles and birds, and they supplement these with an array of insects and arachnids as well as most available pulpy fruits. These animals do not howl like coyotes, but when curious or provoked they can utter a startlingly loud, coarse bark.

Watch for a shadow-animal melting into the brush anywhere along the Tour Loop. If you can glimpse its large trailing tail, you may have seen about as much as a gray fox ever reveals of itself.

Wild cats are remarkably like domestic cats in both appearance and behaviour. They have supple bodies, keen eyes with vertical pupils, exceptionally sensitive ears, retractile claws, a twitching tail, an absolutely silent tred, lightning reflexes and they are masters of both the stealthy stalk and the patient ambush. They scent-mark their territories against feline interlopers. They bury their feces. And like domestic cats, you can never be quite sure what they are going to do next.

Wild cats are notorious for avoiding observation until--for no apparent reason--one of them perversely breaks cover and strolls insouciantly along the roadside in broad daylight or stares quietly into the beam of an oncoming headlight.

At least off and on, the Aransas harbors three native species of cats. If ocelots do in fact occur here, they will boost the number to four. The **jaguarundi** and the **ocelot** are considered in Chapter 6. That leaves the bobcat and the cougar.

The **bobcat** is by far the commonest cat on the Refuge. It is most frequently seen by Refuge personnel on night patrol, but visitor sightings are not unusual. Most of the latter are incidental glimpses from vehicles or at drying waterholes.

The bobcat population was exceptionally high in 1983, and sightings have continued to be numerous going into 1986. Back in the predator control days in 1956, 52 bobcats were trapped on the Refuge over a four-month interval, which indicates a very high density for a top-level carnivore.

Bobcats are unmistakably feline in general anatomy, and they are the only local cat with a short tail. When seen from the side, their hindquarters project above the level of the powerful forequarters, causing the profile to slope down from the rump to the shoulders. The pelage is beige with washes of russet and it is dappled with dusky smudges and bars. Amidst

grass clumps or in sunflecked undergrowth a bobcat is
virtually invisible.

These cats feed mainly on mammals and birds. For them
all of the local rodents and rabbits are prime game. Cotton
rats and cottontails are staples. Bobcats also take white-tail
fawns and piglets of javelinas and feral hogs when they can.
An adult cat can kill a grown deer if caught at a disadvantage.
Because the nocturnal bobcat climbs with ease, it claims birds
with regularity. These animals are even agile enough to make
a calculated leap from the ground and waylay a low flying
dove or quail in midair.

Like most carnivores, bobcats will also take what they can
get: an occasional snake, a stranded fish, a fat grasshopper, a
fly-blown deer carcass. They have the uncatlike habit of
readily sloshing through shallow water and they are among
the many creatures which stalk the tidal flats and beaches at
night in search of blue crabs, fiddlers, crayfish and whatever
else presents itself.

Probably more so than any other species, the **cougar** (=
mountain lion = puma = panther) symbolizes nature at its
wildest and most menacing. In addition to being at the top of
the mammalian meat eating food chain, these big cats
embody the multiple intrigues of silent beauty, brooding
temperment and ominous power. This is the stuff of which
legends are spun, and cougars are attended by their share of
yarns.

Because every sighting of this impressive animal on the
Refuge is both thrilling and noteworthy, there is always need
to confirm each occurrence. Observations are typically very
brief, totally without forewarning and in bad light. Add
inherent excitement, uncertainty about field marks, a dole of
wishful thinking and a touch of anxiety. Especially if the
observer does not have much outdoor experience, it is
astoundingly easy to mistake a yearling deer or even a wind
whipped clump of winter brown bluestem grass for a hurrying
cougar. Even professionals are led astray.

The upshot is this. Since its establishment in 1937, through
1985, there have been approximately 65 reported sightings of
cougars on the Aransas National Wildlife Refuge. The first
was in 1948, the most recent in 1986. Nineteen were made by
Refuge employees. The remainder were reported by routine
visitors, hunters, petroleum company employees and
cowhands. Six sightings were confirmed (ie., made by
experienced wildlife personnel).

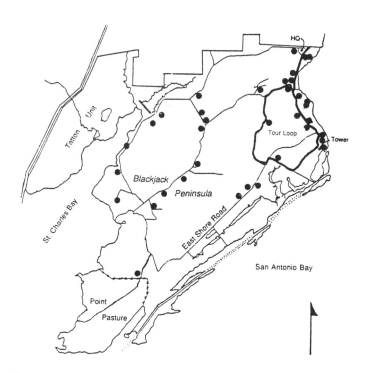

Figure 25 Sightings of cougars on the Refuge through 1985.

The greatest number of annual sightings was eight, made in 1978 and again in 1984. Several visitor sightings have been from the Observation Tower and include reports in 1978, 1979 and 1980 of an unusually dark individual--a "black panther". Occasionally people have reported seeing a pair of cougars together. One of the confirmed sightings was of a cougar stalking a deer. In March, 1981, a freshly killed deer was discovered near the Youth Environmental Training Area with all the earmarks of having just been pulled down by a big cat.

So there definitely are cougars on the Aransas at least now and then. They lie up in the dense brush by day and stalk the abundant white-tailed deer by night; but they are just fickle enough to be occasionally abroad most anytime. These are solitary, retiring, mobile, highly territorial animals. Maybe one, a pair or several routinely include the Aransas in their extensive home ranges.

If you see a cougar, you can count yourself among the privileged few. In this harried age, simply appreciating that you are in good cougar habitat and knowing that one of the great cats may well be dozing securely nearby is a thrill in itself.

Birds

Over 350 species of birds have been recorded from the Aransas National Widlife Refuge. The endangered forms and the game birds are treated in Chapters 6 and 7.

It is beyond the scope of this guidebook to do more than briefly mention some of the common members of the many other groups of birds that reside on or routinely pass across the Refuge. If you intend to seriously study the birds while on the Aransas, ask for a copy of the birding checklist at the desk in the Visitors Center. This brochure lists the kinds of birds known from the Refuge and indicates their seasonal abundance.

There are many books to help you learn to identify birds. The single best one for the Coastal Bend is Peterson's *A Field Guide to the Birds of Texas and Adjacent States.* If you can recognize the coastal birds and desire supplementary information, consult Rappole and Blacklock's *Birds of the Texas Coastal Bend.* This volume includes directions to additional birding sites along the local coast.

Proper identification is merely the first step in getting to know a species of bird. You should also become familiar with its habitat. In which of the communities listed in Chapter 3 is the bird usually found? At what season of the year is it on the Aransas? If it leaves, where does it go? Does it nest here? If so, in what sort of site? If not here, then where does it nest? Can you recognize the bird solely by its call notes? In spring plumage and winter plumage? What is the bird's niche--what does it eat and what eats the bird? How is its anatomy correlated with its niche: its feet, its legs, wings, bill, coloration? By what sorts of sounds and gestures do individuals of the same species communicate with each other?

Consider the last question--bird body language. Take the least sandpiper, for instance, the lowly "mud peep" that is so common on the tidal flats on the Refuge at all seasons except the middle of summer.

Most visitors seldom even bother to distinguish these unassuming little birds from the look-alike western sandpipers which also probe for fly larvae and chase amphipods almost all year long. But let's say that you have taken the time to recognize a mud peep when you see one: the very small, unmistakably sandpipery body; the brown back; the rather pronounced streaked breast band; the yellow-green legs; the short, thin bill. And so on.

Now that you can identify a mud peep you are ready to watch them converse. Find a flock (You almost never see a solitary mud peep--another field trait.) feeding on the tidal flat at the end of the Boardwalk. The individuals will be rather evenly spaced, each with its own traveling square foot of exposed mud to probe. Observe what happens when two birds drift too close together.   Up go their tails, exposing the white undersides.   You can see these bright little semaphores flickering continually across the flat as the birds try to maintain their feeding territories.

Any least sandpiper that fails to heed the warning signal gets chased to the edge of the flock. Sometimes two adjacent birds come to a standoff in a boundary dispute. Then each one freezes in a rigid horizontal position with its bill pointed at its neighbor. After a few seconds of ritualized staring they proceed to feed again, presumably each one better aware of the limits of the other's feeding space.

What other fragments of mud peep talk can you pick up? Here is a whole new dimension to birding--getting better acquainted with old feathered friends as a welcome supplement to ceaselessly searching for new ones.

However, there is no denying the pleasure and satisfaction which derive from observing a large number of different kinds of birds on a single outing. A long and varied trip list, perhaps enhanced by an addition to one's lifelist, is the record of an enjoyable excursion. For such a venture, the Aransas Refuge is made to order. It is one of the perennial birding hotspots in the nation.

When searching for birds nothing can compare with dumb luck for boosting your success, but careful planning is what most frequently puts you in the right place at the right time. The Aransas offers three exceptional callings for birders:

whooping cranes, spring/fall transients and winter residents. To see whoopers visit the Refuge from late October through early April. (A better guarantee is November-March. For further comments see Chapter 5.)

Spring migrants pass across the Aransas from March through May with peak numbers from mid-April through mid-May. Shorebirds and waterfowl usually move early in this interval. The spectacular kettles of soaring raptors and the frenzy of northbound warblers soon follow. The passage of miscellaneous passerines is often heralded by the appearance of blue-gray gnatcatchers in the trees and darting groups of barn swallows in the sky.

The fall migration begins with the sky call of upland sandpiper and the arrival of the first blue-winged teal in late August. Southbound bird movement is in high gear from mid-September through mid-October. While shorebirds and raptors capture the attention, warblers usually either wing across the open Gulf or slip by in scattered nocturnal flights.

The great array of winter residents is ordinarily on the Refuge from November through February.

HERONS AND EGRETS

This is one of the most evident and easily recognized group of birds on the Refuge. All species are large and distinctively colored, and most of them stalk the shallows on long legs, ready to stab after prey with rapier bill and long supple neck. In flight these birds fold their necks onto their chests and trail their outstretched legs. They are either silent or utter hoarse squawks and croaks. Most prefer to nest in crowded colonies called rookeries. Large rookeries containing half a dozen species of herons and egrets along with several kinds of gulls, terns and other waterbirds form on small islets in San Antonio Bay within two miles of Blackjack Peninsula.

Twelve species of herons and egrets occur in North America and the Aransas Refuge hosts them all. Ten of these are permanent residents.

Watch for **great blue herons** at all seasons around all brackish and freshwater sites. These are the largest of their clan, and they seem to have the grumpiest demeanor. Great blues are proficient fishermen but they will thrust after everything from cottonmouth moccasins and young alligators to blue crabs and rice rats. You will be astounded at the large size of some of the fish these birds can manhandle and cram down their expandable gullets.

The **little blue heron** is seen occasionally on the margins of freshwater ponds and sloughs and brackish tidal flats until it moves to inland swamps to nest in the springtime. The pretty slate-blue adults are distinctive. Yearlings are white, and second year birds are white with blue-gray splotches. Check bill and leg traits to distinguish them from egrets.

Tricolored herons are quite common on the Refuge all year. They can almost always be observed from the Observation Tower as they stalk the margin of Mustang Lake.

The crow-sized **green-backed heron** prefers more densely vegetated swampland than the Aransas offers, but you might spot one at Thomas Slough or Hog Lake.

Egrets are actually plumed herons, and they paid dearly for that distinction during the plume hunting days in the early 1900's. The two commonest species are the **great** and the **snowy egrets**. The first of these is the most noticeable large white wader on the tidal flats and it is the bird most often mistaken for a whooping crane by many visitors. The smaller snowy egret has a black bill (yellow bill in the great egret) and sports bright yellow feet.

Reddish egrets are not common birds, but their lively feeding behaviour makes them stand out in any crowd of brackish water waders. Watch one of these birds prance and whirl with wings partly spread as it tries to scare up small fishes along the edge of San Antonio Bay.

Originally from Africa, the **cattle egret** came to Texas via South and Central America in 1954. The first birds were recorded on the Aransas Refuge in 1959. Although it has since become the most abundant kind of egret in the Coastal Bend, it is not frequently seen in the area of public access on Blackjack Peninsula. Cattle egrets are not wetland feeders. They eat insects, especially grasshoppers, and they are prone to follow cattle and snatch prey items stirred up by the grazing animals. You are most likely to spot small flocks of these white birds in the pasturelands inland of the Refuge.

Species	Number of nests		%Change	12 Year
	1984	1985	1984-85	Average
Great Egret	256	242	-09%	406
Snowy Egret	125	210	+68%	236
Reddish Egret	61	64	+05%	54
Cattle Egret	57	28	-51%	63
Great Blue Heron	72	81	+13%	145
Little Blue Heron	5	0	-100%	-
Tricolored Heron	162	281	+73%	248
Black-crowned Night Heron	23	19	-17%	56
Roseate Spoonbill	30	96	+220%	80
TOTAL WATERBIRDS	800	1021	+28%	1288
Laughing Gull	558	397	-29%	210
Black Skimmer	163	179	+10%	158
American Oystercatcher	3	13	+333%	-
Forster's Tern	198	223	+13%	120
Gull-billed Tern	136	201	+48%	51
Caspian Tern	109	158	+45%	73
Least Tern	17	63	+271%	14
TOTAL GULLS AND TERNS	1184	1234	+4%	626
TOTAL NESTS	1984	2255	+14%	1916

Table 2 Composition of waterbird nesting colonies on offshore islands.

The stocky **black-crowned night heron** is rather common on the Refuge but it is seldom observed because it spends the daytime humped in dense stands of reeds or bulrushes. At night it sallies forth to fish and stalk crayfish and crabs, and night herons will gobble down any unprotected nestling birds they happen across. If you disturb a group of roosting black-crowns, they will flap off in confusion uttering a series of popping "quoks". **Yellow-crowned night herons** are only incidental on the Refuge and they do not nest locally.

Bitterns are secretive herons which seldom stray outside the confines of thick growths of tall reeds, cattails and bulrushes. It takes sharp eyes to discern an occasional **American bittern** in Thomas Slough. The smallest of our herons--the **least bittern**--may be there as well, but it is even more elusive unless it flushes. The least bittern is more easily detected by its gentle "coo-coo-coo-coo", which adds to the rising symphony of intriguing sounds that emanate from the bankside vegetation along Thomas Slough at dusk.

OTHER LARGE WADERS

Both the **white-faced** and the **white ibis** occur on the Aransas. Look for the white-faced on Heron Flats. The less abundant white ibis also occurs there and small flocks often use the brackish flats at Mustang Lake. The white-faced ibis will appear black until it wheels in the sun. Then you get a brilliant display of iridescent bronze-green from its back. Both species fly with neck outstretched and decurved bill well exposed.

Wood storks nest in Mexico and move up the Texas coast each summer. These are large, heavy set, archaic-looking birds. Watch for high-soaring flocks as well as small groups hunkered vulture-like on dead tree limbs. These storks are especially attracted by the stranded fishes and other small creatures which are exposed when Hog and Jones lakes begin to dry up.

If a **roseate spoonbill** crosses your horizon, you will not miss its unmatchable pink plumage, which is rendered even more radiant when the sun is low. Spoonbills can be seen the year round on the Refuge, but they are more abundant in the summer and fall. Watch for small groups winging rapidly high across the tidal flats. The Observation Tower is the best vantage for observing the strange sidewise feeding movements of spoonbills. (Do not join the crowd who claim to be viewing flamingos!)

BIRD	1976	1977	1978	1979	1980	1981	1982	1983	1984	1985	TOTAL SEEN	10 YR AVG	TIMES SEEN
Great Blue Heron	70	43	73	133	205	170	75	137	105	78	1089	108	10
Green Backed Heron	0	0	0	0	1	0	0	0	0	0	1	0	1
Little Blue Heron	10	3	4	2	6	6	6	12	4	7	60	6	10
Cattle Egret	3	0	1	6	0	23	2	1	1	0	37	4	7
Reddish Egret	3	1	2	19	14	3	7	3	13	14	79	8	10
Great Egret	49	45	86	151	30	138	32	101	67	56	755	76	10
Snowy Egret	55	23	42	35	37	50	11	60	8	54	85	38	10
Tricolored Heron	19	8	10	18	22	34	12	6	11	24	164	16	10
Blk-crowned Night Heron	4	2	11	20	5	42	2	37	4	35	162	16	10
Least Bittern	0	0	0	0	1	1	0	0	0	0	2	0	2
American Bittern	1	2	1	0	5	5	1	1	0	0	16	2	2
White-faced Ibis	0	26	11	640	0	223	28	15	0	25	968	97	7
White Ibis	0	0	2	135	31	19	2	91	34	124	438	44	8
Roseate Spoonbill	36	11	22	44	28	71	29	6	6	6	259	26	10
Whooping Crane	33	65	23	50	56	30	42	28	44	31	402	40	10
Sandhill Crane	523	660	621	3674	288	475	247	1540	836	75	8939	894	10
	806	889	909	4927	729	1290	496	2038	1143	529			

Table 3 Large waders seen in 10 years of Audubon Christmas Counts.

BIRD	1976	1977	1978	1979	1980	1981	1982	1983	1984	1985	TOTAL SEEN	10 YR AVG	TIMES SEEN
Herring Gull	5	8	11	5	15	100	13	33	35	11	236	24	10
Ring-billed Gull	164	143	81	189	72	85	640	141	204	108	1827	183	10
Laughing Gull	8	28	65	161	79	312	57	110	135	119	1074	107	10
Bonapart's Gull	1	0	0	1	1	0	0	1	1	2	7	1	6
Franklin's Gull	0	1	0	0	0	0	0	0	0	0	1	0	1
Gull-billed Tern	2	0	8	1	0	1	6	3	2	0	23	2	7
Forster's Tern	13	21	12	62	297	154	76	72	40	135	882	88	10
Common Tern	0	0	2	0	2	1	1	0	0	0	6	1	4
Royal Tern	8	2	19	11	16	12	10	11	7	13	109	11	10
Sandwich Tern	0	0	0	0	2	1	0	0	0	0	3	0	2
Caspian Tern	7	90	39	104	40	51	104	136	17	21	609	61	10
Black Skimmer	0	39	40	172	69	130	71	0	0	60	581	58	7
	208	332	277	706	593	847	978	507	441	469			

Table 4 Gulls and terns seen in 10 years of Audubon Christmas Counts.

GULLS AND TERNS

Watch for gulls winging along over San Antonio Bay and for terns hovering and diving into the bay. Both kinds of birds rest on pilings, exposed reefs and the bay shore. The Bay Overlook, Dagger Point, the Observation Tower and the adjacent Boardwalk all offer excellent viewing sites.

In the wintertime the **ring-billed gull** is the most frequent large white gull on the Refuge.

The resident **laughing gull** is the commonest local species of its medium-sized group. Beginning in late March, one is seldom out of earshot of the maniacal calls of the laughing gulls. You might spot flocks of these gulls feeding in the wakes of boats on the Gulf Intracoastal Waterway. These birds nest on the fringe of the heron rookeries on the islands in San Antonio Bay. **Franklin's gulls** pass across the Refuge in spring and fall.

From the Observation Tower you can regularly see the large, red-billed **Caspian terns** fly by individually and in pairs. Be sure you distinguish them from the less common **royal terns.** The most abundant terns plummeting into Mustang Lake are **Forster's** and **gull-billed terns.** You should see the dainty **least terns** during the spring and summer all along San Antonio Bay. These little terns nest on the offshore islets and on the old airfield runways on Matagorda Island.

Black terns are beautiful birds with a jet black head and breast and soft silvery wings and back. There are usually at least a few of them on the Refuge at all seasons except midwinter. Watch for these graceful fliers as they swoop swallow-like to pluck insects from the tips of tidal flat plants.

SHOREBIRDS

The endangered eskimo curlew and piping plover are considered in Chapter 6, the common snipe and American Woodcock, with open hunting seasons, in Chapter 7.

This large and diverse group of birds encompasses a shifting mix of species according to the seasons. The greatest variety is usually on the Refuge in the spring and fall, but there is a large array of winter residents. Summer is the slack season for shorebirds on the Aransas.

Most species are small to moderate-sized, thin-legged and make their living by probing and plucking along the shorelines and mudflats of both brackish and fresh water. The majority tends to feed, rest and fly in flocks. The two largest groups are the plovers and sandpipers.

Six species breed locally: **snowy plover, Wilson's plover, killdeer, willet, American avocet** and **black-necked stilt**. Some, such as the killdeer, willet, **greater** and **lesser yellowlegs, least** and **western sandpipers, black-bellied plover, dunlin, long-billed dowitcher,** and **sanderling** are among the most frequently seen birds on the Refuge during all seasons except summertime.

The **long-billed curlew** is also a prominent member of this coterie. Watch for this bird at the water's edge along San Antonio Bay and on the mudflat in Mustang Lake. You cannot miss the namesake seven-inch downcurved bill that gives the bird an advantage in probing for marine worms and snagging mud shrimp from their burrows. If you flush curlews watch for their cinnamon wing linings and learn their distinctive two-syllable alarm note.

Other shorebirds, like the **solitary** and **stilt sandpipers**, pause only briefly in spring and fall; yet others, like the **lesser golden plover**, are seen only in the spring (in the fall, these birds stream south directly across the Gulf of Mexico.)

The **upland sandpiper** nests in the northern U.S. and Canada, and winters on the pampas of Argentina. It passes over the Aransas in August-September and March-April, and small flocks occasionally set down on the open grasslands of

BIRD	1976	1977	1978	1979	1980	1981	1982	1983	1984	1985	TOTAL SEEN	10 YR AVG	TIMES SEEN
King Rail	1	0	3	1	2	1	0	0	0	0	8	1	5
Clapper Rail	2	0	0	0	1	3	1	0	0	0	7	1	4
Virginia Rail	0	0	0	0	1	0	0	0	0	0	1	0	1
Sora	0	2	4	4	7	3	1	4	2	5	32	3	9
Yellow Rail	0	0	0	0	0	1	0	0	0	0	1	0	1
Common Moorhen	4	5	21	41	12	32	12	19	5	7	158	16	10
Purple Gallinule	0	0	0	0	0	0	0	0	1	0	1	0	1
American Coot	353	1000	522	5490	265	2282	87	403	376	523	11301	1130	10
American Oystercatcher	1	3	1	2	10	4	2	2	6	4	35	4	10
Semipalmated Plover	4	0	2	2	28	5	17	0	0	0	58	6	6
Piping Plover	12	0	0	35	0	4	5	0	0	0	56	6	4
Snowy Plover	3	0	1	0	0	32	33	0	20	0	89	9	4
Wilson's Plover	4	1	0	0	1	0	0	0	0	0	6	1	3
Killdeer	73	104	90	153	81	75	50	126	21	70	843	84	10
Black-bellied Plover	23	3	20	104	47	94	58	27	6	11	393	39	10
Ruddy Turnstone	2	0	0	0	6	0	1	0	16	2	27	3	5
American Woodcock	0	0	0	0	0	0	0	8	0	0	8	1	1
Common Snipe	24	26	8	83	10	14	2	37	1	7	212	21	10
Long-billed Curlew	13	7	8	11	33	50	10	13	27	16	188	19	10
Spotted Sandpiper	4	1	4	5	4	3	1	3	4	3	32	3	10
Willet	12	16	13	34	71	35	92	21	30	29	353	35	10
Greater Yellowlegs	24	56	29	43	28	28	20	54	11	51	344	34	10
Lesser Yellowlegs	7	13	2	34	11	10	15	6	0	0	98	10	8
Baird's Sandpiper	0	0	0	0	0	5	0	0	0	0	5	1	1
Least Sandpiper	56	0	63	27	15	8	84	35	1	0	289	28	8
Dunlin	199	0	101	12	91	69	178	86	200	18	954	95	10
Short-billed Dowitcher	90	1	0	1	0	31	0	51	0	0	174	17	5
Long-billed Dowitcher	19	144	203	317	902	40	20	121	11	1	1778	176	10
Semipalmated Sandpiper	4	0	0	1	0	0	0	3	0	0	8	1	3
Western Sandpiper	256	3	225	20	204	65	169	90	1200	1	2333	233	10
Red-breasted Merganser	0	0	1	0	3	0	0	2	0	0	6	1	3
Sanderling	7	0	20	18	103	31	31	19	14	12	255	26	9
American Avocet	101	0	52	25	66	3	147	176	47	99	716	72	9
Black-necked Stilt	0	0	0	0	0	0	0	0	0	1	1	0	1
Wilson's Phalarope	0	0	0	0	0	0	2	0	0	0	2	0	1
	1298	1385	1393	6463	2002	3028	1038	1306	1999	860			

Table 5 Shorebirds seen in 10 years of Audubon Christmas Counts.

the Tatton and Matagorda units. Even if you do not spot this thimble-headed bird, listen for its sweetly whistled sky call. The urgent notes are unfailing harbingers of the thousands of birds which will soon be funneling along the Central Flyway.

Nonbreeding individuals of shorebird species which routinely nest in the north often hold over on the Refuge, so you may see a few of these oddballs almost any time of the year.

Although not notable for their songs, many shorebirds have distinctive alarm notes and sky calls. The rapidly repeated "pill-will-willet" of the willet can be heard all across the tidal flats in late March and April. In June the nervous "keck" of a nesting black-necked stilt can drive you to distraction.

All of these birds can be observed along the edge of San Antonio Bay. Although the Observation Tower is the single best spot, the smaller species are better viewed from the end of

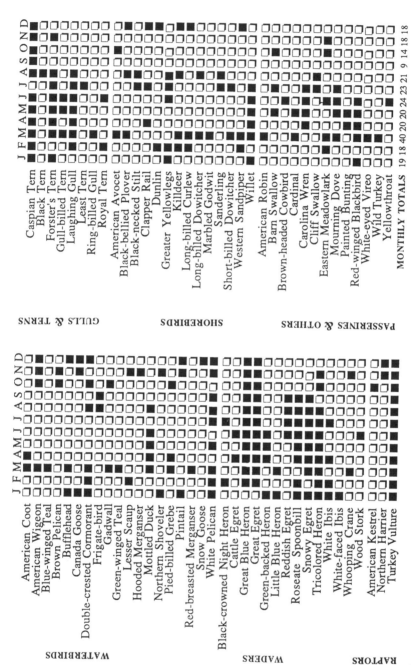

Figure 26 Bird species seen during a monthly 30 minute interval on the Observation Tower, 1985-86.

the Boardwalk, at Dagger Point and opposite the picnic area. Heron Flats is also often very productive and an afternoon sun there makes for excellent viewing.

We have included two separate sets of data to give you an idea of what shorebirds you can expect to see on the Aransas. The Tower Count reveals the species of birds seen from the Observation Tower during a 30-minute interval each month throughout the year. This includes more than shorebirds, and it suggests what an unskilled but informed individual can anticipate.

The Audubon Christmas Count reveals the numbers of each species of shorebird seen on the Refuge by a group of skilled birders during one 12-hour period near the end of the year. The results from 1975-85 indicate annual trends and variation, and the composite list encompasses the winter resident species.

OTHER WATERBIRDS

Anytime during the winter look for pairs and small groups of sleek **common loons** riding the waves and diving deeply for fish well out from shore in San Antonio Bay.

The Aransas routinely hosts three grebes. All dive for small fish, crustaceans and molluscs and swim energetically while under water. Distinguish them from ducks by their stubbier bodies and more chicken-like bills. Watch one of these birds when it becomes suspicious or feels threatened. Without appearing to move a muscle, it will slowly sink vertically in the water until only its head is visible. Then it will disappear entirely, straight down. How do you suppose it manages to submerge so subtly?

The **pied-billed grebe** can almost always be found in the brackish shallows near the Observation Tower and the Boardwalk except in the summertime when they move to inland waters to nest. **Eared grebes** can be expected on Mustang Lake during the winter. The Aransas Refuge is on the northern edge of the range of the **least grebe**, but these little slate-gray, red-eyed divers are occasional in the wintertime. Look for them in pairs in any freshwater pond or slough.

White pelicans can usually be seen in small fishing flotillas on San Antonio Bay and Mustang Lake. The exposed oyster reefs offshore from the picnic area and the edge of False Live Oak Point are favored resting sites. If you spot a flock of these birds flap-gliding through the air, marvel at their effortless

grace. On the water, watch their rhymthic head movements as they seine for fish, drain their pouches and gobble down their catch, so different from the feeding habits of brown pelicans. (See Chapter 6).

Wintering **double-crested cormorants** can sometimes be seen by the hundreds from the Observation Tower as they feed and loaf near False Live Oak Point. They haul out in the spring. Although they breed locally, **olivaceous cormorants** are far less commonly seen on the Refuge. These birds prefer inland freshwater sites.

High-soaring kettles of **anhingas** pass over the Refuge during their spring and fall migrations. A few birds nest in local freshwater sites, so you might find one at any season. One of the real delights of an idle walk along Thomas Slough is seeing the keen-billed profile of one of these water turkeys suddenly break the surface. The birds swim completely submerged or with the head and long neck exposed. They frequently perch on overhanging willow branches while they preen and dry their feathers.

The **black skimmer** is a unique and highly specialized waterbird. Since it is a resident and nests on islets in the local bays, you can expect to see it the year round. Skimmers are at their best when feeding. They prefer quiet bayside water and are frequently most active at dusk and into the night when small fishes and crustaceans are near the surface. The birds' peculiar bills and exceptionally long wings make good adaptive sense only when you watch them expertly cleaving the water's surface with their lower mandibles.

Can you imagine slipping the blade of an oyster knife into a feeding oyster and severing its adductor muscle before the creature can clamp its shells closed? The **American oystercatcher** routinely uses its flattened red bill to turn that trick. It also feeds on mussels, crustaceans and marine worms. The birds are not common. Watch for them on exposed oyster reefs at low tide.

Do not be surprised to hear the dry rattle of a **belted kingfisher** from any freshwater site or at Mustang Lake, especially during the wintertime. Probably because of the lack of suitable nesting sites, kingfishers are scarce on the Refuge in spring and summer.

RAPTORS

The birds of prey constitute a large group with a varying set of component species on the Aransas Refuge. All have a hooked beak designed for grasping, tearing and snipping meat. Except for the vultures and the caracara, each species is equipped with sharp talons and a sure grip for seizing and holding live prey. Keen eyesight, dive-bombing attack and an alert, wary nature also characterize the group. Because they exist at the top of the food web, raptors are usually not abundant, but the few individuals serve critical roles in maintaining the balance between producers and consumers.

To see raptors, you need to keep a sharp eye out and scan both the sky and potential perching sites as far ahead as your binoculars will allow. Your best bet is a slow, alert drive around the Tour Loop. Wintertime is the best season for perching and hunting birds.

The **American kestrel** is probably the most commonly observed of the overwintering raptors. These colorful little falcons can be found perching, hovering or winging swiftly along the roadsides. You might detect them first by their excited "killy-killy-killy" warning call. You may see a kestrel drop on a grasshopper. They also take mice and they are agile enough to knock small passerine birds from the air. Kestrels are even quick enough to include dragonflys in their routine fare, and that means *very* quick indeed.

BIRD	1976	1977	1978	1979	1980	1981	1982	1983	1984	1985	TOTAL SEEN	10 YR AVG	TIMES SEEN
Turkey Vulture	217	222	236	192	582	176	236	360	217	234	2672	267	10
Black Vulture	45	79	43	119	77	111	107	79	60	136	856	86	10
Black Shouldered Kite	2	7	0	7	2	8	8	7	3	10	54	5	9
Sharp-shinned Hawk	2	0	2	0	6	4	0	2	2	2	20	2	7
Cooper's Hawk	2	1	0	1	2	0	1	1	0	0	8	1	6
Red-tailed Hawk	17	8	21	22	20	13	11	27	22	22	183	18	10
Red-shouldered Hawk	1	1	3	5	17	4	6	8	9	1	55	6	10
Broad-winged Hawk	0	0	0	0	1	0	0	0	0	0	1	0	1
White-tailed Hawk	9	7	6	10	7	0	3	7	12	5	66	7	9
Ferruginous Hawk	1	0	1	0	0	0	0	0	0	0	2	0	2
Harris' Hawk	0	0	0	0	1	0	0	0	0	0	1	0	1
Bald Eagle	2	0	0	1	0	1	0	1	0	0	5	1	4
Northern Harrier	39	33	41	51	42	48	40	66	27	31	418	42	10
Osprey	1	0	0	0	0	1	0	0	1	1	4	0	4
Caracara	1	14	0	5	1	2	1	4	7	2	37	4	9
Merlin	3	0	0	1	1	1	1	0	0	2	9	1	6
American Kestrel	47	52	104	82	109	141	51	37	56	63	742	74	10
	389	424	457	496	868	510	465	599	416	509			

Table 6 Raptors seen in 10 years of Audubon Christmas Counts.

Migrating **merlin** occasionally stop over, but they are never numerous. Check your field guide to distinguish them from kestrels. The other falcons--the endangered **peregrine** and **aplomado**--are considered in Chapter 6.

A step up in size from the small falcons are the two crow-sized accipiters: **Cooper's hawk** and the **sharp-shinned hawk**. Expect both species in the winter and during migration. These broad-winged, long-tailed raptors are adept at navigating amid the tangle of the oak thickets. With a quick maneuver and a burst of speed they are deadly in their pursuit of small birds. They usually offer a startled observer only a blurred silhouette.

The **red-tailed hawk** is the commonest of the large hawks that you are apt to see perching on a dead branch or soaring aloft on a winter afternoon. Watch for the brick-red tail which is its hallmark, and listen for its hissing squeal of disapproval at your presence. The red-tail nests infrequently on the Refuge.

The **white-tailed hawk** is less abundant and less versatile than the red-tail. It is only seen soaring over open grassland. These hawks not only cruise over freshly burned tracts, they often actively work the line of flames for the flush of rodents. White-tails occasionally nest on Blackjack Peninsula. They, like the coyote and the jackrabbit, were apparently more abundant when the peninsula was more open.

The Aransas Refuge lies on the northeastern edge of the range of the **Harris hawk**. If you spot one of these brushland raptors, enjoy its rich chocolate plumage with handsome chestnut shoulders and bright white rump band.

When hundreds of hawks pass across the Coastal Bend in spring and fall, most are probably **broad-winged hawks**. The larger **Swainson's hawk** migrate at the same time and sometimes also appear in large silent flocks.

Kites are the most graceful raptors. Watch for an occasional **black-shouldered kite** hovering buoyantly over open areas along the Tour Loop in the wintertime. They also occur on the Tatton and Matagorda units. You may see these birds more commonly over pastures and roadsides inland of the Refuge. **Mississippi kites** are mostly seen as high-flying migrants. **Swallow-tailed kites** appear only as rare spring migrants. The best year ever for Refuge sightings was in 1981, when for a three week span in March, these acrobatic birds were seen almost daily.

The **northern harrier** can usually be spotted from the Observation Tower or along the Tour Loop at all seasons except summer. Of all the birds of prey this long-winged, long-tailed hawk seems to be the best adapted to gliding at grasstop level regardless of coastal wind or blustery norther.

The **osprey** is another long-limbed raptor. Individuals stop over during the spring and fall migrations and an occasional bird winters on the Refuge. Watch for one from the Observation Tower or the Bay Overlook. If you are lucky, you may see an osprey plunge feet-first into San Antonio Bay and then labor into the air with a mullet in its talons. The bird may feed on the wing or seek out a high perch to devour its prey. In an attempt to attract nesting ospreys, tall poles surmounted by open platforms were erected on the Refuge at eight sites in 1978. (One of these is visible on the bayshore opposite the Heron Flats Trail.) To date the birds have spurned these offers.

The first **golden eagle** was seen on the Refuge in December, 1964. Since then there have been half a dozen additional sightings, the most recent one in 1972. All of the birds have been immature. The **bald eagle** is discussed in Chapter 6.

You may have flushed a **crested caracara** from a road kill while you were enroute to the Aransas. These handsome "Mexican eagles" may be seen at any season winging swiftly overland along the Tour Loop, and they consort with vultures on carrion. Caracaras are residents. They prefer the more open, mesquite-studded terrain on the Tatton Unit for nesting.

Both the **turkey vulture** and the **black vulture** are numerous enough to border on being pestiferous on the Refuge. Turkey vultures outnumber the blacks by about five to one. Both species roost in the live oaks at the picnic area and near the Big Tree trail, and scattered individuals can be found resting on dead limbs along the Tour Loop. They enjoy spreading their wings to the morning sunshine. Vultures prefer to soar on rising parcels of warm air, but they will zoom along on buffeting north winds if they must. Their infallible scavenger service meshes well with the natural food web.

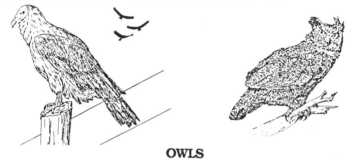

OWLS

Six species of owls have been recorded on the Aransas Refuge. Two of these, the **eastern screech owl** and the **barred owl**, prefer riparian woodlands and occur on Blackjack Peninsula only incidentally. Two others, the **burrowing owl** and the **short-eared owl** are uncommon winter visitors to the open terrain on the Tatton and Matagorda units. The **barn owl** is rarely seen on the peninsula but it is the common resident owl on Matagorda Island.

The **great-horned owl** is without question the commonest nocturnal raptor on the Aransas, and except for the scavenging vultures it is the commonest resident bird of prey. Indeed, great-horned owls rank among the most important predatory animals on the Refuge. These big owls are rare only on the Matagorda Unit.

As predators, great-horned owls are implacable and insatiable. Each night they take a heavy toll among the cotton rats, gophers, cottontails, roosting waterbirds, skunks, young opossums and raccoons, snakes and even stranded fish. Remains of pied-bill grebes, American coots, purple gallinules, black-crowned night herons, snowy egrets, cattle egrets and bobwhite quail have been recovered from the nests of great-horned owls on the Refuge.

These owls lay their eggs in abandoned hawk nests in January. For the past several years a pair has nested near the Headquarters.

Watch for the distinctive silhouettes of great-horned owls in roadside trees at dusk along the Tour Loop. Their beguilingly gentle, six-parted hooting begins at dusk and is most often heard in January and February. Almost invariably the call of one member of a pair will be answered by its partner.

We have included a table of raptor sightings from the Christmas Bird Counts held on the Aransas Refuge between 1975-85.

WARBLERS

Thirty-four species of these colorful passerines are on the current Refuge checklist. Only three--the **orange-crowned warbler**, the **yellow-rumped warbler**, and the **common yellowthroat**--are reliable winter residents. Only the common yellowthroat stays to nest.

Northbound warblers begin to move across the Aransas Refuge in late March, when the first **yellow-throated warblers, black-and-white warblers**, and **northern parulas** arrive. Soon thereafter the Refuge will ring with the "witchity-witchity-witch" of the common yellowthroats. In a routine year the others pass through, sometimes in brief noticeable waves, sometimes in prolonged cryptic trickles. The intermittent flurry continues through midMay.

When a cell of bad weather sweeps across the Coastal Bend and collides with peak waves of migrating warblers over the open Gulf, the birds are hard put to make landfall. In fact, many cannot withstand the buffeting headwinds and rain squalls. Windrows of pretty bodies wash up on the beaches of the barrier islands. Those birds that make it are exhausted, ravenous and confused. For several days they regroup and feed. During that brief interval of revitalization the Coastal Bend experiences a "warbler fallout" when all of the trees are abustle and all of the birders are afield.

To see warblers on the Aransas come in midApril. To experience a fallout you must simply be lucky. (Notable recent fallouts occurred in 1972, 1979 and 1982.) In either case, the large live oaks along the Big Tree Trail, at the picnic area and around Headquarters are the best places to search. If you are on Matagorda Island, the rows of oleanders and the thickets of tamarisk trees are usually very productive.

Mourning Dove	1	Black-and-white warbler	*
Inca dove	1	Worm-eating warbler	2
Roadrunner	1	Golden-winged warbler	3
Paraque	3	Tennessee warbler	4
Common nighthawk	5	Yellow warbler	*
Ruby-throated hummingbird	1	Magnolia warbler	*
Eastern kingbird	*	Black-throated green warbler	10
Western kingbird	1	Blackburnian warbler	*
Scissortailed flycatcher	4	Chestnut-sided warbler	*
Brown-crested flycatcher	2	Bay-breasted warbler	*
Eastern wood pewee	12	Ovenbird	6
Tree swallow	**	Northern waterthrush	5
Bank swallow	**	Kentucky warbler	5
Rough-winged swallow	**	Yellowthroat	3
Barn swallow	***	American redstart	*
Cliff swallow	*	Eastern meadowlark	*
Purple martin	**	Red-winged blackbird	*
Black-crested titmouse	1	Boat-tailed grackle	*
House wren	1	Brown-headed cowbird	3
Mockingbird	1	Scarlet tanager	6
Catbird	*	Summer tanager	*
Brown thrasher	4	Cardinal	*
Wood thrush	1	Rose-breasted grosbeak	1
Swainson's thrush	*	Blue grosbeak	2
Gray-cheeked thrush	3	Indigo bunting	*
White-eyed vireo	3	Painted bunting	3
Red-eyed vireo	3	Savannah sparrow	1
Philadelphia vireo	6	Lark sparrow	4

Table 7 Bird list for May 7, 1972. * indicates 50-100 individuals, ** 100-200, and *** 200+.

To give you an idea of the frenzied bird action on the Aransas in a good warbler year, we have included one staff member's list for May 7, 1972.

CUCKOOS

Yellow-billed cuckoos arrive in the spring and remain through the summer to nest. Watch for these slender, long-tailed birds searching for hairy caterpillars in the live oaks and learn their melodious bell-like call. **Black-billed cuckoos** are rarely spotted as they pass through headed north.

Grooved-billed anis are Mexican birds at the northern limit of their range in the Coastal Bend. They move in small flocks and appear irregularly on the Refuge, mostly in the wintertime. Look for them in the brush on the middle ridge of the Heron Flats Trail. Do not mistake these long-tailed black birds for grackles. Their bulbous beaks quickly identify them.

Although the **greater roadrunner** is a resident throughout Texas, it is currently notably rare on the Aransas Refuge. During the 1940's and through the drought years of the 1950's, when Blackjack Peninsula was much more open, roadrunners were common. The spread of live oak thickets and tall bunch grasses has apparently forced an exodus of this species. Isolated sightings are still made along the northern and western boundaries of the peninsula, and in 1973, a roadrunner was seen at the Youth Environmental Training Area.   The birds occur in the mesquite and prickly pear community on the Tatton Unit and they probably nest there.

GOATSUCKERS

Six species of these weird, night-flying birds have been recorded on the Refuge.   You may startle up a resting individual from the leaf litter along one of the trails through the oak mottes. While leaving the Refuge at dusk, watch for the glowing red eyes of a nighthawk in the beam of your headlights and listen for their variety of distinctive calls which contribute to the semitropical aura of the Coastal Bend.

The **chuck-will's-widow** and the **whip-poor-will** pause only long enough to punctuate early spring evenings with their easily recognizable calls.   Both the **poorwill** and the **lesser nighthawk** are more at home in the brushland southwest of the Refuge, so they are rare spring and summer stragglers.

The **common nighthawk** is the most frequently observed member of the group.   These birds arrive in April, nest on bare open ground and remain until fall.   During the heat of the day you might see resting individuals with eyes closed to slits hunkered on dead branches and atop posts and snags.   Late in the afternoon they take to the air and fly a high, erratic course as they hawk for insects, uttering their nasal "peent" all the while.   Most Texans call these birds bull bats.

The **pauraque**("pav-RAH-kay") is the giant of the clan.   It is another of the Mexican birds that reaches its northern limit on the Aransas Refuge.   These nighthawks are residents.   They haunt the live oak mottes and are most frequently observed around the picnic area and the Youth Environmental Training Area.   Watch for them on the road at dusk and listen for their rasping "pic-pic-p'YEER".

SWIFTS AND SWALLOWS

These are birds of the open sky.   The chittering of **chimney swifts** verifies that spring migration is in full swing. Although these birds are common in the Coastal Bend throughout the summer, a scarcity of nesting sites may account for their relative rarity on the Aransas.   **White-throated swifts** are western birds. The few spring sightings over Headquarters were surely of displaced transients.

Three of the six recorded species of swallows hurry across the Refuge in spring and fall: the **tree, bank** and **rough-winged swallows**. The other three--the **barn** and **cliff swallows** and the **purple martin**--linger through the summer, but the absence of adequate nest sites probably accounts for the erratic occurrence of these birds on the Aransas.

The commonest species, the barn swallow, is often seen hawking low over the tidal flats. You may have noticed an occasional whirling group of cliff swallows while you were enroute to the Refuge. These birds commonly nest under bridge culverts, and a small nesting colony uses a comparable structure at Burgentine Lake. Purple martins occasionally utilize the houses erected for them at Headquarters and at the picnic area. Unhappily, despite propaganda to the contrary, none of these birds is especially prone to feed on mosquitoes.

HUMMINGBIRDS

The **ruby-throated humminbgird** is the only species which makes a reliable appearance each spring. Since 1978, **buff-bellied hummingbirds** have apparently extended their range into the Coastal Bend. Both species may be seen occasionally through the summer, but the withering coastal heat apparently forces most of them to inland riparian forests to nest. Always check the bright red flowers of turk's cap for hummers. The thicket at the parking site beside the Bay Overlook seems to be a favored spot. Also scan the trumpet creeper flowers on the Heron Flats Trail. The watered area around Headquarters may also yield some hummers, and a feeder there lures in migrants.

Hummingbirds frequently pause to refuel on the Aransas before starting south. Besides the two kinds just mentioned, occasional **black-chinned, rufous,** and even a **broad-tailed hummingbird** have been seen in the fall. Doubtless others zip through undetected.

WOODPECKERS

Despite its oaks, the Aransas Refuge does not have the diverse and abundant standing crop of dead branches which attract woodpeckers. If you spot a small woodpecker in the live oaks it will likely be the resident **ladder-backed woodpecker**. **Red-bellied woodpeckers** drift in from the local riparian forests to the north, but they rarely stay. Likewise, **golden-fronted woodpeckers** invade Blackjack Peninsula from the brushland to the southwest. Again, they rarely stay except for a thriving population in the mesquite and prickly pear community on the Tatton Unit.

In the wintertime **northern flickers** come and go. Rarely a displaced **red-headed woodpecker** will put in a brief wintertime appearance, as will an occasional **yellow-bellied sapsucker** and **downy woodpecker**.

MISCELLANEOUS COMMON PASSERINES

The **cardnal** is the commonest resident songbird on the Aransas Refuge. It occurs wherever woody cover is at hand. Cardinals forage in flocks during the wintertime.

Mockingbirds are most at home in the vast brushy interior of Blackjack Peninsula. A slow drive around the Tour Loop in the springtime should make you aware of their cheek-by-jowl nesting territories. In the wintertime watch the mockers work themselves into a frenzy trying to defend their favorite yaupon thickets against an invasion of **American robins**.

During most winters the live oak thickets along the Tour Loop harbor enough **brown thrashers** so that dawn and dusk are enlivened by their low churring calls.

The **scissor-tailed flycatcher** is one of the most eyecatching and delicately pretty summer residents on the Refuge. The arrival of the cheerful, twittering scissortails on or about March 15, sets the mood for springtime on the Aransas. They stay until midNovember.

The **loggerhead shrike** is a permanent resident but it is most often observed in the fall and winter. Watch for it perched on dead branches along the Tour Loop. Despite its small size, the shrike is an energetic predator on insects, mice, lizards and small snakes and birds. Shrikes have been seen with freshly killed horned larks, mockingbirds, warblers and sparrows. This species earns the name "butcher bird" by killing lizards and grasshoppers and impaling the bodies on mesquite thorns until it is ready to consume them.

Most of the meadowlarks on the tidal flats, roadsides and recently burned tracts are **eastern meadowlarks**. Their lilting songs can be heard on sunny mornings throughout the spring and early summer. **Western meadowlarks** move into the Tatton Unit during most dry winters and a few invade Blackjack Peninsula. If you are a birder, you know that the ear is better than the eye for distinguishing the two, but in the wintertime the birds seldom sing.

Horned larks are almost always seen in pairs. Watch for them on open ground on the roadside and in sandy or silty clearings on the tidal flats, where they like to walk along nibbling the fresh tips of the glasswort. Horned larks are especially common on Matagorda Island.

Dickcissels arrive in April, and in most years there is a heavy nesting population of these cheery birds on the open portion of Blackjack Peninsula and all over the Tatton Unit.

You will see **red-winged blackbirds** and both **boat-tailed** and **great-tailed grackles** in the vegetation around most permanent freshwater. If the redwings are nesting, be sure to watch the males announcing their nesting territories by singing and displaying their colorful epaulets. **Common grackles** nest occasionally on the Tatton.

The commonest wren on the Refuge is the resident **Carolina wren.** You can locate it in most thickets and oak mottes around Headquarters and on the Big Tree and Dagger Point trails. It is most easily detected by its song.

Marsh wrens and an occasional **sedge wren** will scold at you during the wintertime at Thomas Slough and from the bulrushes at Hog and Jones lakes. **House wrens** take up the task of winter chiding from the thickets around the Tour Loop. Both **Bewick's** and **cactus wrens** are residents limited to the mesquite and prickly pear community on the Tatton unit and the scattered chaparral communities.

White-eyed vireos are common residents on Blackjack Peninsula and **Bell's vireos** nest on the Tatton.

Most of the twenty species of sparrows recorded from the Aransas are transient or occasional winter residents.   The absence of extensive open, short grass savannah probably limits winter sparrow numbers. The **savannah sparrow** is the common winter resident in the grassy clearings and on the roadsides.   **Vesper** and **field sparrows** show up wherever mesquites dot the grassland. **Lincoln's sparrows** skulk in the green briar thickets in the wintertime, and **swamp sparrows** do likewise in dense bankside vegetation. The resident **lark sparrows** become more evident in spring and summer and this is the season when **Cassin's sparrows** sing and skylark on the Tatton Unit. Watch for **seaside sparrows** amidst the sea ox-eye on the tidal flats at any time of the year.

Species	Number of Individuals in			Total
	'83	'84	'85	'83-'85
Laughing Gull	416	37	6	459
Cardinal	159	69	121	349
Red-wnged Blackbird	114	42	49	205
Mourning Dove	99	53	30	182
Eastern Meadowlark	60	48	43	151
Carolina Wren	36	65	11	112
White-faced Ibis	14	7	86	107
Dickcissel	25	38	31	94
Mottled Duck	13	3	47	63
Bobwhite Quail	22	16	25	63
Common Nighthawk	30	20	11	61
White-eyed Vireo	20	5	33	58
Snowy Egret	17	37	0	54
Painted Bunting	12	4	37	53
Turkey Vulture	30	13	9	52
Black-necked Stilt	20	13	11	44
Killdeer	10	15	11	36
White Ibis	0	0	34	34
Geat-tailed Grackle	24	0	9	33
Great Blue Heron	17	5	9	31
Common Moorhen	15	8	7	30
Yellowthroat	1	6	15	22
Scissortailed Flycatcher	8	4	8	20
Roseate Spoonbill	2	13	2	17
Caspian Tern	6	6	5	17

Table 8 Breeding bird survey.

BREEDING BIRDS

The Aransas Biologist conducts a survey of breeding birds on the Refuge during the first week in June.   The accompanying table presents data for the 25 most common species recorded.   Such a summer survey tallies several hundred individuals of about 45 species. In contrast, a one-day Christmas Count may document thousands of birds of over 125 species.

INCIDENTALS

Just for birders, we include a few Refuge entries calculated to set you on edge.

- **Western grebe**--12 seen off picnic area, February '87.
- **Magnificent frigate-bird**--10 seen over San Antonio Bay after Hurricane Fern, Sept '71; 9 over East Shore Road, Nov '73; 8 sighted, late summer, '83; 2 over Bill Mott Bayou, May '86; 6 sailing over Tower, Aug '86.
- **Whistling swan**--1 seen Dec '46; 2 seen '57; 4 in Feb '70 and 2 in Dec '70.
- **Old squaw**--1 sighting, St. Charles Bay, Nov '77.
- **White-winged scoter**--1 sighting, St. Charles Bay, Nov '77; 1 seen, Jan '86.
- **Zone-tailed hawk**--1 sighting, associated w/vultures, Nov '72.
- **Rough-legged hawk**--1 seen at Patrol Station, Oct '71; 1 on Tatton, Feb '75.
- **Ferruginous hawk**--1 on East Shore Road, Mar '76.
- **Aplomado falcon**--1 seen at East Shore Road & Tour Loop, Nov '72; 1 at Alamo Mill, Feb '73; 2 seen East Shore Road & Tour Loop, Mar '73.
- **Green kingfisher**--1 seen at Tule Lake, Feb '73.
- **Great kiskadee**--1 along North Boundary Road, Oct '72.
- **Brown-crested flycatcher**--2 at HQ, May, '72; 1 in Point Pasture, Nov '85; 1 seen, June '86.
- **Olive-sided flycatcher**--9 on Tour Loop, Aug, '72.
- **Olivaceous flycatcher**--1 sighting at HQ, June '72.
- **Red-breasted nuthatch**--1 sighting, 1941.
- **Long-billed thrasher**--nesting, 1961.
- **Veery**--flock on Big Tree trail, Apr '72.
- **Phainopepla**--1 sighting, Jan '73.
- **Golden-winged warbler**--2 on Big Tree Trail, Apr '72; 1 on Big Tree Trail, May '73.
- **Pyrrhuloxia**--20 seen on Tour Loop, Jan '72.
- **Rose-breasted grosbeak**--1 on Big Tree Trail, Apr '72; 1 at picnic area, May '72.
- **Black-headed grosbeak**--1 on Big Tree Trail, Apr '72.
- **Olive sparrow**--1 on Bludworth Island, May '86.
- **Green-tailed towhee**--1 sighting, '72; 1 seen, Dec '83.
- **Clay-colored sparrow**--6 seen on Tour Loop, May '72.
- **Golden-crowned sparrow**--1 sighting on Tour Loop, Feb '73.
- **Tree sparrow**--1 sighting, '72.

Herptiles

Herpetology is the formal study of amphibians and reptiles, so the two groups collectively are referred to as herptiles. The single best manual for the identification of these creatures is *A Field Guide to Reptiles and Amphibians of Eastern and Central North America*, by Roger Conant.

Herptiles have backbones, but they lack the ability to regulate their internal body temperature, so we call them cold-blooded. On cool days herptiles bask in the sun; on hot days they conduct their business early or late, or they go abroad at night. Most herptiles become semi-dormant during cold spells and their low metabolic rate allows them to survive without eating throughout the cool season. Because of the moderate climate in the Coastal Bend, at least a few species of these cold-blooded creatures can be found astir in every month of the year.

Herptiles are mostly carnivores, and they are ecologically important not only as predators but also because they are themselves prey for a great number of higher-order predators. Herptiles are important links in almost all of the major food chains on the Aransas.

AMPHIBIANS

Amphibians are easily distinguished from reptiles by their moist, scaleless skin. Also, they must lay their eggs in the water and pass through an aquatic larval stage before metamorphosing into an adult. Because of their delicate skin, amphibians cannot tolerate brackish water and are apt to dehydrate in dry air. Consequently, these creatures concentrate in moist swales and around freshwater and are most active during warm, rainy weather.

Amphibian populations follow a boom-or-bust pattern: great abundance and reproductive succcess in wet years; a low-profile, nonbreeding status in dry years. Some species of amphibians may not be seen on the Refuge for a decade or more if conditions remain unfavorable for them. With its searing summers, periodic droughts and occasional overwashes of saltwater, the Aransas does not always present an easy environment for the three kinds of salamanders and 14 species of frogs and toads known to reside here.

Salamanders

None of these creatures is apt to be seen by the casual visitor. Two kinds-the **eastern tiger salamander** and the **small-mouthed salamander** spend practically all of their adult lives underground or beneath surface debris. The former species is rare and the latter has been collected only once, in 1981. Both kinds breed in late winter or early spring while the water is still quite cool. Their larvae are most likely to be seined up from freshwater ponds which do not have large populations of predatory fish.

The **lesser siren** is the most abundant salamander on the Refuge, although it too is seldom discovered without a special effort with dipnet or seine. These animals are permanently aquatic. They have 20-inch long, eel-like bodies, external gills and only one pair of legs--the tiny forelegs. Sirens spend the day nestled in the bottom muck. At night they swim about foraging for crayfish, aquatic worms and insect larvae. They are the only kind of salamander known to communicate vocally by producing a series of sharp clicks. (Look to Greek myth for the derivation of "siren", not to fire trucks.)

Sirens live in the nearly permanent water in Thomas Slough. They also manage to survive in freshwater ponds and ditches that dry up completely by burrowing into the wet mud and secreting a cocoon-like mass of mucous around their bodies. There they lie entombed, sometimes for months, awaiting the return of life-giving rains.

Frogs and Toads

The semiaquatic frogs and the more terrestrial toads lead similar lifestyles. All are mainly nocturnal insect-eaters that use their extensible tongues to capture prey. They have enlarged hindlegs with which they attempt to leap away from their numerous predators. On warm moist nights in the spring and early summer the males aggregate in noisy choruses to coax the females to the breeding pools. The eggs hatch into tadpoles which feed on aquatic vegetation until they metamorphose.

Many snakes, birds and mammals feed on the adults and larvae. Tadpoles trapped in drying puddles and waves of emerging froglets provide windfall feasts for watersnakes, cottonmouths, herons, egrets, grackles, raccoons and feral hogs. Sometimes tadpoles are even killed and consumed by predaceous water bugs. Alligators snap up all the adults and tadpoles they come upon. The piercing shriek of a predator-caught frog is a common sound on the Aransas.

One of the most frequently observed and certainly the most appealing frog on the Aransas is the **green treefrog**. This is the little leaf green frog which is often found hunkered on the shady side of a bulrush stem or a palmetto leaf with its legs tucked beneath its body. Sometimes a cluster of individuals waits out the day on the moist concrete walls at the Observation Tower, on buildings at Headquarters or on the protected side of Refuge signs.

Each evening from late spring throughout the summer the bell-like calls of green treefrogs ring from well vegetated freshwater sites. In warm wet weather their huge nighttime choruses sound from a distance like the clangor of a factory.

You should be able to spot a green treefrog hugging a bulrush or cattail stem along the margin of Thomas Slough or Hog Lake. Also listen for the occasional individual which gets inspired enough to suddenly peal out a series of duck-like yarps from his daytime perch.

The **squirrel treefrog** is also common on the Refuge, but it is less prone than the green treefrog to settle for the day in an exposed position. Its call is a series of raspy quacks.

The **spotted chorus frog** is hardly ever noticed until heavy rains fill the roadside ditches. Then the males produce their tinkling mating calls that sound like a thumb being drawn across the teeth of a comb. **Strecker's chorus frog** produces a series of clear, high-pitched whistles and is most frequently heard during wet weather in mid-winter.

Blanchard's cricket frog is moderately common on the Refuge in wet years, but the population dwindles to extinction during a series of dry years. None has been seen during the mid'80's. If they are present, cricket frogs will be startled from their resting sites on the banksides of freshwater ponds and sloughs. Their calls sound like pebbles being rapidly clicked together.

The Aransas Refuge lies on the junction between the ranges of the **Rio Grande leopard frog** coming up the coast and the **southern leopard frog** coming down the coast. Although some local specimens have intermediate traits, the bulk of them are Southern leopard frogs. For most visitors, however, the subtle distinction will not matter. The very common, medium-sized greenish frog with numerous brown blotches frequently encountered around all freshwater sites is definitely a leopard frog.

Leopard frogs often congregate at windmill overflows and they travel widely overland in wet weather so they are often seen on the roadways. Because of their size and abundance, leopard frogs are a very important prey species for many kinds of snakes, the alligator, all wading birds, many raptors and raccoons. Many other birds and mammals will take a leopard frog if they have the opportunity.

Almost everyone will recognize the deep and resonant "jug-o-rum" of the **bullfrog** booming out of the thick vegetation in Thomas Slough on a balmy afternoon. It is quite a feat to spot one of these wary beasts. Stalk the sound. Use your binoculars. Scan not only the bankside but the emergent vegetation which breaks the water's surface. You may see only a large green head poking up.

If you do see a bullfrog, you can determine its sex by the size of its eardrum: larger than the eye in males; smaller than the eye in females. Of course, if you actually see your frog calling, you have its sex pegged. Only males call.

Frogs are basically insectivores, but because they are so large bullfrogs frequently snap up bigger prey: crayfish, sunfish, tadpoles and frogs, watersnakes, young turtles, and even mice and shrews. It is very likely that on the Aransas bullfrogs occasionally gulp down hatchling alligators as well as displaced nestling and recently fledged birds.

Watch the shallows in the pools along the Heron Flats Trail for bullfrog tadpoles lolling in the sun on submerged vegetation. Older ones may be as broad as the palm of your hand.

Both the **eastern** and the **great plains narrow-mouthed toads** occur on the Refuge. The latter is more common. Both are plump, brown, wet-skinned little creatures with pointed snouts. They are seldom seen unless one is uncovered when a log or board is rolled aside. Their favorite prey is termites and ants.

When summer rains fill all the depressions, narrow-mouthed toads aggregate and the males, submerged except for their little turret heads, produce insect-like buzzing calls. The call of the eastern narrowmouth is deeper and coarser than the clean buzzing whine of the Great Plains species.

The commonest true toad in the Coastal Bend is the **Gulf Coast toad.** These medium-sized, warty amphibians are not often seen in the daytime, but they are abundant around Thomas Slough and the watered lawns at Headquarters. At night they often feed on insects beneath the lights. In chorus the males emit a penetrating trilled call. After a successful breeding season, hordes of insect-sized toadlets can be seen scampering across the roads.

After exceptionally heavy summer rains the rapidly repeated, riveting trills of **Texas toads** can occasionally be heard on the western side of Blackjack Peninsula and on the Tatton Unit. These toads have been reported from St. Joseph Island, so they might occur on Matagorda Island as well, but they have not been documented there.

The Aransas Refuge has two species of the peculiar spadefoot toads: **Couch's spadefoot** and **Hurter's spadefoot**. They are named for the shovel-like tubercle on their heel which they use to dig backward into the sand.

Spadefoots are fat-bodied, smooth-skinned creatures. Their eyes have vertical pupils and their skin secretes an irritating mucous.

Spadefoot toads spend most of their time underground. On the Refuge they have been unearthed from pocket gopher burrows. They are most evident during and immediately following hard summer rains. The males call lustily, producing an agonized, groaning bleat. The eggs hatch quickly and the tadpoles develop rapidly, so spadefoots can breed successfully in temporary rainpools. They thus avoid competition with other species which demand more permanent water.

At least four other kinds of frogs and toads could reasonably be expected to occur on the Aransas, but to date none of these has been reliably documented: gray treefrog, upland chorus frog, Fowler's toad and eastern green toad.

REPTILES

Reptiles are most readily distinguished from amphibians by their dry, scaly skin. Most of them deposit eggs in the soil, but a few kinds bear live young. None has a larval stage. Although some kinds live in and around water, many others survive in the driest portions of the Refuge.

Reptiles are generally carnivorous, but some turtles live principally on plant material. In contrast to amphibians, most reptiles are silent or only hiss when provoked. A few species are venomous. The group contains many important predatory and prey species.

The **alligator** and the **sea turtles** are discussed in Chapter 6.

Turtles

The Aransas Wildlife Refuge presents a rather hostile environment to turtles. Recurrent drought reduces or eliminates freshwater sites. The dense population of raccoons is adept at digging up turtle eggs and the numerous alligators are ever-ready to chomp up juvenile and adult turtles. Yet, six species of turtles manage to beat the odds.

The **red-eared turtle** is certainly the kind that visitors are most likely to see. Look for it basking on the bank or out in the water with only its head exposed at Jones Lake, Thomas Slough and the ponds along the Heron Flats Trail.

You might see an **ornate box turtle** crossing the road around Headquarters or on the Tour Loop, although the animals are not common on the peninsula. Be sure you give it the right of way. This terrestrial species feeds on dewberries, yaupon and green briar fruits, fresh greenery and whatever insects it can catch. When provoked it can pull in its legs and fold the edge of its bottom shell tightly against its top shell for protection. Perhaps because they are free of feral hog predation, box turtles are more abundant on the barrier islands and even on some of the offshore islets than they are on the mainland.

The **yellow mud turtle** is occasionally seen on Blackjack Peninsula and the related **Mississippi mud turtle** occurs on the Matagorda Unit. Both prefer freshwater ponds with muddy bottoms, where they forage for aquatic insect larvae, crustaceans, worms and fish. The yellow mud turtle is most often noticed when it crosses the roads after rains.

The **common snapping turtle** has been seen only in the ponds on Matagorda Island, but it probably occurs in Thomas Slough and perhaps in other semipermanent bodies of freshwater on Blackjack Peninsula. These large turtles are omnivores powerful enough to clamp down on any small or medium-sized vertebrate that wanders within reach of their wicked jaws, and they also eat aquatic insects, submerged vegetation and carrion.

The **Texas diamondback terrapin** fills the ecological niche between true sea turtles and freshwater turtles. Diamondback terrapins, named for the sculptured scutes on their carapace, are most at home in the brackish shallows along the shoreline of the mainland, the lee sides of the barrier islands and the margins of the islets scattered throughout the bays.

Diamondbacks feed on marine crustaceans, worms, molluscs and small fish. These turtles are not common locally. On Blackjack Peninsula about the best you can hope for is to find a shell or several of the distinctive scutes washed up on the beach along San Antonio Bay.

Two other turtles bear mention. The **spiny softshell turtle** is seen now and then in the local bays. This is a river species that occasionally gets flushed into the brackish environment, and individuals have been observed on the Refuge around Burgentine Lake. Since this is an alert and secretive species, it may be more widespread than Refuge records indicate.

There are a few vague references to **Texas tortoises** on Blackjack Peninsula. The Aransas Refuge lies on the northern edge of the range of this southern tortoise. Although the dense vegetation on the peninsula would probably not be to their liking, these creatures would not be out of their element on the Tatton Unit. The Texas tortoise is accorded threatened status by the State.

Lizards

The **green anole** (commonly called a chameleon because of its ability to change from green to brown) occurs sparingly in the larger oak mottes and the oak-bay forest on Blackjack Peninsula, and it lives around the buildings on the Matagorda Unit.

The best place to look for an anole on the peninsula is around the residences at Headquarters and amidst the tangle of vines and shrubs where the Heron Flats Trail borders Thomas Slough. If you spot one of these pretty lizards slinking along a branch in the springtime, watch for a male to pause periodically to pump its forequarters and erect the pink bib beneath its throat. That colorful little flag is a no-trespass sign to neighboring anoles. Your own bright clothing might stimulate the lizard to display.

Two kinds of spiny lizards occur on the Refuge. The **Texas spiny lizard** is rare. It prefers more open and diversified forests. The **southern fence lizard** is quite at home in the oak mottes and it ranges through the oak thickets and even onto the treeless tidal flats. This is probably the most widespread lizard on Blackjack Peninsula. It causes many of the rustles you hear along the trailsides, and you may see one basking or searching for insects on the roadside.

The southern fence lizard is well camouflaged in grays and browns, but you may see a male raise the side of his body to reveal a bright streak of metallic blue. That is his way of attracting a female and of warning other males to keep their distance.

The **prairie racerunner** is the striped lizard with the long tail which runs rapidly across the open ground along the roadsides in the summertime. It is also fairly common in mowed grassy places around the picnic area and at Headquarters and it skitters across the sunny stretches of the Heron Flats Trail. Racerunners are very common on Matagorda Island.

Prairie racerunners chase down all sorts of ground-living insects and arachnids and they scratch for termites and ants.

These alert lizards are best observed with binoculars. You will recognize a male by his exceptional coloration: besides his pattern of black and pale yellow stripes, his head is a powder blue and the front third of his body bears a bright chartreuse wash. The closely related but less colorful **spotted whiptail** occurs on the Tatton Unit.

Skinks are ground-living lizards with such small shiny scales that they are often mistaken for salamanders. These active little lizards live in the deep leaf litter in the live oak mottes and the oak-bay forest, and they are often uncovered when logs or boards are lifted from the ground. They feed on small insects and arachnids.

The Aransas hosts two kinds of skinks. The **five-lined skink** has been seen only in the vicinity of Headquarters. The **ground skink** is most common under trees, but it ranges through the grassland and onto the tidal flats and frequents the watered area at Headquarters. Rather than actually see a ground skink, you are more likely to hear its gentle rustling in the debris on the trailsides. They are especially common along the Big Tree Trail.

The **Texas horned lizard** is rare on Blackjack Peninsula. (The numbers of this reptilian symbol of Texas have dropped so alarmingly that it was placed on the State's threatened list in 1967.) It is occasionally seen on the more open Tatton Unit. However, along the roadways of packed shell and across the sparsely grassed, sandy wastes of the Matagorda Unit, horned lizards are still delightfully common. The best way to find one is to walk along on a sunny afternoon and wait for a patch of ground to suddenly erupt at your feet and go spraddle-legging off ahead. Keep your eye on it until it stops. Then ease up for a close look.

Slender glass lizards are legless animals often mistaken for snakes. They are well adapted to sliding through the dense tangle of stems on the tidal flat and in all grassy areas on the peninsula, and they either slide over or wriggle through the loose sand on Matagorda Island. Glass lizards prey on all sorts of ground-living insects and arachnids.

An adult glass lizard is about 20 inches long. At least 12 of those inches are tail. When leaped upon by a predator, the glass lizard lives up to its name by readily disjointing its tail into several twitching pieces. While the predator is temporarily distracted the eight-inch lizard body slips quietly away to safety. The lizard can regenerate another tail. (Legend has it that when danger is past, the lizard returns and rejoins its tail segments to its body. What do you think?)

Slender glass lizards are common on Blackjack Peninsula. You may see one on the open stretches of the Heron Flats or the Heritage trails. Also watch the ground along the Boardwalk. These lizards frequently move across the paved roads late in the afternoon and they often pause on the warm asphalt. When disturbed, their movement on the pavement is much less sinuous than that of a snake.

The **Mediterranean gecko** is an Old World lizard that has been spread widely to warm seaports because of its habit of tucking into cargoes of lumber and plants. These lizards are nocturnal, and they frequently appear on walls and ceilings to harvest insects at lights. There are beachhead populations all along the Texas Coast, but on the Aransas geckos have so far been found only in the buildings on the Matagorda Unit.

Two other species of lizards should be mentioned in passing. The southern prairie skink is to be looked for in the same habitat as the ground skink. And one of the real biogeographic mysteries of the Aransas is the absence of the keeled earless lizard, a species adapted to coastal sands. Although this lizard is abundant on Padre and Mustang islands, it has not been seen on Matagorda Island, nor is it known from the extensive sands on Blackjack Peninsula.

Snakes

Thirty-two kinds of snakes (over 40% of the species native to Texas) have been documented on the Aransas National Wildlife Refuge. Many of these are small, secretive and seldom seen. The several common larger kinds are most often noticed crossing the roadways, where you can observe them from your car window.

Four small resident snakes spend most of their time underground or beneath surface debris, and are seen abroad only at night after summer rainshowers. The **Texas blind snake** is the smallest species on the Refuge. Adults are sometimes mistaken for earthworms. These little pinkish-brown serpents burrow through the sand in search of termites and ant larvae. Armadillos and moles routinely dig them up and eat them. The **flat-headed snake**, **Texas brown snake** and **rough earth snake** each attains a length of about 10 inches. They live beneath logs and in leaf litter and feed on earthworms, crickets, ground spiders, centipedes and the like.

Three kinds of garter snakes live on the Refuge. The adults are about 24 inches long. They are almost always found around freshwater or in damp swales. Garter snakes feed on frogs, tadpoles, fishes and insects, and these snakes are in turn preyed upon by all wading birds, most raptors and a variety of mammals. Even bullfrogs, alligators and other snakes enjoy a garter snake meal.

While the **Texas garter snake** and the **checkered garter snake** are relatively rare, the **Gulf Coast ribbon snake** is the most abundant snake on the Aransas. When you see a medium-sized striped snake slither away from the edge of Jones Lake or when you hear the shriek of a snake-caught frog in the damp grass, a Gulf Coast ribbon snake is very likely the culprit.

The water snakes are stout-bodied serpents that bask on the bankside and enter the water for protection and to search for food: amphibians, fish, crayfish and aquatic insects. Water snakes are often found in considerable numbers around drying water holes where they feast on all manner of stranded aquatic creatures. Although these snakes have nasty dispositions and readily bite if handled, they are all nonvenemous.

Five kinds of water snakes have been found on the Aransas Refuge. The **diamond-backed water snake** is the commonest member of the group around freshwater sites. The **green water snake** is occasionally seen, but it is much less abundant. **Graham's water snake** has been observed only twice on the northern edge of Blackjack Peninsula. A single specimen of the colorful **broad-banded water snake** was seen crossing the road along the Tour Loop in 1981.

The **Gulf salt marsh snake** is the only species which prefers a brackish water habitat. This brownish serpent with straw-colored lines down its body and brown half-moons on its belly is the commonest water snake in the tidal flat community. Watch for it from the Boardwalk and around the clumps of reeds on the edge of San Antonio Bay. These snakes forage along the inner perimeter of the tidal flat for frogs and crayfish and frequently take advantage of mullet and killifishes trapped in tidal pools.

The **western mud snake** is not closely related to the water snakes, but it does live in the same freshwater habitat. This snake prefers heavily vegetated pools with a thick layer of muck on the bottom. It burrows through the ooze in search of its favorite prey: crayfish and lesser sirens. Mud snakes are among the prettiest species on the Refuge, but they are seldom observed. They are a shining, iridescent black above and a startlingly bright carmine below. Most sightings have been at Burgentine Lake on the western side of Blackjack Peninsula, but Thomas Slough is bound to be well populated with this species.

The **rough green snake** is one of the most frequently observed and most appealing snakes on the Aransas. It takes a sharp eye to spot one; look for them amid the shrubs and vines along the Heron Flats Trail. These slender serpents move slowly along the branches in search of caterpillars, katydids, grasshoppers and spiders. They have the neat habit of sipping dew drops from leaves to satisfy their thirst.

Green snakes are commonly killed by vehicles when they try to cross the roads. Watch out for them, and if you do see a dead one pause for a second look. Soon after death their mint green begins to transform into a turquoise blue.

Kingsnakes are medium-sized reptiles that are known especially for their habit of feeding on other snakes, including venomous species. (They are immune to the venom.) Kingsnakes also eat lizards and rodents and they consume the eggs of birds and reptiles. These snakes subdue their prey by constriction. Four kinds of kingsnakes occur on the Refuge.

The **speckled kingsnake** is not only the commonest representative of its group on the Aransas, it is one of the most handsome large serpents in the Coastal Bend. Each black scale bears a gleaming yellow dot giving the snake a luminous salt-and-pepper appearance. Watch for this slow-moving, rather docile snake on the tidal flat and in grassy swales.

The Refuge is on the eastern edge of the range of the closely related **desert kingsnake**. It has been taken on the dry upland on the Tatton Unit. Both the speckled and the desert kingsnakes also inhabit Matagorda Island.

Only one **prairie kingsnake** has been seen on the Refuge, in the short grass upland on the Tatton Unit. The species may be more common there than the single record suggests.

Despite its common name, the **Louisiana milk snake** is another kind of kingsnake. (If you like to pursue myths, see if you can find out how milk snakes got their name.) This secretive species is occasionally found by turning driftwood along the strand line on the margins of the bays. Individuals are sometimes seen abroad on warm rainy nights, but they spend much time burrowing through the sand and cordgrass tussocks.

The prettily ringed milk snake somewhat resembles the coral snake. Remember: red and yellow kill a fellow; red and black, venom lack. Milk snakes have the red-and-black combination. Besides that, where the coral snake has a bright yellow band the milk snake has a cream colored one.

The **Texas scarlet snake** is also brightly ringed in red, cream and black. As with the Louisiana milk snake, the red and black bands are adjacent, announcing the scarlet snake's harmless nature. Another good mark is its red snout (black in the coral snake).

The scarlet snake spends most of its life burrowing through the loose coastal sand in search of reptile eggs which seem to be its dietary staple. Only a few specimens have been found in Coastal Texas and four of these were discovered on the Aransas Refuge. The deep sand of the oak-bay forest between the Youth Environmental Training Area and the Big Tree Trail is the preferred habitat of the scarlet snake.

Two species of rat snakes are known from the Refuge. The **great plains rat snake** is fairly common. It prefers short grass prairie and is most often seen on the Tatton Unit and in the ridge-and-swale community on Blackjack Peninsula.

The **Texas rat snake** is quite common and can be expected in all communities. This is one of the largest snakes on the Refuge. Adults routinely grow six feet long. These lithe constrictors prowl across all types of terrain and they spend much time in trees and shrubs. Texas rat snakes are relentless predators of rodents and birds and they are particularly adept at discovering rodent, rabbit and bird nests. It is their fondness for eggs that has earned these serpents the local name of "chicken snake".

Your best chance to see a Texas rat snake is when an individual crosses the road on the Tour Loop. They are slow moving, so give them time to pass across.

Racers are slender, alert and very fast-moving snakes that hunt the grassland and low shrubbery for lizards, mice, birds' nests and grasshoppers. They are usually abroad during the hottest part of the day. Racers are best seen as they dash across the road. An encounter afoot is often no more than a startled glance and a quick rustle before the speedy reptile has disappeared.

The **western coachwhip** is a pale brown racer, and the sharp outlines of its scales give it an attractive braided appearance. Coachwhips prefer the short grass habitat of the Tatton and Matagorda units, while the **eastern yellow-bellied racer** ranges throughout the dry interior of the Refuge. This is the olive-brown to blue-gray snake that occasionally streaks across the paved roads ahead of your vehicle. A closely related variety, the **Mexican racer**, reaches its northern limit on the Aransas. It cannot be easily distinguished from the eastern yellow-bellied racer in the field. Both of these snakes are locally called blue racers.

Only one specimen of the **bullsnake** has been seen on the Refuge. This large and powerful constrictor (the one individual discovered in a building at Headquarters in 1974, was seven feet long) prefers more open terrain than is offered on Blackjack Peninsula. The species may be a routine resident on the Tatton Unit. Bullsnakes are arch predators on all rodents and ground-living birds.

The loose sandy terrain of the Aransas Refuge is prime habitat for two very interesting species of snakes: the **western hog-nosed snake** and the more common **eastern hog-nosed snake**.

These harmless snakes are known for their entertaining defensive behaviour. When startled they coil, flatten the body, hiss wickedly and even engage in sham striking behaviour. If this bluff fails, the snakes suddenly go into writhing contortions as though mortally wounded. The act ends with the snake on its back, mouth agape and tongue dragging in the sand. When the source of provocation departs the serpent cautiously rights itself and glides away.

Hognosed snakes use their up-curved snouts to dig through the sand for resting toads and lizards. How does a hognose snake swallow a defensive toad puffed up with air? Simple. It pops the toad with a special pair of long teeth located in the back of its mouth.

Five species of venomous snakes have been definitely recorded from the Aransas Refuge. Only two of these need be of concern for routine visitors. Remember, even poisonous snakes are protected here. You are performing no useful service and you may endanger yourself if you molest one of these serpents. Observe it; admire it; and let it be.

The **Texas coral snake** is rather common on Blackjack Peninsula, but because of its secretive nature it is seldom seen. This serpent spends most of its time beneath surface debris or in the tangle of roots and maze of rodent burrows beneath the sand. There it ferrets after its favorite prey--small snakes and lizards.

Coral snakes are most commonly encountered abroad early or late in the day after summer rains. On the Refuge most specimens have been found around the watered lawns at Headquarters.

These slender, brightly ringed snakes (red and yellow kill a fellow) pack a potent venom, but unless he picks one up the likelihood of a person being bitten is virtually nil. Educate the children and you need no further precaution.

The remaining four species of venomous snakes are pit vipers. They all possess a pit in front of each eye leading to a unique heat sensing organ which allows the snake to detect warm-blooded prey in the dark. Pit vipers have a large pair of fangs folded in the roof of the mouth. These are erected when the snake strikes, and conduct the venom into the flesh of the prey or predator, or into a careless person. Unlike the coral snake, pit vipers bear camouflage colors. Because they routinely lie in ambush for their prey, they are apt to be encountered at close range by oblivious hikers.

Most visitors never see a poisonous snake on the Refuge. The best guarantee for avoiding an encounter is to stay on the marked trails and scan heavily vegetated trailsides before proceeding. Be particularly careful around the margins of roadside pools and lakes. Moist warm weather after a prolonged dry spell brings out the wildlife on the Aransas, and that includes the snakes. Your safest and most likely confrontation will be to see a poisonous snake crossing one of the roads. Get a good look from your vehicle window and resist any temptation to run over the reptile.

Despite the ample litter of oak leaves, the environment on Blackjack Peninsula is apparently too sandy and dry for copperheads. The **broad-banded copperhead** has been rarely seen on the northern edge of the Refuge. The moist and shaded woods along the first half of the Heron Flats Trail look like good habitat for this snake, but only one individual has been sighted there.

Whereas the copperhead is rare, the closely related **western cottonmouth moccasin** is the most abundant poisonous snake on the Aransas. These fat-bodied pit vipers are most often seen in and around brackish or freshwater sites, but they can be expected on any well vegetated area, and they are frequently seen crossing the roads. Cottonmouths disperse across the entire Refuge in wet years and concentrate around the lakes and on the tidal flats in dry years.

Moccasins are prone to remain quietly coiled unless approached closely. Then they may vibrate the tail and cock their head back while gaping widely to reveal the white lining of their mouth. Some individuals strike wickedly if further provoked. Others either remain immobile or attempt to slither into the vegetation or the water.

Cottonmouths are probably the most indiscriminant feeders among the snakes on the Aransas. Although they seem best adapted for securing fishes, frogs and crayfish, they will take any creature that their venom will stop and their jaws can engulf.

A stomach analysis of 34 cottonmouths collected on the nearby Welder Wildlife Refuge revealed that the predominant food item was birds. Among the 13 bird species were red-winged blackbirds and brown-headed cowbirds, which roost in bulrushes, and eastern meadowlarks, which inhabit tidal flats and grassy swales. The young of American coots, soras and common moorhens were eaten. Even mockingbirds and cardinals were taken, probably when the birds were attempting to drink. Other snakes ranked high, mostly water snakes and garter snakes, but one cottonmouth had consumed a diamondback rattlesnake. Certainly the most amazing record was of a 41-inch cottonmouth which had managed to swallow a 49-inch Great Plains rat snake. How's that for gluttony?

The food list continued through lesser sirens, green treefrogs, pigmy mice and least shrews and even extended to snails, grasshoppers, caterpillars and sundry aquatic insects. Besides that, cottonmouths occasionally consume fishes and amphibians which have died in drying waterholes.

Two species of rattlesnakes are known to occur on the Aransas: the **western massasauga** and the **western diamondback**. The little massasauga ("mass-ah-SAW-gah"; an adult is seldom over two feet long) is only occasionally seen on Blackjack Peninsula. It prefers the grassy uplands on the Tatton Unit and the interior of the Matagorda Unit. These snakes lie up in animal burrows and in clumps of bluestem grass by day and hunt at night for mice, shrews, frogs and other snakes. Although massasaugas frequent damp swales and stands of Gulf cordgrass, they generally avoid boggy saline terrain.

The western diamondback rattlesnake is at once the best known and the most systematically persecuted snake in Texas. Certainly it deserves respect. Western diamondbacks are large, dangerously poisonous and if pressured, readily defend themselves.

There are few natural sights more thrilling and ominously beautiful than a cornered diamondback with the forepart of its huge body drawn into a high S-shaped curve, its black tongue testing the air and its rattles sending out a dry whine that sets every nerve on edge. The alert snake swivels to follow every movement and it can instantly strike half its body length. Most of the poisonous snake bites that occur annually in Texas are due to encounters with this truly spectacular creature.

Western diamondbacks range throughout the Refuge. They can be expected in all communities, although they are rare in the oak-bay forest and the interiors of large live oak mottes. The species is especially common in the cordgrass areas that border the tidal flats, among the mesquite and prickly pears on the Tatton Unit and across the grassy interior of the Matagorda Unit. Although they must be watched for, rattlers are not overly abundant in that part of the Refuge open to public access.

Diamondbacks are not prone to climb, but they do not hesitate to swim across pools and lakes and individuals occasionally strike out across the bays. During high water a rattlesnake can coil into a buoyant mass and float until it makes landfall.

Rattlers tend to move into armadillo burrows and brushy hideaways in the uplands of Blackjack Peninsula during January and February. Even at this time these snakes are not completely dormant. Individuals often emerge to bask in the winter sun and they have been found crawling about when the temperature was a chilly 40° F. Rattlesnakes are very frequently seen crossing the Refuge roads in the springtime when they begin moving to their preferred foraging grounds in the cordgrass meadows. As summer progresses the reptiles lie up during the day and hunt for food at night.

Despite their broad habitat tolerance, western diamondbacks are rather restricted in prey selection. They feed mainly on rodents. On Blackjack Peninsula their staples are cotton rats and rice rats. On the Tatton they certainly take advantage of another favorite, the south plains wood rat. Doubtless rattlers also consume significant numbers of pocket gophers and whatever smaller rodents they come across. They also take small cottontail rabbits as well as meadowlarks, bobwhite quail and other ground-living birds.

Although adult rattlers can fend for themselves, juveniles are commonly killed and eaten by most carnivorous mammals, also feral hogs, javelinas, wading birds, raptorial birds, kingsnakes and alligators.

Because of its multifarious ecological ties, the western diamondback rattlesnake plays a critical role in the natural balance on the Aransas. If you see one, give it the consideration it so much deserves but so seldom receives.

The Aransas Refuge is on the extreme southern edge of the known range of the western pigmy rattlesnake, and there is actually one Refuge record for this species, but the documentation is vague.

Judging by their known distributions in Texas, at least 10 other species of snakes could eventually be added to the Refuge list: indigo snake, long-nosed snake, Schott's whipsnake, Texas glossy snake, Texas night snake, ground snake, black-headed snake, Texas patch-nosed snake, blotched water snake and canebreak rattlesnake.

Fishes

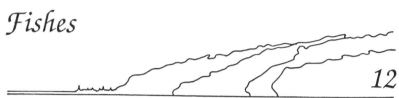

Except for an occasional flash of silver amidst the waves or the wriggle of a tail fin when a Forster's tern makes a successful dive, most visitors to the Aransas Refuge seldom actually see a fish. Yet, fishes constitute the most abundant and diverse group of backboned creatures in the Coastal Bend. Sixty species are on the Refuge checklist of common kinds. One good haul with a 20-foot minnow seine might net several hundred individual fish, and any enthusiastic high school class can bring in 30 species in an afternoon.

A standard manual for the fishes of the Gulf of Mexico covers over 500 species, the majority of which might be expected to invade, at least occasionally, the proclamation boundary of the Aransas Refuge. When the rivers rise freshwater fishes mix with the saltwater forms. Even when the weather is benign and the waters are serene, the natural mix of salt, brackish and fresh water provides a welter of aquatic habitats that are populated with a wide array of fishes.

Strictly freshwater fishes and several tolerant brackish water forms inhabit the ponds and sloughs which dot the inland parts of the Refuge. These sites are depopulated during droughts and revitalized during years of washover.

All the fishes are subject to the same recurrent stresses. The Coastal Bend is characterized by periods of low rainfall. This means reduced surface runoff which translates into increased salinity in the bays and tidal flat pools. At such times Mustang Lake may get as salty as the Gulf, and Long Lake rises to twice that salinity. Because of salt in their mud bottoms, even freshwater ponds become brackish as they evaporate.

Drought is usually accompanied by elevated temperature. On a torrid August afternoon, knee-deep water in Mustang Lake can reach 95° F. Aside from its direct impact on aquatic creatures, such heat drives virtually all dissolved oxygen from the water. Unless they are especially adapted, fish must seek deeper, cooler water or asphyxiate.

Local waters are shallow; shallow water is subject to rapid changes in quality. Local bottoms are muddy; muddy bottoms are easily swirled to produce muddy water. Muddy water hinders the penetration of sunlight; less sunlight means fewer submerged green plants. Also, shallow muddy bottoms, constantly shifted by waves and currents, provide poor footing for rooted aquatic plants. Fewer plants means skimpier food chains and harder times for herbivorous creatures and consequent belt-tightening for carnivores. The ecological rules are the same for aquatic communities as for terrestrial ones.

Routine stresses can be aggravated by a blue norther with its wind-whipped tides and plunging temperatures. Or a hurricane may dash seawater into freshwater basins and inundate vast stretches of coastline. Runoff from hurricane-spawned rains restructures local drainage channels and transforms the bays into freshwater lakes for weeks on end. Local flooding brings a plethora of agricultural chemicals into Burgentine Lake, and an uncharted array of pollutants flushes coastward from the Gulf Intracoastal Waterway.

Yet, the fishes thrive. They eat and are eaten and so compose a vital portion of the food web that succors the Aransas.

Think about fish connections. A striped mullet scoops a mouthful of organic muck from the bottom of San Antonio Bay. A Gulf salt marsh snake corners and consumes the mullet. That night the snake falls prey to a raccoon. The 'coon runs afoul of a young alligator, manages to pull away but later dies from its wounds. Turkey vultures quickly find the body and leave only skin and bones. Later you see one of these same scavengers wheeling on a rising parcel of warm air high over Headquarters, but because the natural cycles are intricate and subtle, you may never suspect that mullet calories are helping keep the bird aloft.

We shall mention only the few fishes that you are likely to observe or hear about. To learn more, we recommend *Fishes of the Gulf of Mexico* by Hoese and Moore. Many of the local species are on display in the aquarium maintained by the Texas Parks and Wildlife Department in Rockport. In Corpus Christi, you may also enjoy a visit to the Museum of Natural History and to the Texas State Aquarium which is expected to open in late 1989.

During a lull in the traffic of birds at the Observation Tower, you might gaze across the surface of Mustang Lake and wonder what sorts of fishes swim beneath the turbid water. One way to find out is to drag a seine along the margin. This would miss the larger, quicker species, but would get a fair sample of the smaller, more common ones. The following table is an outline of what might be caught; it also suggests what sort of prey the wading-and-spearing birds are after.

ABUNDANT	COMMON	OCCASIONAL
sheepshead minnow	bay anchovy	sheepshead
tidewater silverside	silver jenny	dusky pipefish
striped mullet	bayou killifish	black drum
spot	silverperch	naked goby
Gulf killifish	Atlantic croaker	common jack
pinfish	pigfish	hardhead catfish
longnose killifish	gizzard shad	least puffer
Gulf menhaden		skipjack
		Atlantic needlefish
		southern flounder
		blackcheek tonguefish
		speckled trout
		redfish

The catch from seining a freshwater pond will be more difficult to predict. Each pond has its own history, water quality, type of vegetation and assemblage of resident predators. If the site has not dried up in recent years and is not routinely invaded by saltwater, then you could expect such fishes as the following.

FISH FROM FRESHWATER POND

sailfin molly	carp	sheepshead minnow
spotted gar	mosquito fish	rainwater killifish
warmouth	bluegill sunfish	golden topminnow
redear sunfish	yellow bullhead	longear sunfish
	bantam sunfish	

KILLIFISH

Killifishes, collectively called mud minnows, constitute a dominant and usually the most abundant group of small fishes in protected shallow waters throughout the Coastal Bend. Adults seldom exceed six inches in length from the tip of their protruding lower jaws to the edge of their squared-off tail fins. They are ecologically important because of their abundance and their position low in the food chain.

Most species of killifish are omnivores; they graze the phytoplankton, nibble the bottom-living algae, sort through the muck, snap at amphipods, crunch up small snails and avidly tear into bits of carrion. And almost every carnivore gobbles up killifish.

The most remarkable trait of killifishes is their indestructability. Of all the local fishes, the killifishes can tolerate (and even thrive on) the greatest extremes in salt concentration, oxygen depletion and elevated temperature. Although not remarkably cold hardy, they can secrete sugar into their bloodstream to give it an antifreeze quality, and then burrow into the bottom mud until the water temperature rises.

Seven species of killifishes are resident on the Aransas. Three--the **bayou killifish**, the **golden topminnow** and the **rainwater killifish**--prefer fresh to slightly brackish water and occur in Thomas Slough and several inland freshwater sites. Another three like distinctly brackish water. The **longnose killifish**, **gulf killifish** and the **diamond killifish** live in Mustang Lake and in the vegetated shallows around the perimeter of Blackjack Peninsula.

The seventh species of killifish, the **sheepshead minnow**, is versatile enough to live in every aquatic habitat on the Refuge. In a group renowned for its toughness, this is the toughest. If you see small fishes anywhere, they are most likely to be this kind. The shallow tidal pool near the end of the Boardwalk, even when reduced to just a fetid puddle, is often aswarm with happy sheepsheads. As the water evaporates the salinity rises to extraordinary levels and the fishes' backs protrude from the ooze. Still they manage. They continue to wriggle valiantly until a raccoon scoops them up or the saline mud finally solidifies around them. Tough to the end!

From late March through midMay, look closely into the pools between the middle and outer ridges on the Heron Flats Trail. (Mollie Pond and Killifish Pond in Figure #23.) There the male sheepshead minnows and **sailfin mollies** will be engaged in setting up breeding territories and in courting females.

The peacock blue backs of the male sheepsheads flash in the sun as the energetic little fish dash about. High-male mollies are less frenzied and even more colorful. They continually sidle up to each other and erect their large dorsal fins to reveal resplendent blues, washes of orange and contrasting rows of black dots. While watching these fish you may notice the silvery, quick-darting, male **mosquito fish** chasing after their own corpulent females in these same pools. Most visitors pass obliviously by this silent, frantic spectacle.

If you ease up beside Thomas Slough and sit quietly where you can peer into clear water, you may see one or more of the species of sunfishes appear from the submerged vegetation. **Bluegills** and **redear sunfishes** are common and can usually be seen at the alligator observation site across the road from the Visitors Center.

Consider yourself privileged if one of the neatest predatory fishes on the Refuge slips into view and begins to drift very slowly toward a preoccupied sunfish. The **spotted gar** is well camouflaged with olive-brown blotches. It is an intriguing fish with strange bony scales, a functional lung, a mouth full of needle sharp teeth and an immensely old ancestry. Hold your breath as the distance between gar and sunfish gradually shortens. The sunfish may spook. The gar may get close enough to make a lightning-fast sidewise snap. Either way you will have had a revealing experience.

On a larger predatory scale, in Jones Lake, the big **alligator gars** stalk **carp**. And when the water level drops so they can get at them, alligators feast on both carp and alligator gars. With a further drop in water level the feral hogs wade in and chomp up the stranded fish. As the water is gradually replaced by hard-baked mud wading birds, raccoons, cottonmouths, vultures, scavenger beetles and microbes reroute the dwindling aquatic resources into the terrestrial food chains.

Invertebrates

In this catchall chapter we include the multitude of creatures without backbones--everything from crayfish to crickets and flies to fritillaries.

Invertebrates are immensely varied in appearance and behaviour, rich in numbers of species, countless in numbers of individuals and mostly small in size. Their huge populations are explained in part by body size and diversity. Small, adaptable bodies make small demands on natural resources: little food, little water, little oxygen, little space. A nook or cranny and a crumb or dew drop will suffice. (How many grasshoppers can live on an acre of ridge-and-swale compared to how many deer on that same area?)

The short lifetime that usually goes with small size is compensated by rapid development and prolific reproduction. When a favorable season rolls around, the invertebrates rapidly rise to the occasion. And when times get hard they can disappear into dormant stages.

Because they live everywhere and in profusion, invertebrates are involved in practically every aspect of the ecology of the Aransas Refuge. Though only a few species can be ranked as dominant forms, it is the cumulative impact of groups of species that counts--all the crabs, all the beetles, all the spiders, all the ants.

Within these groups there are herbivores, carnivores, omnivores, detritivores, scavengers and parasites. Some kinds filter water; others eat mud; a great number munch up greenery or suck plant sap. Lots of them fly; many climb; others hop, crawl or wriggle. Most constitute important fodder, by whatever circuitous food chain, for the backboned residents on the Refuge. (Try imagining a food chain that links a cricket with a bobcat; a doodlebug with a red-tailed hawk.)

Although the great diversity among invertebrates makes them endlessly fascinating, that same diversity presents a problem. In a general guidebook we can mention only a small fraction of the forms known to occur on the Aransas Refuge. We have chosen those that you are most likely to notice (some perhaps as nuisances) during your visit, a few that are ecologically important and some that are just downright interesting.   Coverage is further limited by touching only lightly on aquatic habitats.

To study the terrestrial invertebrates in more depth, begin with *The Audubon Society Field Guide to North American Insects and Spiders*, by Lorus and Margery Milne. Borror and White's *A Field Guide to the Insects* is also a good introductory manual.

Because the number of kinds of invertebrates is so large, there are no widely accepted common names for them all. This makes accurate communication difficult. But every species does have a unique scientific name composed of two Latinized terms. Therefore, by following a common name with the scientific name in parentheses we can correctly refer to each kind of organism: **carolina wolf spider** (*Lycosa carolinensis*) or **angular-winged katydid** (*Microcentrum rhombifolium*).

If you do not care about the exact species (and many visitors will not), then skip over the scientific name. No harm done. But if you want to do further reading about some invertebrate, then the scientific name provides you with a reliable starting point. So, use the scientific names or ignore them as you will.

CRUSTACEANS

Although these creatures are mostly aquatic in habit, several kinds are frequently observed or leave noticeable evidence of their occurrence. A few species make significant links between the aquatic and terrestrial food webs.

The Aransas has at least two species of **crayfish** (called crawfish locally): *Procambarus clarki* and *Cambarus hedgpethi.* You may not see a crayfish during your visit, but a large population exists in the freshwater sloughs and ponds and in scattered burrows which extend down to the water table. Entrances to burrows can be found in the black mud around the margins of Jones and Hog lakes and at the edges of roadside puddles. These are holes about as large in diameter as your index finger and usually rimmed with a low platform composed of excavated mud.

As you drive the Tour Loop watch in low-lying grassy areas for crayfish chimneys: vertical tubes 4-6 inches tall constructed of mud pellets hauled up from extensive burrows. Such hardened mud chimneys stand out boldly where a swale has been recently burned. Chimneys can be found on the inland fringes of the tidal flats, but they do not extend into the saline mud. Holes and mud pellets around brackish water are the work of fiddler crabs.

Crayfish are key industry species on the Aransas. They are numerous, widespread, and occupy the interfaces between water/land and brackish/fresh water, so they figure in a wide variety of food chains. Although mostly herbivorous, crayfish will eat most small aquatic creatures and also work through detritus, so they convert a large array of organic materials into animal protoplasm. And virtually every larger animal regards crayfish protoplasm as delicious. From fishes, snakes and alligators to raccoons, herons and whooping cranes, they actively seek and probe for crayfish. The Refuge simply would not be the same without this important crustacean.

The **blue crab** (*Callinectes sapidus*) is the ecologically important marine analog of the crayfish. Although they must spawn in saltwater, juvenile and adult blue crabs live throughout the brackish water community and frequently invade freshwater ponds and streams. During wet weather or high tides these crabs even move overland so they often populate inland ditches and ponds on Blackjack Peninsula.

From early summer into midwinter, there is a steady and plentiful supply of succulent young blue crabs entering the back bays all along the Coastal Bend. These form a staple in the diets of many denizens of the tidal flats. Every bird you see stalking the margin of Mustang Lake would welcome an opportunity to gobble up a tender young blue crab.

The Aransas harbors two common species of fiddler crab. The **mud fiddler** (*Uca pugnax*) prefers a muddy substrate and is usually found among stalks of sea ox-eye at the bay's edge. The

sand fiddler (*Uca pugilator*) is partial to wet sand and ranges across the tidal flat. Mud fiddlers are larger and their carapaces are aquamarine; the smaller sand fiddlers are cryptically sand-colored. Both species dig vertical holes and scatter the pellets of excavated material around the entrance. Fiddlers do not build chimneys like crayfish do.

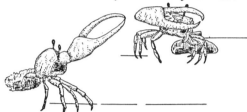

During the warm part of the year you can count on seeing sand fiddler burrows at the end of the Boardwalk. At low tide you may see some of the little crabs near their burrows or around the bases of the cordgrass clumps at the edge of the water, sifting the sand and mud for organic matter. Because they have special chambers for holding water around their gills, fiddlers can spend extended periods on the beach and tidal flat. All tidal flat predators eat them.

Fiddler crabs live in colonies and they have interesting social behaviour. If you get the chance, watch them with your binoculars and see if you can figure out how the males communicate with their over-sized pinchers.

At low tide, note the many small volcano-like turrets in all stages of collapse in the muddy sand of the bayshore off the Boardwalk. Each one was constructed by a **mud shrimp** (*Calianassa jamaicense*). These burrowing crustaceans, so very common across the shallow bay margin and in all brackish pools, are one of the delicacies for which many bird bills probe.

The numerous unadorned pinholes in the sand between the mud shrimp burrows are made by several kinds of **marine worms** (*Marphysa sanguinea* is the most common one), and there are bird bills capable of extracting these slender morsels. Other holes in the mud are made by marine clams, mostly the **common rangia** (*Rangia cuneata*), **stout razor** (*Tagelus plebeius*) and **jackknife clam** (*Ensis minor*). Raccoons are often seen belly-deep in the bay at low tide feeling for these bivalves. The shorebirds that frequent the wet sand off the end of the Boardwalk at low tide are searching for any of the preceding invertebrates, each species according to its own taste and ability.

If you continue your bayside walk, stop at a lavender patch of stranded marine algae. Turn it with your toe to uncover a great number of little hopping amphipods, appropriately called **beach fleas** (*Orchestia gryllus*). Sanderlings and snowy plovers know how to hustle after amphipods.

Beach fleas well illustrate the relationship between small body size and large population numbers. If the clumps of these little crustaceans were spread evenly, there would be about 20 individuals per square inch of beach. Consider one hundred yards of beach some 30 feet wide (say, from the Boardwalk to the Big Tree Trail at medium low tide). That stretch of apparently barren silty sand is home for more than 25 million beach fleas which collectively weigh over 2 tons! No wonder they attract the birds.

As you move along the beach looking ahead at the strand line, you may spot what appears to be a wave of cockroaches scurrying away from patches of shade cast by driftwood. These are crustaceans akin to pillbugs and aptly named **sea roaches** (*Ligia exotica*). They wet their gills in saltwater occasionally, but they live and breed at the water's edge. Like household cockroaches, these sea roaches are insatiable scavengers.

If you turn over pieces of debris along the strand line (the upper limit of routine high tide), you will surely uncover groups of **sowbugs** (*Porcellionides pruinosus*). Like the sea roaches, these animals are relatives of the common pillbug, but when provoked they scurry for cover rather than rolling into a ball. Sowbugs come out at night to feed on decomposing plant and animal matter thrown up by the waves.

INSECTS
Dragonflies

These fast flying insects are very common on the Refuge. Adults spend the day cruising or darting through the air or perching on the extreme tips of reeds and branches. They hawk after all sorts of flying insects (mosquitoes are favored prey), which they catch with their legs and snip to bits with their strong mouthparts. Some feed on the wing while others return to a favored perch for a leisurely meal.

The aquatic dragonfly larvae ambush freshwater insects and tadpoles, which they grasp with a remarkable set of quickly extensible mouthparts.

The large **brown-spotted yellow-wing** (*Celithemis eponina*) with pale yellow wings shot through with red veins and overlaid with large brown blotches is one of the most eye-catching of the dragonflies seen around the ponds on the Heron Flats Trail. But the most common kind during the summer is the little **skimmer** (*Sympetrum danae*). The black males and burnt-orange females patrol the tidal flats and swales, often in immense numbers.

Beetles

Of the welter of beetles on the Aransas, the ones most apt to catch your eye are the **tiger beetles** (*Megacephala carolina* and *Cicindella spp.*) that scatter across the beach before your advancing footsteps. These fast-moving predators on small insects and amphipods run in short spurts but can fly when pressed. Adults are strikingly colored in metallic green or in copper with enamel white comma-shaped marks. The grub-like larvae live in vertical burrows in the sand where they lurk in the openings to snatch passing insects.

Butterflies

Butterflies brighten the landscape; they also cross-pollinate flowers in their search for nectar. Their caterpillars munch leaves and serve as prey for a variety of insects, spiders and birds.

You can identify quite a few butterflies from your vehicle. (Pictures of all species mentioned here are in *The Audubon*

Society Field Guide to North American Butterflys, by Pyle.) The common large black species with blue-green iridescense on the hindwings is the **pipevine swallowtail** (*Battus philenor*). It dallies over roadside flowers throughout the spring and summer. Its caterpillar, brick red with rows of fleshy tubercules, feeds on pipevines from which it absorbs bitter compounds. These compounds, passed on to the adult , render it distasteful to most birds.

When the lavender-flowered thistles and mist flowers bloom in the spring, the large brown-and-yellow **palamedes swallowtails** (*Papilio palamedes*) flutter over them in great numbers. The mint green palamedes caterpillars, which feed almost exclusively on red bay leaves, have a pair of spots, bright orange with black centers, on the humped thorax. These baleful eyespots probably intimidate some predators.

As the summer progresses, **eastern tiger swallowtails** (*Papilio glaucus*), **eastern black swallowtails** (*Papilio polyxenes*), and **giant swallowtails** (*Papilio cresphontes*) appear. The giant swallowtail is the state's largest butterfly, with a wingspan over five inches. Its brownish larva, splotched with biege, bears a striking resemblance to a splatter of bird droppings.

You may have to stop and observe them at rest to see the distinctive marks of the fast flitting yellow butterflies common along the roadsides. Among the most abundant are the medium-sized **orange sulphur** (*Colias eurythemi*), **clouded sulphur** (*Colias philodice*) and the **dogface butterfly** (*Zerene cesonia*), the last one named for the black figure on its forewings, complete with eye, muzzle and ear. Look for the larger yellow **cloudless sulphur** (*Phoebis sennae*) and orangish **orange-barred sulphur** (*Phoebis philea*) flying high and fast between flowers.

In the early spring the white flowers of several wild mustards bring out a cloud of **cabbage whites** (*Pieris rapae*). You might think of this as a pretty example of a natural association, but cabbage whites were unintentionally introduced from Europe over a century ago and have spread across the continent. Watch also for the native **checkered whites** (*Pieris protodice*). By early summer the **great southern whites** (*Ascia monuste*) will be attending the flowers of sea ox-eye on the tidal flats.

The **gulf fritillary** (*Agraulis vanillae*), rich russet above with large silver dashes outlined in black on its underwing, is common in summer. The smaller, tawny brown **variegated fritillary** (*Euptoieta claudia*) is overlaid with an intricate pattern of black lines and spots but its underwings are not boldly marked.

Hackberry butterflies (*Asterocampa celtis*) may invite themselves to your picnic; salad dressing is irresistably attractive to them. Put a daub off to one side and watch the butterfly take a sample with its watchspring tongue.

Of the few butterflies that overwinter as adults, two live on the Aransas. You might see either the **red admiral** (*Vanessa* *atalanta*) or the **buckeye** (*Junonia coenia*) basking in the cold winter sun. Both are bright colored and distinctively patterned. Two related species, the **painted lady** (*Vanessa cardui*) and the **American painted lady** (*Vanessa virginiensis*) are also cold hardy and are occasionally sighted in the wintertime. All four species can be expected on the Refuge during the warm part of the year too, when they are joined by the **West Indian buckeye** (*Junonia evarete*).

You might suppose that only a serious lepidopterist would be motivated to identify any of the confusing array of little checkered butterflies that flits among the roadside daisys. Yet, with a fieldguide and a little patience you can distinguish the common species: the **silvery checkerspot** (*Chlosyne nycteis*), **Scudder's patched** (*Chlosyne lacinia*), **Texan crescent** (*Phyciodes texana*), and the diminutive **pearl crescent** (*Phyciodes tharos*). These make dainty additions to anyone's life list.

The hairstreaks are a group of small (less than two inches), fast flying butterflies of particular beauty. Once one stops on a flower it will allow you to approach slowly for a closeup view. On the hindwing are two pairs of hair-thin tails which are kept in constant twiddling motion.

These little butterflies rest with wings folded over their bodies so you can get a good look at the tracery of red, silver and black decorating the underside of the hindwing that is used to identify the species. With a fieldguide in hand, kneel beside a hairstreak sipping nectar and see if you can distinguish the four common kinds: **red-banded** (*Calycopsis cecrops*), **dusky blue** (*Calycopsis isobeon*), **southern** (*Euristrymon ontario*) and **gray** (*Strymon melinus*).

Now and then you will spot a hairstreak resting in an odd posture on a flower. Odder still, it does not fly even when you touch it. Look closely. The little butterfly is probably being held in the clutches of either a **bristly flower spider** (*Misumenops asperatus*) or a squatty **ambush bug** (*Phymata erosa*.) You have stumbled upon an unsung fascination of the Aransas--the intricate community of small creatures that lives on and within flowers. Indian blankets, thistles, mist flowers and sunflowers are especially well populated.

The predator will be clinging to the butterfly's head. With your magnifying glass (which you should bring as faithfully as you bring binoculars) study the floral world of bees, beetles, spiders, butterflies and caterpillars. You may look up to find other visitors curiously watching you, wondering what secret you have discovered.

One other hairstreak, the **great purple** (*Atlides halesus*) is less common but claims attention. The underwings of both sexes are purple-gray with red and metallic blue markings; the upper wings of males are a brilliant, iridescent turquoise, and even the abdomen is showy--blue above and bright red below. The caterpillars of this species feed on mistletoe.

Most butterflies prefer open sun, but in the shady oak mottes in springtime or after early summer rains, a flutter of **little wood satyrs** (*Megisto cymela*) may be startled from the leaf litter. In the fall of a good year you may encounter the **zebra longwing** (*Heliconius charitonius*), an animated spangle of sunshine wafting slowly through the trailside gloom.

The migratory **monarch** (*Danaus plexippus*) passes across the Refuge, northbound in late March, southbound in late October and early November. Sometimes monarchs filter through in unimpressive dozens. At other times they arrive by the thousands.

Unlike a bird, no individual monarch makes a roundtrip from the wintering grounds in Mexico to the northern edge of the summer range in Canada and back again. Eggs are laid, larvae grow and pupae metamorphose along the way and several generations transpire during the annual cycle. In mild years a few weather-beaten adult monarchs overwinter on the Aransas.

The **queen** (*Danaus gilippus*),a nonmigratory relative of the monarch, is common on the Aransas throughout the warm part of the year.

Although not a close relative, the summertime resident **viceroy** (*Limenitis archippus*) resembles the monarch. This is an apparent example of mimicry. Monarch caterpillars pick up foul-tasting chemicals from the milkweeds on which they feed. This repulsive quality is retained by the adult and apparently causes potential bird predators to avoid monarchs. The viceroy, which actually does not taste bad, takes advantage of the situation by resembling the monarch closely enough to fool some predators.

Snout butterflies (*Libytheana bachmanii*) are not migratory like monarchs, but they do form northbound waves when there has been a good hatch in South Texas. During these outbursts, usually in July-August, snouts pass across the Coastal Bend by the hundreds of thousands daily for a week or more.

The many small to medium sized butterflies called skippers are recognized by their widely spaced antennae terminating in curved, knobbed tips. The kinds of skippers are not easily distinguished, but two very common dusky species are the **funereal dusky-wing** (*Erynnis funeralis*) and the **common sooty-wing** (*Pholisora catullus*). A brighter one is the aptly named **long-tailed skipper** (*Urbanus proteus*). All three visit a variety of wildflowers.

Moths

The Aransas supports a rich fauna of moths with larvae and adults involved in many ecological relationships: high-flying adults are among the staples for nighthawks and bats; many larvae are caught by wasps which feed them to their own developing offspring; and small birds search out both adults and larvae. But because moths are mainly night flyers, we shall pass over the group with mention only of some caterpillars that might catch your attention.

At one time or another you are likely to see a wooly bear caterpillar (named for its covering of black hairs) hustling across the road; in some years they become a nuisance. The commonest one, the **saltmarsh caterpillar** (*Estigmene acraea*), is not restricted to the bay margin as its name implies. It feeds on a variety of plants throughout the ridge-and-swale community and metamorphoses into a furry-bodied white moth with a two inch wingspan.

In the springtime the handrail of the ramp to the Observation Tower is sometimes alive with fuzzy caterpillars of the **hickory tiger moth** (*Halisidota caryae*), that feed on live oaks. Their tufts of hair look like they might sting. They do not, but beware, some species of look-alike tussock moth caterpillars do have stinging hairs. Best observe and not touch.

Watch for **bagworms** (*Thyridopteryx ephemeraeformis*) attached to the willows along the Heron Flats and Heritage trails. These tough sacks, one to two inches long and covered with small sticks, contain caterpillars or wingless females of a nondescript little moth.

Bees and Wasps

You will recognize honeybees and bumblebees on any springtime or summertime walk. How about leafcutter bees and carpenter bees?

The medium-sized **leafcutter bees** (*Megachile spp.*) visit flowers to collect pollen which they carry beneath their abdomens, rather than on the hind legs like honey bees. You may already have noticed evidence of their remarkable habit for provisioning their nests.

These bees lay their eggs in holes in the sand, lined and partitioned with bits of leaves and stocked with pollen. Pieces are cut from the leaves of various shrubs. Each kind of leafcutter bee probably has its own preferred plant. On the Aransas, the red bay trees along the Dagger Point Trail are heavily used. Examine the bay leaves. If the bees have been at work, half to full circles will be neatly snipped from their edges. Some leaves may have their entire margin disfigured.

You can also see extensive leaf cutting on rattlepods beside the pier at Jones Lake, but this is beetle work, not bee work. **Broad-nosed weevils** (*Eudiagogus pulcher*) feed on the edges of the rattlepod leaflets. In late May or early June you can find the little black-and-pink beetles munching away. If you touch a branch the weevils will quickly twirl to the far side or drop off.

Eastern carpenter bees (*Xylocopa virginica*) lay their eggs in galleries gouged in solid wood and provisioned with pollen. These large, robust bees resemble bumblebees as they zoom around their nest site, buzzing loudly. Such a colony sounds aggressive, but the bees will not sting unless they are handled.

Carpenter bees will burrow in dead branches, but they seem to prefer the smooth surface of planks, and they always place their entrance hole in the underside of the plank. For several years a group of carpenter bees has used the split rail barriers on the Heron Flats Trail and at the alligator observation point across from the Visitors Center. Another colony lives at the corral on the Heritage Trail.

You may find a nest of **paper wasps**--called yellow jackets locally--(*Polistes exclamans*) attached to a tree branch or beneath an overhang around the Refuge buildings. These natural paper combs are constructed of chewed wood pulp and saliva. What do you suppose paper wasps bring to their developing larvae for food?

At least one kind of **hornet** (*Vespula squamosa*) occurs on the Aransas. In 1985, a volleyball-sized nest was discovered beneath a clump of Gulf cordgrass on the Heron Flats Trail.

At the base of the ramp to the Observation Tower, look up at the ceiling spotted with blobs of dried mud. These are the workings of two species of **mud dauber wasps** (*Sceliphron cementarium* and *Chalybion californicum*). The energy required to haul so much mud is amazing enough. At least as remarkable is the fact that each of the several cells of every mud nest is provisioned with at a dozen or more paralyzed spiders to serve as food for a wasp larva. That's a lot of spiders.

Galls are abnormal plant growths caused by the introduction of a chemical substance. Several groups of tiny insects induce these growths and deposit their eggs inside so their larvae can feed on the gall tissue.

One kind of **gall wasp** (*Holcaspis cinerosus*) leaves abundant evidence of itself in spherical woody galls on live oak trees. Once the wasp larva metamorphoses and leaves, the gall may become the home of small spiders or of specialized species of carpenter ants. (See Chapter 3.)

The only other plant gall that is abundant enough on the Refuge to be noticeable is not caused by a wasp, but it is convenient to mention it here. Almost every red bay tree has many leaves with abnormal swellings on their margins. In springtime these leaf galls are lavender; later they turn brown. If you slice open a fresh gall and look inside with your hand magnifier you can make out a colony of tiny cottony white insects. These **jumping plant lice** (*Trizoa sp.*) do not appear to affect the host tree.

Flies

Flies of one kind or another are everywhere you look: houseflies attend your picnic; **March flies** (*Plecia nearctica*), popularly called lovebugs, smudge your windshield; **shore flies** (*Ephydra spp.*) skitter along the muddy edges of brackish tidepools; **dance flies** (*Empididae*) hover in seething swarms over the cordgrass. But for all visitors, all personnel and most wildlife there is only one important fly on the Aransas Wildlife Refuge--the **mosquito**

Important, of course, from our point of view; mosquitoes are arch nuisances and potential carriers of disease. But mosquitoes are also ecologically significant. Their teeming aquatic larvae transform microbes, protozoa, algae and suspended detritus into animal protein to be consumed by the next higher link in the food chain. Many creatures, from spiders and dragonflies to frogs and birds, consume the flying adults.

Whatever you may think of them, you cannot ignore mosquitoes. At peak seasons the impact of hordes of blood-hungry mosquitoes is enough to alter the habits of both wildlife and men. Deer, birds and even herptiles engage in whatever escape behaviour they can to avoid the misery of repeated mosquito bites. Visitors use chemical sprays and protective clothing or plan to avoid predictable outbreaks and favored feeding times. For the unwary or the unbelieving, what might have been a pleasant hour's ramble along the Heron Flats Trail can become a 10-minute, leg-slapping dash for the car.

At least a few mosquitoes are active during every month of the year on the Aransas. Numbers drop precipitously in January and February but resurge with the earliest spring warmup and remain bothersome until the first strong northers in late November and early December. Throughout the long mosquito season, day to day abundance depends on rainfall. Wet years spawn unsuppressed multitudes; a string of dry months fosters a truce, immediately broken at the first rainshower or unusually high tide. Strong breezes inhibit the flying adults; calms set them loose in force. Even on windy days, mosquitoes are quick to emerge from the grass and find the downwind side of an exposed patch of skin.

Though at times it seems that every one of Texas' 76 species of mosquitoes must be on the Aransas Refuge, no systematic survey has been made. Judging by proximity to the tropics, mild winters, convenient sloughs and exposure to the Gulf weather systems, the mosquito fauna should be diverse. However, the majority of the ones that whine around visitors and wildlife belong to just two saltmarsh species: *Aedes sollicitans* and *A. taeniorhynchus*. These are occasionally supplemented by several species of *Psorophora*.

The saltmarsh mosquito you swat at today may well have begun life six months ago as one of the fertilized eggs sprinkled across dry depressions in the tidal flats and swales—places which catch temporary puddles after rainshowers or high tides. The embryos develop rapidly until they are ready to hatch; then they cease all activity and wait.

The eggs with their full-term embryos may lie dormant in the soil for weeks. (This is how most survive the winter months.) Finally, inevitably, the water comes. The puddle fills, and within ten minutes active little mosquito wrigglers have popped from their eggshells and begun to feed. In only three to four days, the larvae develop to pupae and two days later, the pupae metamorphose.

With all the water in the bays and lakes, why do saltmarsh mosquitoes use ephemeral puddles? The big reward is avoidance of predatory killifish and mosquito fish. Another is a rich source of food confined in a quiet cache free from competition. But the price they must pay is that they have to hurry. The wrigglers' lives are a race against evaporation. However, they do have a safety net. Some of the eggs do not hatch on cue. If the puddle disappears too rapidly, these tardy eggs will have a chance to hatch when the puddle fills the next time.

Five to six days after rain or tide, in brackish pools and grassy puddles all across the Refuge, thousands of adult saltmarsh mosquitos split their floating pupal cases, test their wings and fly off to shady spots to harden their new cuticles. After a day of rest the newly emerged mosquitoes are hungry. Sugar from flower nectar gives them energy. They mate. Soon the females, swelling with eggs, are possessed with the urge to have a blood meal. Protein from blood is necessary for viable eggs.

So, we have a blood-famished female saltmarsh mosquito clinging to a blade of Gulf cordgrass on the edge of the Heron Flats Trail, and here you come. She prefers to fly at dusk or dawn, but, startled from rest in midafternoon, she rouses to the opportunity. She can see you dimly against the sky as she rises and circles downwind. Her antennae bring her vital information: a waft of your carbon dioxide-laden breath, a stream of warm moist air from your active body; and she zig-zags quickly upwind following your spoor.

Guided now by eye, the mosquito closes in. Lactic acid from your pores leads her to a patch of exposed skin where she settles gently. If she is lucky, her proboscis will find a capillary without stimulating a pain receptor and she will gorge in 20 seconds and fly heavily away. If she is unlucky you will spook her or swat her.

If things go well for her, two days after her encounter with you, the mosquito will be scattering components of your blood, neatly encapsuled in little spindle-shaped eggshells, across the tidal flat. Then the waiting begins again.

If you believe the only good mosquito is a dead one you should learn about the largest, loudest, most fierce-looking mosquito on the Aransas Refuge. It has no common name so we must refer to it by its tongue-twisting scientific name: *Toxorhynchites rutilis* ("Tox-o-rin-KITE-eez ROOT-ti-lis").

This beautiful insect, resplendently decked in metallic blues, violets and coppers is uncommon, but sometimes wanders into automobiles and gets trapped against the windshield. Will you refrain from swatting it when you learn that it never sucks blood and that its larvae feed only on other mosquito larvae?

Grasshoppers and their Kin

This large and important group is herbivorous. Most kinds are seasonally abundant. Being staple in the diets of many vertebrates, arachnids and other insects, their ecological associations are diverse.

On any summertime walk, watch for flashes of bright color as grasshoppers take to the air; and notice how these insects abruptly disappear when they fold their wings and crash-land. On sunny stretches of the Heron Flats Trail each footstep may startle the little **sulphur-winged grasshopper** (*Arphia sulphurea*) into crackly-winged flight. The golden-yellow wings of the **mottled sand grasshopper** (*Spharagemon collare*) and the delicate orange ones of **Caudell's long-horned grasshopper** (*Psinidia amplicornis*) bear a contrasting black band near the tip.

In the tall grass along the Heritage Trail the large **Carolina grasshoppers** (*Dissosteira carolina*) and the high-flying **bird grasshoppers** (*Schistocerca americana* and *S. alutacea*) occur. Many of the grasshoppers of the road and trailsides belong to the large group of **spur-throated grasshoppers** (*Melanoplus spp.*).

Grasshoppers have quite an array of social mannerisms. Courting males are particularly interesting. Some raise their legs or wings to display bright colors; others produce subtle squeaks, clicks and chatters. A few engage in brief shuffling dances. Stand still and eavesdrop on them.

As you walk in shaded or moist areas, keep an ear cocked. Many kinds of mostly green and arboreal katydids and grasshoppers with long, hair-like antennae make sounds by day and by night.

Round-winged katydids (*Amblycorypha rotundifolia*) produce a series of soft "tsips". **Angular-winged katydids** (*Microcentrum rhombifolium*) click. At dusk, the **leaf katydids** (*Pterophylla camellifolia*) high in oak trees begin their repetitious stuttering calls. Because of its ventriloquil quality, it may be difficult to locate the penetrating buzz of the **cone-headed grasshopper** (*Neoconocephalus triops*) perched in tall grass.

The daytime call of **saltmarsh grasshoppers** (*Orchelimum spp.*) is a measured sequence of trills and clicks. Don't confuse this sound from the depths of cordgrass clumps with the nearly continual, dry rasping trills of the **dogday cicadas** (*Tibicen spp.*) which come from the willows along Thomas Slough

At night the crickets tune up: **tree crickets** (*Oecanthus angustipennis* and *O. exclamationis*) in the willows; **field crickets** (*Gryllus pennsylvanicus*) on the ground and a range of singing cousins in between.

Many visitors see, but few appreciate the widespread evidence of the peculiar **mole cricket** (*Gryllotalpa hexadactyla*). These burrowing insects leave little meandering ridges in the moist soil at the edges of freshwater ponds. If you move quietly you may hear a mole cricket producing its subdued groaning chirp from the security of its burrow. Not one person in a thousand even knows these unique little creatures exist. Yet, they are common on the Aransas.

Ants

These insects, abundant in every community type and eaten by a variety of animals (prairie racerunners, horned lizards and armadillos are especially fond of them), are ecologically most significant as consumers.

The Coastal Bend is rich in ant species, but no one has formally surveyed the kinds on the Refuge. Loose sand is poor substrate for tunnelling and level land is subject to swamping and saltwater washover. The Aransas offers few suitable microhabitats--no rocks, no ledges, no cracks, few logs; yet there are plenty of ants and you can hardly fail to notice some either interesting or pestiferous ones.

Everyone knows that ants love picnics. Is that why the picnic area harbors as great an array of ant species as anywhere on the Refuge? Probably not. The ants are more likely attracted by the elevated ground, a tight mixture of shell and sand and the convenient access to grasses, weeds and shrubs. Your picnic crumbs are simply an added attraction for them. It is a fact, however, that most of the kinds of ants that we shall mention can be found within a few minutes' stroll from the picnic area.

The **harvester ants** (*Pogonomyrmex barbatus*), the most conspicuous of the seed eaters, are what most people call red ants. A more affectionate nickname is "pogo". An individual harvester ant is not long-lived, but a colony may last for years, so nest sites in favorable spots are semipermanent. There are several pogo mounds near the picnic area, another on the slope beside the Visitors Center, and a venerable one midway along the Heron Flats Trail.

Pogos are large enough to be observed from a discrete distance with binoculars. Watch the constant streams of workers moving on broad pathways out into the grass and back to the nest with seeds to be stored in underground chambers. Continual busy excavating, hauling, scraping, clipping, and grooming goes on even in winter, and this keeps the mound neatly paved with small particles and a wide circle around it free of greenery. Maybe you can spot a red-and-yellow **assassin bug** (*Apiomerus sessipes*) perched on a weed waiting to reach down and snatch up a hapless pogo from a passing column.

Look for a second species of harvester ant (*Pogonomyrmex occidentalis*) hurrying across the hot sand at the head of the Dagger Point Trail. These ants live in deep sand and do not make a mound at the nest entrance.

Check the mowed roadside on the slope just north of the picnic area for a veritable ant city. The dozen or more craters of excavated sand pellets are the work of a colony of **Texas leaf-cutter ants** (*Atta texana*). Other cities are established along the Big Tree Trail and at the ramp leading to the Observation Tower.

Leaf-cutters are most active at night, but they work on overcast days and even in sunshine in the springtime when new leaves are growing. Workers climb into a variety of shrubs, (yaupon is a favorite), to snip fresh greenery and early fruits. Long columns of workers carry the plant bits into the nest where they are finely minced and spread out in carefully tended chambers. The ant colony feeds on the fruiting bodies of a special fungus that grows in this subterranean garden. When a new queen sets out she tucks a pellet of the vital fungus into a special cavity in her mouth as seed-stock for the garden of a new colony.

Here and there in the grassy expanse between the picnic site and the bay, you can find the shoetop-high craters of the widespread **pyramid ant** (*Conomyrma insana*). These ants feed mainly on plant sap and nectar, and will tank up on any sweet liquid spilled at a picnic table.

Sooner or later everyone who goes outdoors in the Coastal Bend runs afoul of fire ants. Most aggressive is the **imported red fire ant** (*Solenopsis invicta*), a native of Brazil that invaded the Refuge in the 1960's. However, two native species-- the **tropical fire ant** (*S. geminata*) and the **southern fire ant** (*S. xyloni*)--are equally defensive of their nests. Beware of the low, irregular fire ant domes scattered abundantly along all trailsides and roadsides.

The burning sensation is immediate when a fire ant pinches up a bit of skin with its mandibles and plunges in its stinger. If the sting is from an imported fire ant, a pustule usually appears the next day. This may become infected if scratched, and one person in a hundred develops clinical hypersensitivity to the stings.

Fire ants do not have a sweet tooth. They feed on live and dead insect larvae, soft-bodied adult insects, spiders, centipedes, pillbugs, earthworms; whatever they encounter and can overcome. They are attracted to oils and tissue fluids and quickly find freshly killed creatures. To survive hard times, they will even eat their own brood. Although accounts are often exaggerated, fire ants will occasionally attack pipping eggs and unfeathered young birds. They can be a menace to nesting bird colonies on the offshore islands.

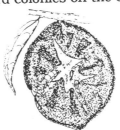

Several kinds of ants live in the spherical woody galls that adorn the branches of most live oak trees. (The wasp that induces the galls was mentioned earlier.) One **gall ant** (*Camponotus rasilis*) occupies several kinds of plant crevices including galls, but the **corkheaded ant** (*Camponotus etiolata*) is adapted especially to the galls. In a few members of the colony, the head is shaped like a bottle cork and one of these ants dutifully plugs the single entrance hole in the gall until a sister ant, returning to the nest, twiddles the corked head with her antennae, bidding the animated portal to open.

The Aransas Refuge even has one species of **army ant** (*Neivamyrmex pilosum*) that sends out columns of eyeless but efficient soldiers to raid the nests of other ants.

SPIDERS AND THEIR KIN

The most abundant and diversified group of predators on the Aransas is the spiders. On a foggy spring morning, the omnipresence of moisture laden spiderwebs adorning the shrubs, trees, and weedstalks and spread over the grass suggests their abundance. And these webs represent only a fraction of the spiders on the area; many spiders build webs out of sight or too small to notice and others make no web at all.

Sample the treetops, the tidal flat or the roadside --spiders everywhere. A few sweeps with an insect net or a sift through a handful of leaf litter will have the same result: almost as many tiny spiders as insects.

All spiders are carnivores, and insects are their principal prey. The collective impact of hundreds of thousands of hungry spiders forges one of the most significant links in the food web on the Aransas.

When a creature finds a new and successful means of making a living (as a spider using webbing), many variations on the same theme soon evolve. The resulting diversification is called *adaptive radiation*--related species pursuing the same essential lifestyle, each in a slightly different way.

Recognizing adaptive radiation when you see it is both instructive and fun. The varied ways that spiders use to bring down their prey offers a classic opportunity. Any time you see a spider during your visit, see if you can classify its feeding style. Most ground-living species are wandering hunters. They pounce-and-grapple without resorting to a web. Jumping spiders leap-and-grab. Flower spiders rely on an ambush strategy. Then there are the web makers: vertical webs, horizontal webs, funnel webs, sheet webs, domed webs, maze webs and many more. Each web type is designed to capture insects with certain habits. Observe, speculate and enjoy as you walk.

On a morning with fog or heavy dew the commonest medium-sized vertical orb webs that glisten on the weed tops are made by the **star-bellied spider** (*Acanthepeira stellata*) and the **hump-backed orbweaver** (*Eustala anastera*). In the shubbery the clusters of peculiar webs resembling inverted bowls are made by the **basilica spider** (*Mecynogea lemniscata*). **Grass spiders** (*Agelenopsis spp.*) deck the roadsides and shortgrass meadows with their horizontal sheet webs. And on the stalks of smooth cordgrass at the end of the Boardwalk the **elongate stilt spiders** (*Tetragnatha elongata*) spin their webs to catch dance flies and mosquitoes.

In the summertime you will see large vertical orb webs with a zigzag white zipper in the center strung high in the tops of tall weeds and shrubs. These are spun by **black-and-yellow garden spiders** (*Argiope aurantia*). The related **banded garden spiders** (*A. trifasciata*) spin a smaller web nearer the ground. It is thought that the purpose of the zipper is to keep small birds from crashing through the web.

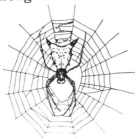

Watch for spiderwebs in the shade along the Heron Flats Trail. Here one of the prettiest spiders on the Refuge spins her snare. The **orchard spider** (*Leucauge venusta*) is richly colored in red, yellow and bright silver. The grotesque **spiny-bellied orb weaver** (*Micrathena gracilis*) and **arrow-bellied orb weaver** (*M. sagittata*) also string webs in the trailside shrubbery. Each has long spines on its enameled abdomen. The curious little **caudate orb weaver** (*Cylosa caroli*) builds a web at knee-level. In the center, where it fixes a jumble of debris, it sits quietly camouflaged. Poke a finger at the litter and the spider will forego its ruse and drop to the ground.

Although the population comes and goes depending upon weather and winds, in some years the large webs of the subtropical **golden-silk spider** (*Nephila clavipes*) are common on shady trails. These webs are made of strong, sticky yellow silk, and several of the hairy-legged female spiders commonly string their orbs next to each other.

Of the spiders that do not capture prey in a web, the most common are **wolf spiders** (*Lycosa carolina* and others). You will see many of these ground dwellers at the inner edge of the tidal flat and throughout the grassland, moving around searching for insects to pounce upon. At night their eyes glow like green gems in the beam of a flashlight.

Often colored to blend with their surroundings, **flower spiders** (*Misumenops asperatus, Misumena vatia,* and *Misumenoides formosipes*) crouch in flowers to ambush insects attracted there. The **green lynx spider** (*Peucetia viridans*) lurks in the foliage with the same purpose.

The largest of the many species of **jumping spiders** on the Refuge is *Phiddipus audax*. This is a hairy black spider with white markings on its abdomen and metallic green mouthparts. These arachnids commonly live on prickly pear pads and you may notice their cottony retreats nestled among the thorns.

Two species of North American spiders are dangerously poisonous to man. Both of them catch prey in messy tangles of web spun across crevices and amid plant litter. Both occur on the Aransas, but they live secretive, retiring lives and are not likely to be encountered on a routine visit.

The **black widow** (*Latrodectus mactans*) is common beneath logs and in cracks on standing stumps. The shiny black female has a bulbous abdomen, long thin legs and a distinctive red hourglass mark on the belly. Although these spiders usually snare insects, one was observed to catch and overpower a newly metamorphosed toad.

The **brown recluse** (*Loxosceles reclusa*) is only occasionally encountered, mostly in surface litter and abandoned dwellings or outbuildings. This medium-sized, long-legged brown spider is rather plain. The slightly darker brown, violin-shaped mark on its back that is supposed to distinguish it is not nearly so clear as the red hourglass of the black widow.

Only one species of **scorpion** (*Centruroides vittatus*) has been recorded from the Aransas. It is moderately common beneath surface debris throughout the dry inland areas and along the strand line at the edge of the bay.

With a heavy population of mammals, it is not surprising that the Refuge harbors several species of ticks. The **lone star tick** (*Amblyomma americanum*) and the **gulf coast tick** (*A. maculatum*) are the commonest species.

The lone star tick is indiscriminate in its choice of hosts. It attaches to any mammal and has also been recorded on forty species of birds. Larvae of the gulf coast tick infest ground-living birds, especially the eastern meadowlark, but adults shift to such larger mammals as feral hogs and white-tailed deer. Both species readily parasitize man, and if you should brush against the wrong leaf, you may have the demoralizing experience of picking up a load of several hundred "seed ticks" (larval ticks).

If you sit in or walk through tall grass you can anticipate an infestation of another pestiferous arachnid--the **chigger mite** ("redbug", *Trombicula spp.*).

Many other kinds of invertebrates live on the Refuge, from doodlebugs to earthworms and centipedes to land snails. If you keep alert for them every walk can become an adventure.

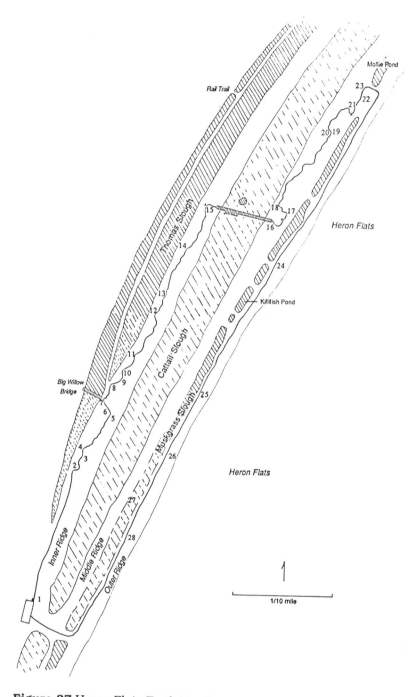

Figure 27 Heron Flats Trail. Numbered stakes are correlated with a brochure available at the Vistors Center.

Woody Plants

Most of us realize that plants constitute the critical producer level of the food web. Through photosynthesis, green things tap the energy in sunshine and with it manufacture the life-stuff upon which they and ultimately all animals depend. Plants also produce oxygen, provide shade and shelter, hold soil, and influence rainfall and wind currents. In addition, plants have their own secrets, lifestyles and beauty that make them worthy of attention.

Over 1500 kinds of native plants grow in the Coastal Bend. The current Refuge file lists 457 species, and it is continually being adjusted and expanded. Of these, we mention only a few conspicuous and ecologically important ones in this and the following two chapters. Chapter 8 covers those alien plants which were deliberately introduced. The spontaneous appearences of alien weeds, grasses and herbs, even those recognizably due to Man's activity, are too frequent and widespread for more than passing comment.

Names of plants present the same problem as names of invertebrates. We have met it in the same way, by providing a Latin name along with our choice of a common name.

To indicate areas where various plants can be located on the Refuge, we frequently refer to the biotic communities described in Chapter 3. On the Heron Flats Trail some individual plants are marked with numbered posts to match the commentary in a brochure (available at the Visitors Center). Where appropriate, we have referred to these station numbers to direct you to a particular plant.

None of the many illustrated books about woody plants deals specifically with those of the Texas Coastal Bend, but for the trees we recommend *Trees of North America*, by Brockman. The single best reference to all of the plants of the region is *Flora of the Texas Coastal Bend*, by Jones, but this work is sparsely illustrated and the text is written for the serious botanical enthusiast.

TREES

The loose porous sand, occasional washover by the sea and recurrent dry spells combine to limit the Aransas to a meager 20 species of native trees. Actually, you can describe 98% of the tree cover on the Refuge with one three-letter word: oak.

Hands down, the most abundant and important tree on the Aransas Wildlife Refuge is the **live oak** (*Quercus virginiana*). In previous chapters we have frequently mentioned the outstanding value of live oaks to wildlife and we commented on the problem of controlling the spread of shrubby oaks. We should also pay homage to these trees' critical role in holding the sand against the buffeting of wind and wave. And certainly one of the live oak's most appealing attributes is its innate beauty. Mottes of live oaks with their spreading branches and alluring shade; the tiers of wind-pruned trees that march across the peninsula; the picturesque oaks clinging tenaciously to the tip of Dagger Point: these constitute the pleasant backdrop for every Aransas experience.

Growing among the live oaks, **laurel oaks** (*Quercus hemisphaerica*) are distinguished by leaf or acorn. Live oak leaves are stiff and leathery, dark green above and silvery-green beneath; the columnar acorn gradually tapers to the tip. Leaves of the laurel oak are thinner and pale green both above and below; the short fat acorn forms a rounded dome. Laurel oaks never attain the venerable, spreading stature of live oaks.

Scattered **blackjack oaks** (*Quercus marilandica*) are recognized by black, chunky bark and wide, three-lobed leaves. In the fall, the purple and reddish-brown of the dying leaves of blackjacks stand out amid the evergreen live oaks and laurel oaks. Watch for them in the oak-bay forest to the

east of the road between Dagger Point and the Tower. The peninsula was named for this oak, probably because of its distinctive appearance rather than its abundance.

You can see all three of these oaks on the Dagger Point Trail. The Heron Flats and Big Tree trails wend through groves of large live oaks, and the Headquarters and picnic site are located in others. Wind sculptured oaks are best viewed from the Observation Tower. The Tour Loop meanders through ridge-and-swale clothed mostly with live oaks and laurel oaks.

Although we will not bother to distinguish them, there are two more kinds of low-growing oaks on the Refuge (*Quercus minima* and *Q. fusiformis*). There are also a few **post oaks** (*Q. stellata*) in the interior of the peninsula and several **Durand's oaks** (*Q. sinuata*) at the Youth Environmental Training Area.

When crushed, the lance shaped, lustrous green leaves of the **red bay** (*Persea borbonia*), emit a spicy aroma. Clusters of small yellow-white flowers bloom in May and develop by autumn into round fruits with a large pit covered by a thin shell of black pulp. In most of the fruits you can find the small round exit hole of a seed weevil. The swellings on the edges of the leaves are galls mentioned in Chapter 13. Red bays are at their finest in the oak-bay forest community, best seen on the Dagger Point Trail.

Large **netleaf hackberries** (*Celtis reticulata*) grow beside the Observation Tower ramp and smaller ones are on the Heron Flats Trail (Station #19). **Sugar hackberries** (*Celtis laevigata*), with larger, much thinner leaves, are less common. **Black willows** (*Salix nigra*, Station #7) line Thomas Slough. The **anaqua** (*Ehretia anacua*) at Station #3 is now dead, but these trees occur in isolated clumps in the interior of the peninsula. Their dark, olive-green leaves are sandpaper rough both above and below. Birds are fond of their yellow fruits.

Several species of small trees can be seen on the Heron Flats Trail. **Mexican persimmon** (*Diospyros texana*, Station #5) has white flowers in the spring, round green fruits by early summer and edible, fuzzy black fruits by late summer. Opossums, raccoons, deer and even armadillos eat the juicy persimmons. Although they are messy to peel, you can try a sweet ripe persimmon for yourself. If you like to speculate on how plants get distributed, notice the flat red-brown persimmon seeds in the animal feces along the trail.

Honey mesquite ("meh-SKEET", *Prosopis glandulosa*, Station #25) grows thickly in the mesquite-prickly pear community on the Tatton Unit and it is a member of the chaparral community. Mesquites are occasional along the middle and outer ridges of the Heron Flats Trail where you can get a close look at their lacy light green foliage, cylindrical creamy flower spikes and woody bean pods. Deer, javelina, coyotes and rodents crunch up fresh mesquite pods.

In the shade along the inside ridges crush a leaf of **lime prickly ash** (*Zanthoxylum fagara*, Station #21) and inhale the uplifting citrus odor. Or enjoy the pink flowers and pendant, three-lobed capsules of the **Spanish buckeye** (*Ungnadia speciosa*, Station #8). In the fall buckeye leaves turn lemon yellow before they drop.

One **retama** ("rey-TAH-mah", *Parkinsonia aculeata*) grows between the outer ridge and Heron Flats about thirty feet south of Mollie Pond, but it is easier to observe the specimen planted at the Visitors Center. Retama has a smooth green trunk, thorny green branches and long drooping leaves with many small green leaflets. In the summertime it produces clusters of bright yellow flowers that eventually transform into thin brown bean pods. On the Aransas retamas are most common in the chaparral and the mesquite-prickly pear communities.

A few rather anemic **huisache** ("WEE-satch", *Acacia farnesiana*, Station #22) occur on the inner and middle ridges. On the firmer inland soils of the Coastal Prairie huisache is abundant and makes a respectable 20-foot tree. It grows sparingly on shell, but this species does not do well on deep sand. It is uncommon on the Refuge.

Salt cedar (*Tamarix gallica*) is actually native to Western Europe. In the Coastal Bend it has escaped cultivation to grow in thick clumps along bayshores, around fresh and brackish pools, and along roadside ditches. Salt cedars growing on the shoreline of Blackjack Peninsula and several of the islands in San Antonio Bay serve to soften the erosive impact of the waves and they provide nesting and resting sites for birds. You can observe a clump of salt cedars at Station #27 on the Heron Flats Trail. A second clump grows on the bayshore between the Boardwalk and the Big Tree Trail.

Just before you recross Cattail Slough, at the exit end of the Heron Flats Trail, the last tree on the south side of the path is a **prickly ash** (*Zanthoxylum clava-herculis*.) These pale barked trees with cat-claw prickles on branches and twigs are scattered on sandy mounds across the peninsula, where white-tailed deer browse the shining aromatic foliage and bobwhite quail eat the small round fruits. Occasionally, a trunk will have spine-tipped corky projections.

SHRUBS

Yaupon ("YO-pahn", *Ilex vomitoria*) is the commonest shrub on the Refuge. It has firm, evergreen leaves with scalloped edges and clusters of white flowers in spring. By autumn the orange-red berries brighten the undergrowth of the oak mottes and feed many mammals and birds.

The less abundant **American beauty berry** (*Callicarpa americana*) shares the understory habitat with yaupon. In early summer, clusters of lilac flowers bloom at the bases of the leaves, and by late summer the pairs of thin, ovate leaves are surrounded by globular masses of bright lavender berries. Both yaupons and beautyberries line portions of the Big Tree Trail.

Tree huckleberry (*Vaccinium arboreum*) reaches the western edge of its range here. In late April bell-shaped white flowers dangle among the ovate leaves at the ends of sprangly twigs; by autumn they have matured into edible (but not tasty) black fruits. The best spot for tree huckleberries is along Blueberry Ridge on the Green Branch of the Dagger Point Trail where they are easily spotted in the winter by their rich wine-red foliage.

Several shrubs most characteristic of the chaparral community form a dense woody screen along portions of the Heron Flats Trail. **Tanglewood** (*Forestiera angustifolia*, Station #18) anticipates spring in mid-February when its clusters of tiny greenish-yellow flowers with red anthers sprout directly from the still leafless twigs. From a distance a tanglewood in flower has a fuzzy appearance. Later, the stiff, crooked stems are densely covered with narrow leaves in small clusters or opposite one another. The fruits are pear-shaped, black and about 3/8" long.

By early March the bright yellow flowers of **agarito** ("ag-ah-REE-tow", *Berberis trifoliata*, Station #15) will scent the outer ridge. Each stiff agarito leaf has three spiny margined leaflets. **Spiny hackberry** (*Celtis pallida* Station #16) and **brasil** (*Condalia hookeri*, labeled "bluewood" near Station #18) both have thorny stems. In late summer spiny hackberry has round, clear orange fruits 1/4" in diameter; brasil sets slightly smaller juicy black fruits. **Texas torchwood** (*Amyris texana*, Station #20) is a densly branched shrub with numerous shiny dark green leaves, each made up of three small leaflets. If you crush a leaf you can detect a distinctive aroma.

Where freshwater regularly stands, the **rattlepod** (*Sesbania drummondii*), is likely to grow. This perennial sprouts from a woody base, often making a small tree. Its fine-cut green leaves are brightened in early summer by drooping sprays of golden-yellow, bonnet-shaped flowers and later by flat three-inch pods with four membranous ridges. At Jones Lake and along Thomas Slough, you can hear the summer breezes rattle the dangling dry pods.

Coffee bean (*Sesbania macrocarpa*), with thin 8" long pods, and **bagpod** (*S. vesicaria*) with two seeds in each short inflated pod, are infrequent annuals in low moist sites.

Buttonbush (*Cephalanthus occidentalis*), another perennial of pond margins and moist depressions, has large leaves (to eight inches) arising from the stem in pairs or triplets. In June you can spot the fuzzy white ping-pong balls of buttonbush flowers between the Bay Overlook and the Dagger Point turnoff.

Wax myrtle (*Myrica cerifera*) is a holdover from the late Pleistocene when the Aransas was much wetter than it is today. This is a waist-high shrub with thin, yellow-green leaves. It is moderately common but spotty; several plants grow near the beginning of the Big Tree Trail. With a magnifying glass, you can see the tiny orange-yellow wax glands which profusely dot the undersides of the leaves. In the fall wax myrtle branches are covered with clusters of small round, frosted-gray fruits.

Groundsel (*Baccharis halimifolia*) may grow to 10 feet tall with abundant narrow leaves and late summer clusters of fuzzy white flowers. Often surrounded by water, groundsels are favored nesting sites of red-winged blackbirds and great-tailed grackles. Groundsels border the bridge across Cattail Slough and grow along the inland edge of Heron Flats. The closely related **bush baccharis** (*Baccharis texana*) is a lower, more dry adapted species with small, dark green leaves. It grows along the middle and outer ridges on the Heron Flats Trail.

Marsh elder (*Iva frutescens*) closely resembles groundsel, and grows in the same habitat. Distinguish between the two by the arrangement of their leaves: in pairs along the stem in marsh elder; singly in groundsel.

SUBSHRUBS
Five species of ankle to knee-high plants with weak woody stems that dominate the tidal flat community can be seen at close range from the Boardwalk.

Most of the gray-tinted growth around Mustang Lake is **bushy sea ox-eye** (*Borrichia frutescens*). This very common plant grows in nearly pure stands across the tidal flats where it serves as a natural breakwater, a shelter for marine organisms and a nest site for seaside sparrows and such shorebirds as the willet. The succulent, gray-green leaves are arranged in pairs along the pale stems. Sea ox-eye blooms throughout the summer, but a few plants can usually be found at any time of the year bearing yellow daisy flowers with spiny bases. After the petals fall, the spherical spiny heads remain on the stem tips for weeks.

Whereas sea ox-eye grows in heavy silt, glassworts poke their brittle, leafless stems through the saline sand. Two species of glassworts grow on the tidal flat. The yellow-green stem joints of the upright, sparsly branched **annual glasswort** (*Salicornia bigelovii*) are much longer than thick. The profusely branching **perennial glasswort** (*S. virginica*) has gray-green stem joints about as long as thick. In early summer a sparkling yellow dust of pollen on the sand is a clue to look for glasswort flowers, tiny yellow dots at the prominent stem joints. In the fall the somber tidal flat is brightened when the perennial glasswort turns shades of rose and carmine.

The prostrate stems and erect branchlets of **saltwort** (*Batis maritima*) snake across the sand among the glassworts. Its paired, pale green jellybean-shaped leaves are interspersed in summer with pea-sized lumpy yellow fruits. Whooping cranes feed heavily on the leaves.

Scattered through the bushy sea ox-eye zone is **Carolina wolfberry** (*Lycium carolinianum*), a straggly, drooping plant with sharp thorns and thin green leaves. The sporadic blue-lavender flowers produce bright red berries nearly 1/2" across. Look closely at a fruit. Do you see the family resemblance in this miniature pepper? Geese, whooping cranes, and other birds eat these berries, and coyote feces are sometimes full of the thin yellow seeds. The related **Berlandier's wolfberry** (*L. berlandieri*) grows in the chaparral community.

During the first two weeks in April the **coral beans** (*Erythrina herbacea*) burst into spectacular bloom. You cannot miss their spikes of fire truck-red, sword-shaped flowers along the roadside between the Bay Overlook and the Tower. In the summertime their black woody pods split open revealing the red beans which stick to the margins for some time before falling to the ground.

You can find the waxy red flowers of **turk's cap** (*Malvaviscus drummondii*) in the shade of live oaks along the roads and trails. Hummingbirds probe into the twisted petals beside the protruding column of stamens. The small, apple shaped fruits that ripen to bright red in late summer are edible, but rather tasteless.

Lantana (*Lantana horrida*) blooms throughout the summer with flat clusters of small flowers at the tips of spreading, brittle stems. Flowers at the outer edge of the cluster are orange; the younger central flowers are butter-yellow and the balls of round fruits are deep blue-black when ripe. Lantana is occasional on the roadside and it grows near the picnic area.

Wild indigo (*Baptisia leucophaea*) is a knee-high plant widely scattered in swales along the Tour Loop. It has attractive drooping sprays of soft yellow, bonnet-shaped flowers during March and April.

Partridge pea (*Cassia fasciculata*) plants with their lacy foliage may grow from ankle to head high, depending on moisture. In favorable years, they dominate the clearings along the roads. From June to the end of warm weather, bees are busy on the thick, dark-brown anthers of the abundant yellow flowers. Each of the three smaller upper petals of the 1 1/4" flowers has a small red spot at the base. Beans of the partridge pea are favored food for all ground-dwelling birds.

On the Aransas Refuge the **salt marsh-mallow** (*Kosteletskya virginica*) grows only along Thomas Slough from the big willow tree (Station #7) on the Heron Flats Trail to a point about half way to the picnic area. These head-high plants with velvety gray-green leaves produce their large, soft pink hibiscus-like flowers throughout the summer.

VINES

Some 25 kinds of vines twist their way through the vegetation on the Aransas Refuge. Six of these have woody stems.

The largest species is **mustang grape** (*Vitis mustangensis*). This common vine clambers through the canopy of most oak mottes, including the one that shades the picnic area. A specimen is labeled near Station #3 on the Heron Flats Trail, and you can get a close view of the broad leaves with white cobwebby undersides as you ascend the ramp to the Observation Tower. When the purple-black grapes ripen in early summer they are heavily used by wildlife. If you care for a taste, hold a grape between thumb and forefinger and squeeze it until the pink pulp pops into your mouth. Discard the caustic skin and spit out the seeds.

Greenbriar (*Smilax bona-nox*) is the most abundant vine on the Aransas Refuge. Curtains of its prickle-studded, wiry green stems render the undergrowth impenetrable to all but small or low-slung bodies. The spherical clusters of round black fruits that ripen in the fall are relished by the same animals that eat mustang grapes. Although the vine is evergreen, some leaves turn a beautiful orange-bronze in October. You can hardly avoid encountering greenbriar along the Big Tree Trail.

On any summer day the ground at Station #11 on the Heron Flats Trail may be littered with large orange-red, trumpet-shaped flowers fallen from the the high-climbing **trumpet creeper** (*Campsis radicans*). The flowers attract hummingbirds, and the huge olive-green leaves (over a foot long but divided into many leaflets,) have special secretory glands that attract ants. Trumpet creeper is not known elsewhere on the Refuge.

Just before entering the trees at the start of the Heron Flats Trail, the path is bordered with a briar patch of **dewberry** (*Rubus trivialis*) laced through with **pepper-vine** (*Ampelopsis arborea*). The sprawling prickly woody stems, white petaled flowers and edible black fruits of dewberry are easily recognizable as a kind of blackberry. Young leaves at the stem tips of pepper-vine are reddish-bronze; older leaves are dark green. The small round fruits change from green to lavender and finally to shiny black, but they are not good to eat.

Dry summers keep **poison ivy** (*Rhus toxicodendron*) uncommon on the Refuge. It does grow on the Heron Flats Trail, and though the one marked at Station #12 is not always evident, the species is easily identified by its smooth green three-parted leaf, the terminal leaflet on a distinct stalk. As though to atone for its noxious reputation, the tiny pale berries of poison ivy are avidly eaten by most small birds, and in the fall the leaves turn a flame-red before dropping.

SUCCULENTS

The huge **Spanish daggers** (*Yucca treculeana*, Station #24) on the sunny shell ridges of the Heron Flats Trail are impressive at any time of the year, but they are especially so from late February to mid-March when they put up their heavy panicles of white flowers. Each dagger plant supports a thriving community of insects and arachnids which come to feed on the flowers and on each other. A second, smaller species of yucca (*Y. tenuistyla*) is thinly scattered across the tidal shore community.

Prickly pears are easily recognized by their stems of flat oblong pads studded with patches of spines. The large **Texas prickly pear** (*Opuntia lindheimeri*, Station #17) is one of four kinds of cactus that grow on the Aransas. In April its fresh flowers open a clear yellow; day-old ones turn orange-gold. Bumblebees and various beetles are attracted to the flowers. The egg-sized fruits, called tunas ("TOON-ahs"), ripen to a rich burgandy color by late summer. Everything from birds and javelinas to rodents and insects feeds on the juicy tunas. Prickly pears are especially abundant in the mesquite-prickly pear community on the Tatton, where they are a mainstay in the diet of the South Plains woodrat.

Tasajillo ("tah-sah-HEE-yo", *Opuntia leptocaulis*) is occasional in the chaparral community and one clump grows beside the path between stations #17 and #18 on the Heron Flats Trail. Look for waist-high columns of cylindrical green stems covered with stout yellow spines. After summer showers this cactus puts on a few small pale yellow blossoms. The flowers soon transform into bright red, knobby fruits that cling to the stems for weeks. Tasajillo has an efficient means of distributing itself. The spines imbed themselves into the flesh of an animal that brushes against them and the stem segment readily breaks loose. When scraped off by the irritated animal, the segment falls to the ground and roots.

Plains prickly pear (*Opuntia macrorhiza*), a shoetop-high cactus with gray spines, is widespread on clay soil bordering St. Charles Bay. The **devil's head** (*Echinocactus texensis*), a low mound covered with a network of fierce thorns, is common in the mesquite-prickly pear community on the Tatton Unit and along the low clay ridges near Burgentine Lake.

The only native palm on the Aransas is the **dwarf palmetto** (*Sabal minor*). Palmettoes reach a stubby treeform along the coastal river bottoms, but on the Refuge they are little more than sprays of fan-shaped, pleated leaves springing directly from the ground. These leaves are often bicolored: pale brown at the margin and green centrally. This is a consequence of wintertime burning. The brown portion was killed by the fire; the green region is fresh growth. In May palmettoes send up tall slender green stalks of inconspicuous flowers and later have round black fruits. A palmetto is marked at Station #6 and you can find them around Thomas Slough and on the roadside to the Tower.

Herbaceous Plants

Here we cover an assortment of nonwoody flowering plants arranged into seven groups: wildflowers, aquatics, grasses, vines, epiphytes, parasites and extra specials. The book by Jones cited in Chapter 14 covers all of these groups except the grasses. Grasses are well illustrated and described in *Grasses of the Texas Coastal Bend* by Box and Gould. There is no illustrated wildflower book just for the Texas Coast, but three which include many coastal species are *Wildflowers of Texas* by Ajilsvgi, *Texas Wildflowers* by Campbell and Lynn Loughmiller, and *Roadside Flowers of Texas* by Wills and Irwin. You may also find *Plants of the Texas Shore* by Cannatella and Arnold useful.

WILDFLOWERS

To help you find them, we have tabulated the common wildflowers seen each month on the Refuge in three appendices. Appendix A lists wildflowers which routinely appear on the slope beside the Visitors Center; Appendix B lists the main flowering plants along the Heron Flats Trail, and Appendix C covers the roadside between the Visitors Center and the Observation Tower. None of these tables includes all of the species that may be in flower.

Remember: wildflowers are best enjoyed by simply looking at them. Please refrain from picking them.

Most of the plants on the Refuge produce flowers and so could be put into this category, but we have limited the term "wildflower" to its popular use--species which have prominent and usually attractive flowers. Even this restriction leaves well over one hundred kinds. The most eyecatching 65 of these are listed here by flower color.

White Flowers

False garlic (*Nothoscordum bivalve*) has a bouquet of six to twelve white flowers at the tip of a shin-high stem. Its few thin leaves arise directly from a subterranean bulb. Each stalked blossom is about 1" across and has six petal-like parts. This plant closely resembles a small onion, but a crushed leaf lacks the distinctive onion odor. In a wet spring, false garlic lines the roadside between Headquarters and the picnic area.

Several days after good summer rains, legions of **rain lilies** (*Cooperia drummondii*) rim the roadsides, each ephemeral foot-tall stalk bearing one shining white trumpet. The larger **spider lilies** (*Hymenocallis liriosme*) are more enduring, but rare. Their exotic looking white blossom consists of a central cup surrounded by six strap-like segments. Waist high clumps of their long, inch-wide leaves grow in moist depressions; look for one on the edge of the tidal flat between the Heron Flats Trail and the picnic area.

In the fall on the roadside near the entrance to the Heron Flats Trail, watch for the wands of **green lilies** (*Schoenocaulon drummondii*). Each 18" stem terminates in a cylindrical spike of greenish-white flowers followed by small green fruits. The spent black stems may persist for months.

Late February is the time to get down on your hands and knees to examine the tiny white flowers and downy leaves of **whitlow grass** (*Draba cuneifolia*) sprinkled along the Heron Flats Trail. It is among the first of the early-rising mustard family to celebrate springtime. While you are down, check shady spots for **chickweed** (*Stellaria media*). Each of its five white petals is split nearly to the base, making the flower appear to have 10 thin petals. These early species are soon joined by **peppergrass** (*Lepidium virginicum*) which bears its many tiny flowers in shin-level clusters at the ends of the branches.

Old plainsman (*Hymenopappus artemisiaefolius*), like its namesake, stands alone, tall and straight. Look for its waist-high clusters of ivory flowers in the clearing near the picnic area. If the spring is a wet one, **windflowers** (*Anemone heterophylla*) will be common. Each 1½" flower has 10-20 thin petals around a silvery green dome. You may find an occasional lavender windflower.

In early April the shin-high **prairie bluet** (*Hedyotis nigricans*) begins to bloom. One of the most widely distributed wildflowers in the state, it blooms everywhere until winter sets in. Each ³/₈" flower in the loose cluster has four downy, lavender-white petals. If you are on the Aransas in January or February, watch for minute purple-blue dots of **tiny bluets** (*Hedyotis crassifolia*) in moist sandy openings. You will have to bend low to enjoy their delicate beauty

On May mornings **hoary pea** (*Tephrosia onobrychoides*) blooms along the roadside near the Dagger Point turnoff. Each waist-high stalk has several bonnet-shaped flowers; by afternoon the day-old lower ones turn from white to rosy-red.

Beach pimpernel (*Samolus ebracteatus*) is most at home on the tidal flat but it grows profusely in the roadside ditches along the Tour Loop. The ¼" flowers with five flaring, pink tinged lobes dangle from a knee-high stalk. Most of the leaves spread out at ground level.

Summertime white flowers on the Aransas include tall **prickly poppy** (*Argemone sanguinea*), pancake-shaped clusters of **buckwheat** (*Eriogonum multiflorum*), fat cylindrical stalks of **pussyfoot** (*Petalostemum obovatum*) and tiered flower heads of the strong scented **horsemints** (*Monarda maritima* and *M. citriodora*). Two yellow centered white daisies are common. The erect stems and 1³/₄" flowers of **lazy daisy** (*Aphanostephus skirrhobasis*) grow around Headquarters and the Picnic Area. **Fleabane daisy** (*Erigeron myrionactis*) is abundant on the deep sand near Dagger Point and Jones Lake. Its erect pedicels stand up from prostrate stems and bear ³/₄" flowers.

Keep your distance when you inspect the luminous white flowers of **bullnettle** (*Cnidoscolus texanus*); the foliage of these waist-high perennials is covered with fierce stinging hairs. Bullnettles grow from enormous subterranean rootstocks that require deep sand, like that around the picnic area.

The shin-high **green milkweed** (*Asclepias viridis*) produces summertime clusters of numerous green-white flowers. The five petals of each ³/₄" blossom form a shallow dish centered by a purple star-shaped structure incorporating the anthers.

Tiny slits in this structure lead to chambers holding saddlebag-like packets of pollen grains. When an insect steps into a slit, a saddlebag hangs on its leg and is withdrawn when the insect moves on. The fragile bag ruptures while the unwitting insect is visiting another flower, thus effecting cross-pollination.

A second kind of common milkweed, **zizote** ("zeh-ZOH-tay") (*Asclepias oenotheroides*), can be distinguished by its smaller flowers with petals that are bent down at the tips and a greenish-white (rather than purple) central structure. Both species have viscid white sap and seeds with delicate parachutes.

Watch the roadside of the Tour Loop about $1/4$ mile beyond Hog Lake for the impressive head-high stalks of **button snakeroot** (*Eryngium yuccifolium*) standing in moist depressions. A cluster of long, bristly margined leaves is at the base of each stalk and the tiny flowers are nestled in globose spiny heads at the tips the branches.

Throughout the summer, in sunny spots on road and trailsides, **coast germander** (*Teucrium cubense*) blooms. Many flowers open on each leafy vertical branch and each $3/4$" flower has one large tongue-like petal and four shorter ones.

Along some stretches of the Tour Loop the edge of the asphalt is hidden beneath the pale green foliage of a prostrate plant with the unlikely name of **frog fruit** (*Phyla incisa*). A crowd of tiny flowers surrounds each of the $3/8$" nubbins that arise on long slender stalks from the bases of the paired leaves. Where the plants spread on the dark roadway, the flower clusters stand out. Frog fruit is also a common, but less noticeable, trailside plant. (Frogs do not eat the fruit!)

The singularly flanged stems and large rough leaves of **frostweed** (*Verbesina micraptera*) are found in the shade of oak trees. This chest-high perennial blooms in late summer when the wide clusters of $1/2$" flowers above dark green leaves are very attractive to a variety of flies, wasps and butterflies.

Look for the shade loving **rouge plant** (*Rivina humilis*) in nooks along the Heron Flats Trail. The juice of the round, translucent red berries at the bases of the cylindrical flower clusters will stain your fingers. In the fall the leaves of rouge plant turn a striking bronze-red.

Seaside heliotrope (*Heliotropium curassavicum*), a plant of the tidal flat, withstands sun, wind and salt. Its rubbery stems with their thick, gray-green leaves lie prostrate or are weakly ascending. The $1/8$" flowers are arranged along pairs of distinctively coiled stem tips.   You can find seaside heliotropes beside the Boardwalk.

In the fall half a dozen species of asters bloom. All have waist to chest high foliage and flower heads about one-half inch across, with yellow centers and numerous white to pale lavender petals.

Watch along roadside ditches for the weedy growth and lavender-white flowers of **saltmarsh aster** (*Aster subulatus*), the most common one. A thicket of leafless green stems of **spiny aster** (*A. spinosus*) flanks the west end of the bridge across Cattail Slough and it grows in dense stands on low ground along the tidal flats and around ponds. **Saline aster** (*A. tenuifolius*) grows in soft mud subject to tidal flooding. Its fleshy leaves and large lavendar flowers are found sparingly in the tidal flat community. The knee-high prickly green foliage and small flowers of **heath aster** (*Aster ericoides*) are scattered through the inner grasslands.

Pink Flowers

Drummond's wild onion (*Allium drummondii*) is sprinkled along the shell ridges on the Heron Flats Trail in March and April. Ten to twenty-five small flowers, each of six petal-like parts on a short pedicel, are loosely clustered on an ankle-high stalk.   Crush one of the thin leaves to get the characteristic onion odor.

Pink puffball flowers are produced by two different low-growing plants along the roadside and the Heron Flats Trail. To tell them apart, feel the erect pedicel: in **powderpuff** (*Mimosa strigillosa*) it has soft bristles; in **sensitive briar** (*Schrankia latidens*) it is covered with stiff prickles. Have you still got enough child-like interest in nature to run your finger gently along the leaves of these plants and watch them respond by folding their leaflets together?

Meadow pinks (*Sabatia campestris*) are among the most fetching springtime wildflowers on the Aransas.   The blossoms are about $1^1/4$" wide, with five vivid pink petals and a butter-yellow star-shaped center. The related **grass pink** (*Centaurium calycosum*) is a miniature version, about half the size of meadow pinks and with a white centered flower.

Pink primroses (*Oenothera speciosa*), a sure sign of spring nearly throughout Texas, appear on the roadside in February on the Refuge. The nodding, showy flowers are $2^1/2$" across, with four flaring petals and a yellow central spot. The erect flowers of the similar but less common **white primrose** (*Oenothera kunthiana*) are only $1^1/4$" across.

American germander (*Teucrium canadense*) grows in dense clumps in moist spots along the roads. The rigidly upright, waist-high stalks have erect spires of open flowers with many unopened flower buds at their tips. Each flower is about $1/2$" long, with one large tongue-like petal and four smaller ones. The petals are pale pink with lavender spots.

Pink mint (*Stachys drummondii*) blooms on the outer ridge of the Heron flats Trail in March. The flowers are arranged in an attractive terminal spike with unopened buds at the tip. Each flower is $3/8$" long, its basal tube flared into a notched upper lip and a large, lobed lower lip. The edges of the leaves are neatly pinked.

Round, two-toned heads of **rose palafoxia** (*Palafoxia texana*) begin to bloom in the summer but are at their peak after fall rains when they decorate the sandy ridges along the road from the picnic area to the Observation Tower. The widely branched, semi-woody plant may grow to chest-height.

In July, when the **gay feathers** (*Liatris acidota*) bloom in a dense array across the roadside clearings between Dagger Point and the Observation Tower you cannot miss them. Their wide topped spikes of flowers at the ends of erect, knee-high stems look like great plumes stuck in the grass.

Purple and Lavender Flowers

A second species of **gay feather** (*Liatris elegans*) grows in the deep sand along the Dagger Point Road. It has a foot-long spike of lavendar flowers atop a leaning, waist-high stalk.

Several kinds of **wild petunias** bloom on the Refuge in the summertime; all have purple-violet, trumpet-shaped flowers about $1^1/2$" long. The most common one on the trails is *Ruellia yucatana*. If you are in the right place on a hot summer afternoon you may hear pops and clicks as the fruit capsules of petunias burst and fling their tiny seeds several feet away.

The Aransas has several species of spiderworts of which the **stemless spiderwort** (*Tradescantia subacaulis*) is one of the most common. The rosettes of long, veined leaves appear in early spring, and the flowers, varying from deep orchid through lavender to purple and blue-violet, are at their finest in mid-morning.

Although **alophias** (*Alophia drummondii*) are not especially rare, they are so delicately beautiful that it is always a delight

to see them appear after spring showers. Each flower has six petal-like parts: three large outer ones that give the flower a 2" spread; and three small upright central ones. The outer segments are rich purple-violet with a small white, purple-spotted base. The inner segments are purple with darkened bases. You may recognize the alophia for what it is--a member of the iris family.

Three kinds of shin-high clumps of spotted, two-lipped purplish flowers can be confusing. The two skullcaps along the Heron Flats Trail can be picked out by a flattened disk projecting from the upper side of the green tube at the base of the flower. Skullcap flowers have a white blotch on the larger lower lip. **Drummond's skullcap** (*Scutellaria drummondi*) has flowers 1/2" long and leaves no more than 1" long; **egg-leaf skullcap** (*Scutellaria ovata*) has 3/4" flowers and leaves 2" long or more.

Sand brazoria (*Brazoria arenaria*) has a paler colored, wider flower tube with the spots inside it and no projection on the green lower tube. It sends up its shin-high spires of flowers in the clearing at the picnic area in April.

Waist to chest-high stems of vervains with small flowers in vertical spikes at the tops of many branches are frequent on the roadsides in the summertime. **Texas vervain** (*Verbena halei*), has thin, smooth stems and pale 1/4" flowers. **Gulf vervain** (*V. xutha*) has robust, hairy stems and lilac-pink flowers 3/8" wide. Most of the lobed and toothed leaves of vervains are on the lower, unbranched part of the stem.

Upright growth and vertical flower arrangement make **lance leaf loosestrife** (*Lythrum lanceolatum*) resemble vervain; but fewer, larger (1/2"), flowers and untoothed leaves distinguish it. Loosestrife also prefers more moist sites than the vervains. A second species, **western loosestrife** (*L. californicum*), has darker flowers and grows on the perimeter of the tidal flat.

The weak, prostrate or clambering stems of **wine-cup** (*Callirhoe involucrata*) are common around Headquarters in the springtime. The rich burgandy flowers, standing on erect, leafless stalks, are cupped in the early morning, but the five broad petals spread widely by noon.

The flower stalk and each leaf of **purple wood-sorrel** (*Oxalis drummondii*) spring directly from the ground on delicate stalks. Each of the two or three flowers in a cluster has five spreading petals. The shamrock shaped leaves fold up at night.

Low-growing **sandbells** (*Nama hispidum*) thrive on otherwise barren strips of roadside. The pale, 3/8" flowers have a spot of yellow in the throat. Sandy roadside areas are frequently covered by the prostrate foliage of **silver stems** (*Stemodia tomentosa*). The small pale flowers are almost lost in the silvery foliage. The hairy leaves of sandbells and the wooly ones of silver stems are adaptations for reducing water loss.

Both **sand phacelia** (*Phacelia patuliflora*) and **bluecurls** (*P. congesta*) are shade-loving spring bloomers. The ankle-high sand phacelia has many cup-shaped 1" flowers with five white centered violet petals. Bluecurls stand waist-high and have tight coils of numerous small violet-blue flowers and white buds. Flowers of both are spangled with bright yellow pollen sacs on slender, blue filaments.

Despite its coarse name, **toadflax** (*Linaria texana*) is quite delicate. Six or eight pale, 1/2" long flowers are open at a time on the upper portion of the thin, unbranched, knee-high stem. Each flower has two short upright upper petals, a broad, three lobed lower lip, and a long, thin spur that curves beneath the petals. Toadflax blooms in small colonies on the roadside and along the Heron Flats Trail in February and March.

From March through June the large, lilac to cream-colored shaving brush heads of **bull thistle** (*Cirsium horridulum*) attract butterflies in sunny upland spots. The robust, prickly plants stand knee-high. **Texas thistle** (*Cirsium texanum*) is a taller, thinner, less prickly plant with neatly rounded, rose-purple flower heads 1 1/2" wide.

The flat-topped, fuzzy clusters of small lilac flowers of **coast mistflower** (*Eupatorium coelestinum*) are to be seen everywhere on the Aransas throughout the spring and summer. The fleshy leaves are arranged in pairs along the sprawling or semi-erect stems. This is another flower favored by butterflies.

Sea-lavender (*Limonium nashii*) and **saltmarsh gerardia** (*Agalinis maritima*) are tidal flat inhabitants that can be looked for along the Boardwalk and the outer ridge of the Heron Flats Trail. Sea lavender has a rosette of wide leaves at ground level from which a knee-high dense panicle of 1/4" violet flowers rises in late summer. If you look closely, you can see that the little flowers are neatly aligned along one side of each thin flowering branch. Gerardia has simple fleshy leaves and produces pinkish-purple flowers arranged in a few-flowered spike at knee-level. Each 1/2" flower is tubular with five spreading petal lobes, the lower lobes noticeably larger.

Blue Flowers

Not even an indigo bunting can match the blue of the **dayflower** (*Commelina erecta*). Below the two sky blue petals, there is a much smaller translucent white one. Dayflowers wither by midday and are replaced each morning by fresh blossoms from the boat-shaped cup of green leaves around the flower buds.

In a wet spring, the trailsides and roadside ditches of the Aransas are awash with **blue-eyed grass** (*Sisyrinchium pruinosum*). Several flattened, unbranched stems arise together in a shin-high tuft on which the bright flowers make a natural bouquet. Despite the name, this is not grass, but a member of the iris family. Each yellow centered, 3/4" flower has six petal-like parts that terminate in delicate hair-like bristles.

Bluebonnets are not common on the Aransas. **Texas bluebonnet** (*Lupinus texensis*) grows on the dark soil of the Tatton Unit and it has been introduced several times near Headquarters. You may see this species on the roadsides as you approach the Refuge.

On the Tour Loop you will see **blue hearts** (*Buchnera floridana*) all summer and **downy lobelia** (*Lobelia puberula*) in the fall. Blue hearts, with only one or two dark blue-violet flowers open at a time on delicate stems, are hard to spot; but the bright blue spikes of lobelia are conspicuous against the backdrop of faded vegetation worn out by the long hot summer.

Red Flowers

Shoe-top high clumps of **scarlet pimperneL** (*Anagallis arvensis*), a native of Europe that grows widely in South Texas, bloom along the Heron Flats Trail in springtime. The flowers, a peculiar shade of salmon-orange, grow on slender pedicels from the bases of the opposite leaves. An occasional plant has vivid blue flowers.

Erect spikes of the pale brick-red, bonnet-shaped flowers of **scarlet pea** (*Indigofera miniata*) rise from prostrate grayish-green roadside foliage in the summertime. The flowers and leaves of **anil indigo** (*I. suffruticosa*) resemble those of scarlet pea, but the plant is waist-high and shrubby.

Cardinal feather (*Acalypha radians*) is common along roadsides and trailsides all summer; look particularly at the picnic area and the head of the Heron Flats Trail. The plants form ankle-high mounds of round, hairy leaves with lobed margins. The tiny red flowers are densely packed into vertical spikes about an inch long. On female plants the groups of long, silky red styles look like a bird feather. Spikes of male flowers are compact.

Globe mallow (*Sphaeralcea lindheimeri*), is not common on the Refuge, but where it does grow the distinctive rosy-orange color of its 1 1/4" flowers stands out. The sprawling, shin-high plant is covered with white down, and the flowers are widely spaced on the erect stem. Globe mallow occurs sparingly on the slope at the Visitors Center and on sandy sites enroute to the Tower.

The red-orange of **Indian paintbrushes** (*Castilleja indivisa*) is easily recognized on the roadside just beyond Headquarters. A careful examination will show that what appears to be one large flower at the top of each stem is actually a tight cluster of several orange tipped leaf-like bracts. Each bract encloses an inconspicuous greenish yellow flower.

Drummond phlox (*Phlox drummondii*) is the most common phlox and one of the brightest wildflowers on the Aransas. Most of the five parted blossoms are purple-red with a darker central star, but some are pale purple with a white star. Phlox bloom through the spring and into the summertime depending on the rains.

If one wildflower were chosen to be emblematic of the Aransas Wildlife Refuge it might well be the **Indian blanket** (*Gaillardia pulchella*). This showy plant blooms nearly the year round, and in an ordinary summer it grows in truly breath-taking abundance. The flower heads are 2" across, with red-brown centers and numerous red rays tipped with yellow. The proportion of red to yellow varies: many flowers are almost totally red; a rare one is all yellow. If you are sharp-eyed, you may spot one of the curious **flower moths** (*Schinia masoni*) which rest on Indian blankets during the

daytime. The moth has a yellow head and body and crimson wings, and it artfully positions itself so its colors align with those of the flower.

Yellow Flowers

Stinging nettle (*Urtica chamaedryoides*) is a weedy plant with terminal clusters of small, pale greenish-yellow flowers. The paired leaves have toothed margins and the whole plant is covered with irritating hairs. Stinging nettle is among the earliest plants to bloom, beginning on the Refuge in January along the Heron Flats Trail.

The pale yellow flowers of **southern corydalis** ("ko-RID-uh-lis", *Corydalis micrantha*) have a wash of orange-brown at the base. One petal extends into a sac-like appendage so that the flowers appear as slightly arched, $5/8$" tubes positioned horizontally along the upper stems. The bright yellow flowers of **puccoon** (*Lithospermum incisum*) are in clusters and the five spreading petal lobes have crinkled margins. Both bloom in early spring, corydalis around Headquarters; puccoon at the picnic area.

Both of the species of coreopsis ("ko-ree-OP-sis") that begin to flower in April have a red-brown central disc and eight golden-yellow petals with a velvety red-brown spot at the base. The more abundant **goldenmane coreopsis** (*Coreopsis basalis*) has 2" flowers and decks the roadside near the entrance gate and the slope at the Visitors Center throughout the springtime and early summer. **Plains coreopsis** (*C. tinctoria*) has flowers about 1" wide and prefers slightly drier ground. In dry spells, stunted individuals of both species get only 2-3" tall and have flowers scarcely $1/2$" across.

On spring mornings, the bright yellow flowers of **square-bud primrose** (*Calylophus drummondianus*) open early along the outer ridge on the Heron Flats Trail. The larger blooms of **evening primrose** (*Oenothera grandis*) open at dusk, and turn a rich golden-yellow when they close at dawn.

Both **Texas dandelion** (*Pyrrhopappus multicaulis*) and **Carolina dandelion** (*P. carolinianus*) are occasional in roadside depressions. In spring and early summer their 2", pale lemon yellow flowers, composed of overlapping tiers of petals and borne on tips of knee to waist-high stems, open early and close by midday. Texas dandelion has several flowers and its midstem leaves are lobed; Carolina dandelion has a solitary flower and unlobed leaves. Both produce round globes of parachute bearing seeds which invite the passerby to puff them on their way.

Green thread (*Thelesperma filifolium*), like coreopsis, has daisy-like flowers with purple-brown centers and eight golden-yellow rays. But green thread is a larger, more branching plant, sometimes growing chest-high, with leaves dissected into thin green segments. Green thread grows on the outer two ridges of the Heron Flats Trail, where its flowers may be mistaken for those of the shrubs through which the plant clambers.

Bur clover (*Medicago polymorpha*) occurs in all mowed areas at Headquarters and along roadsides and trailsides. The small yellow flowers, dark green leaves and coiled, prickly fruit seldom grow above shoetop level. The related **yellow sweet clover** (*Melilotus indicus*) has numerous $1/8$" flowers in erect spikes on knee-high stems. Both of these clovers are introduced.

Ankle high clumps of the $3/4$" shamrock leaves of **yellow wood-sorrel** (*Oxalis dillenii*) appear sparingly from early spring until the dogdays of summer. The five parted flowers have fine streaks of orange or red in the throat. The green fruits look like tiny okras and have a sharp sour tang.

Head-high stems and large jagged leaves of **wild lettuce** (*Lactuca ludoviciana*) grow along shaded parts of the Heron Flats Trail. The small yellow flowers are unremarkable, but the fleecy $3/4$" spheres of parachute seeds that follow are eyecatching.

The flowers of **queen's delight** (*Stillingia sylvatica*) are not showy enough to get them into wildflower books, but they are worth knowing for their oddity and because they attract a variety of insects and flower spiders. The plants grow to chest height and stand stiffly erect from a thick base. The numerous stems and dark green leaves exude milky sap if broken. The blossom is held above the abundant, upward angled leaves on a stout yellow stalk: several round green female flowers beneath a column of small greenish-yellow male flowers. In late spring, the female flowers develop into marble-sized, three-lobed green fruits. Queen's delight is best seen on the Tour Loop beyond Hog Lake.

The bronze-centered, soft yellow flowers of **wild flax** (*Linum rigidum*) may be first noticed garnishing the ground in the afternoon. The five $1^1/4$" petals are barely joined at the base and fall together by midday. **Pale flax** (*L. alatum*) is similar but lacks the bronze center. Both kinds occur on the Heron Flats Trail and at the picnic area in the springtime.

Along shell ridges you may find another of the several plants with long prostrate stems, numerous small leaflets, and sensitive leaves. The leaves of **yellow-puff** (*Neptunia pubescens*) are dark green with a paler central area and its globose flower heads are bright yellow. Run your finger down a leaf to witness the touch-me-not trait.

As summertime progresses the proportion of yellow flowers on the Refuge increases, and most of them have a daisy-like anatomy: a central disc surrounded by strap-shaped petals called rays.

Camphorweeds (*Heterotheca latifolia* and *H. subaxillaris*) are common on the sand around the picnic area and grow to waist or chest-height with many bright yellow, 1" flowers.

Camphor daisy (*Machaeranthera phyllocephala*) grows on the edge of the tidal flat. You will see its $1^1/4$" flowers, sticky stems and sharp-toothed leaves at the end of the Boardwalk. Bruised leaves of these three plants emit a strong camphor odor, which probably deters some herbivores.

A tall, columnar brown center and drooping, brown-based yellow rays easily distinguish the **Mexican hat** (*Ratibida peduncularis*). The flowers stand head-high on stout leafless stalks; the lobed leaves are mostly on the lower portion of the stem. Some flowers have all yellow rays, and in immature ones the central column is olive-green. In the summertime Mexican hats are common at the end of the Heron Flats Trail.

Rough-hairy, knee-high **brown-eyed susans** (*Rudbeckia hirta*) are common on the roadside all summer. The red-brown central dome of the flower is less than half the height of the center of Mexican hat, and the 20 or so rays are golden-yellow and lack a basal spot. The flower is about 2" across.

Three kinds of sunflowers grow on the Aransas, all with the same general appearance: coarse leaves on stout stalks capped by large flowers with numerous bright yellow rays surrounding a wide dark center. Well watered **common sunflowers** (*Helianthus annuus*) grow over head high and have 2-4" flowers. They like disturbed places, and are particularly abundant near the picnic area.

The **silver-leaved sunflower** (*H. agrophyllus*) looks much like the common sunflower but its very hairy leaves are noticeably gray-green. The hairs probably retard water loss. Although common on the Refuge, it is infrequent in the area of public access. Look for a stand on the roadside about a quarter-mile outside the entrance gate. Well established plants soar to 15 feet tall.

The **coast sunflower** (*Helianthus debilis*), grows to chest height and has $2^{1}/4$", distinctly orange-yellow flowers. It prefers deep sand and can be seen occasionally along the edges of firebreaks.

What appears to be a waist-high sunflower but with a yellow-centered blossom is probably **rosinweed** (*Silphium simpsonii*). These grow sparingly on the roadside between the Visitors Center and the Heron Flats Trail. **Cowpen daisy** (*Verbesina encelioides*) also has yellow rays and a yellow center, but the tips of the rays are deeply notched. The branching plant has toothed, gray-green leaves with basal lobes that clasp the stem. The leaves are aromatic when crushed. Cowpen daisys grow beneath live oaks at the Visitors Center and at the Bay Overlook parking area.

A thin solitary stem branching profusely at knee-level gives **broomweed** (*Xanthocephalum dracunculoides*) its name. The narrow leaves are inconspicuous, while the hundreds of small daisys on the stem tips create a billow of bright yellow dots along firebreaks and roadsides in late summer.

The erect leafy stems of **seacoast goldenrod** (*Solidago sempervirens*) sprout in chest-high clumps from perennial rootstocks. The narrow leaves angle upwards and the numerous small, butter-yellow flowers are clustered in a tight 6" terminal spike. Occasional plants bloom early, but fall (Sept-Nov) is the time to enjoy the bright wands of seacoast goldenrods swaying above the brown grasses along the Tour Loop. The more diffuse, flat-topped flower clusters of **fragrant goldenrod** (*S. odora*) also appear in the fall. The two species readily hybridize, so intermediate plants are common.

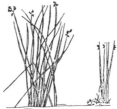

AQUATIC PLANTS

Aquatic vegetation is important as shelter and as a food source for wildlife. It contributes to quality and depth of the water, to firmness and fertility of the bottom and--as the plants wax, wane and change in species composition--to the health and longevity of the aquatic community.

Most of the aquatic plants on the Aransas have flowers, and we have already mentioned those with attractive blossoms. Others can be identified by their growth form or specific growth site. Freshwater plants are best observed along Thomas Slough, from the bridge across Cattail Slough, or from the observation deck at Jones Lake. Brackish water species can be seen at the end of the Boardwalk.

The flat leaves of **cattails** (*Typha domingensis*) erupt thickly from a maze of rhizomes in the rich ooze at the edge of freshwater. There is a small gap between the thick female flower spike and the thinner, terminal male part. By early summer the male flowers will have fallen, leaving a naked stalk extending above the brown, velvety female cluster. In late summer seed-carrying cattail fluff fills the air.

The six-foot tall, slightly curved cylindrical stems of **California bulrush** (*Scirpus californicus*) grow in dense stands in shallow freshwater. Chest high **three-square bulrush** (*S. americanus*), with a sharply three angled stem, grows in shallow water and in moist depressions. Neither of these has evident leaves, but in the summertime both have tufts of brownish flowers near the stem tips. Bulrushes and cattails provide nesting, roosting and feeding sites for red-winged blackbirds, marsh wrens and common moorhens, and their submerged jungle of stems is inhabited by sunfishes, snails, lesser sirens, yellow mud turtles and a host of other creatures.

Common reeds (*Phragmites communis*) grow in dense leafy clumps and send their tall plumed seed heads 12 feet high to sway in the prevailing wind. A prominent growth of reeds can be seen along the edge of the bay between the Heron Flats Trail and the picnic site. In the same area are several head-high clumps of **saw-grass** (*Cladium jamaicense*) with lax panicles of rust-brown flowers and leaf margins armed with sharp teeth that can slice an unwary finger.

Despite the name, saw-grass is actually one of a large group of grassy looking plants called sedges. Most wet places are lined with a diversity of ankle to knee-high kinds of sedges; one that is apt to catch your eye is **white-top sedge** (*Dichromena colorata*). At the top of each knee-high stem is a spray of drooping leaves with chalky white bases that give the appearance of a flower.

On muddy banks and in half dried ponds the ground is covered with the round, umbrella leaves of **penny-wort** (*Hydrocotyl umbellata*) and the small, paired leaves of **water-hyssop** (*Bacopa monnieri*). The tiny flowers of penny-wort are white; water-hyssop has cup-shaped lilac flowers. Standing above these are leafy clumps of **marsh fleabane** (*Pluchea purpurascens*) with dense heads of purple-pink flowers.

The intense yellow, four-petaled flowers of **water primrose** (*Ludwigia linearis*) regularly grace Thomas Slough, and **water lilies** (*Nymphaea elegans*) appear in the more permanent freshwater sites after a series of wet years.

Whenever the Guadalupe River floods, it flushes clumps of **water hyacinth** (*Eichhornia crassipes*) into San Antonio Bay. As they raft across the brackish bay, these freshwater plants slowly die and windrows of them, dead and dying, accumulate along the eastern shore of Blackjack Peninsula. Water hyacinths can be recognized by the spongy enlargements on the leaf stalks that help to keep the plant afloat.

The only emergent herbaceous brackish water species of note is **smooth cordgrass** (*Spartina alterniflora*). This is the dominant species of the Gulf Coast saltmarsh community, but only small stands occur locally. Smooth cordgrass provides both food and shelter for many small marine creatures and it buffers the bayshore against wave erosion. From the end of the Boardwalk you can see this grass growing in San Antonio Bay and from the Tower you can see it lining the immediate edge of Mustang Lake.

GRASSES

Virtually everyone knows a grass when they see one, but few can recognize even half a dozen kinds. Yet, grasses are a large and important fraction of most communities, and on the Gulf Coastal Plain they are vegetative dominants.

Seething generations of insects, arachnids, fungi and microbes live and die without ever leaving the micro-jungle of grass stems. More legions squirm through the grass sod. Even larger creatures like fulvous harvest mice, eastern meadowlarks and Great Plains rat snakes satisfy most of their requirements in grassland.

An array of animals from white-tailed deer and bobwhite quail to grasshoppers and caterpillars consumes fresh grass; and others like savannah sparrows, pigmy mice and harvester ants depend on grass seeds. All of the grass dependent animals in the countless nests, daytime retreats and fur-lined nooks hidden among the innumerable grass clumps on the Aransas work their way into other food chains. The grasses rank as significant members of the producer level in the food web.

Aside from their direct impact on wildlife, grasses mold the terrain by holding topsoil and by inhibiting or at least influencing the growth of woody plants and forbs. Finally, more than any other plant group, grasses have swayed the history and the economy of humans on the Coastal Prairie.

Grasses are flowering plants, but because their wind pollinated flowers do not need insect lures, they are seldom showy or colorful. However, grasses are not lacking in their own beauty: crisp brown winter foliage; waving heads of silver seed fluff; the poetic arc of a clump of seacoast bluestem braced against the steady onshore breeze; the sweep of a hundred unbroken acres of gossamer-laced, dew-laden culms immobilized in the trance of dawn.

About 85 kinds of grasses are known from the Aransas Refuge. We mention only a few prominent and important ones.

Two groups, the bluestems and the cordgrasses, cover more ground on the Aransas than all the other kinds of grasses combined. Bluestems dominate the sandy interior. Cordgrasses take nearly sole possession of the saline flats.

Bluestems

Bluestems are perennial bunch grasses, so-called because of the tint of their foliage, but this distinction is not always evident. About a dozen species grow on the Refuge. They make up most of the grass cover in the clearings along the Tour Loop. Bluestems are at their best in the fall (Oct-Nov) when they have reached full growth and are heavy with seed.

Bushy bluestem (*Andropogon glomeratus*) is one of the most prominent grasses on the Aransas Refuge. It grows prolifically in robust, head-high clumps in all low lying sites along the roadsides. Its whiskbroom-like, shaggy seed heads give it a topheavy appearance. One of the most attractive displays on the Aransas is a glade of bushy bluestem caught at the peak of its straw and russet splendor by the first rays of an October sun.

Broomsedge bluestem (*Andropogon virginicus*) resembles bushy bluestem, but it is a shorter, more delicate plant and prefers drier, upland sites. Its winter stalks are straw colored.

Silver bluestem (*Andropogon saccharoides*) has silvery, tapering seed heads at the ends of thin leafless stalks. Seen against a low sun, an expanse of silver bluestem is dazzling.

The introduced **King Ranch bluestem** (*Andropogon ischaemum*)is common on the Refuge. Look for its thin purple-brown seed heads in the clearing near the picnic area. In the fall, you may notice violet islands in the purple-brown sea of King Ranch bluestem. These are patches of **Roemer tripleawn** (*Aristida roemeriana*), a grass with three whisker-thin hairs attached to each seed. Because of these hairs, the seed heads ripple in the coastal breeze.

Big bluestem (*Andropogon gerardii*) is the giant of its clan. It grows in isolated clumps towering up to 12 feet above the surrounding grasses. The lilac-tinged heads have a crowfoot arrangement of three seed-laden fingers. Big bluestem disappears quickly when grazed by cattle, so it is seldom seen in its full glory anywhere else in the Coastal Bend.

We will not attempt to distinguish among the abundant **seacoast bluestem** (*Schizachyrium scoparius*) and members of groups called dropseeds, paspalums and panic grasses that make up the rest of the knee to waist-high bunch grasses in the swales along the Tour Loop.

To strike pure gold on the Aransas, find an expanse of **Indian grass** (*Sorghastrum nutans*) in full seed in the late afternoon sun.

Patches of misty rose-lavender along the Tour Loop in October are the finely divided seed heads of of **Gulf muhly** (*Muhlebergia capillaris*). These fleecy structures, held above a waist high clump of thin, tough leaves, vie with spiderwebs for glistening with dew drops on cool fall mornings.

Cordgrasses

Each of the three species of cordgrasses on the Refuge has its own growth zone dictated by the salt and moisture content of the soil. Smooth cordgrass, mentioned among the aquatic plants, grows only along regularly inundated bay margins. The tidal shore community is dominated by **marshhay cordgrass** (*Spartina patens*) which begins on the inland perimeter of the tidal flat and extends across all low saline depressions. You can find it on both sides of the path along the outer ridge of the Heron Flats Trail.

A rank, waist-high clump of **Gulf cordgrass** (*S. spartinae*), called sacahuista ("sah-kah-WHEES-tah") by ranchers, makes a vegetative symbol for the Gulf Coast. On favorable saline soils above the reach of high tides, such as on the Tatton Unit,

Gulf cordgrass grows in pure stands. It can be observed from the Boardwalk, from the Observation Tower and along the outer ridge of the Heron Flats Trail. Touch your palm gently against the tips of Gulf cordgrass leaves to appreciate why many old timers called it needle grass.

Marshhay and Gulf cordgrass are not always easy to distinguish from each other. Marshhay is seldom over knee-high and its thin, lax leaves take on a cow-lick curvature, but they are never so evidently bunched like Gulf cordgrass. In seed the two species are easily recognized: marshhay has a slender stalk with half a dozen well-separated fingers of seeds; Gulf cord has a single stout stalk terminating in a long spike of numerous overlapping seed branches.

Other Grasses

Two smaller kinds of tidal flat grasses are readily seen along the Boardwalk. Shin high **seashore saltgrass** (*Distichlis spicata*) thrives in saline muck. It is recognized by the leaves staggered neatly up opposite sides of the stalk. **Shoregrass** (*Monanthochloe littoralis*) forms a prickly green mat only a few inches high on the moist sand.

You may recognize a carpet of **Saint Augustine grass** (*Stenotaphrum secundatum*) beneath some live oak groves. This introduced lawn grass is common in the Coastal Bend and it often survives without care long after the humans who planted it are gone and forgotten.

The common reed, mentioned among the aquatic plants, is actually a huge grass.

If you spend much time walking anywhere on the Refuge, you are sure to get a shoestring or pants cuff full of sticker burs, compliments of the **Gulf Coast sandbur** (*Cenchrus incertus*), a pesky native species of grass.

VINES

The strategy of a vine is to reach the sunshine by climbing up some convenient support, usually another plant. Besides the woody vines mentioned in Chapter 14, there is a welter of climbing, clambering and twining herbaceous vines on the Refuge. The ones which we will describe can all be found along the Heron Flats Trail.

Two morning glorys are easily recognizable. Both have trumpet-shaped flowers. In **Alamo vine** (*Ipomoea sinuata*) the trumpet is bright white with a purple spot inside the throat. This vine has leaves dissected into finger-like lobes, and it sets fleshy turnip-shaped fruits. **Tie vine** (*Ipomoea*

trichocarpa) seldom climbs over chest-high and has lavender trumpets and three-lobed leaves.

You may miss the yellow flowers of **melonette** (*Melothria pendula*) or **globe berry** (*Ibervillea lindheimeri*) but their fruits and their watchspring tendrils are more eyecatching. Melonettes look like inch-long striped watermelons; ripe globe berries look like orange-red ping-pong balls.

The thin, green **Texas nightshade** (*Solanum triquetrum*) vine that scrambles in the understory has white, cupped flowers with five petals and red, tomato-like fruits about $3/8$" in diameter.

There are several different kinds of twining vines with milky sap; all produce bull's horn-shaped fruits that open to release flat, brown seeds on silken parachutes. **Milkweed vine** (*Sarcostemma cynanchoides*) has pairs of soft, heart-shaped leaves and clusters of small white flowers and it bears a smooth pod 4" long. Each solitary, pale green flower of **pearl milkweed** (*Matelea reticulata*) has an opalescent dot in the center. Its 6" pods are prickly. **Dwarf milkweed vine** (*Cynanchum barbigerum*) produces a prodigious number of fragrant, urn-shaped white flowers $1/8$" long, and its smooth pods are less than 2" long.

Snapdragon vine (*Maurandya antirrhiniflora*) has a $3/4$" tubular flower that flares into two upper petals and three larger lower ones. The floral tube is whitish. The petals are purple and there is a raised yellow area in the throat of the tube. Look for the flowers and the triangular leaves on abundant stems, scrambling among the shrubs and bunch grasses along the outer ridge of the Heron Flats Trail. There too, watch at shin-level for the $1^1/4$", pale lavender spoon-shaped flowers of **butterfly pea** (*Centrosema virginianum*). Before the heat of midday you can also spot them from your vehicle along the Tour Loop.

Three species of low twining beans with small, yellow bonnet-shaped flowers and curved bean pods are common on the Refuge. Both **Texas snoutbean** (*Rhynchosia texana*), with 1-3 flowers rising from the leaf base, and **least snoutbean** (*R. minima*), with a delicate spike of flowers from the leaf base, have leaves divided into three leaflets. **American snoutbean** (*R. americana*), which often sprawls along the edge of the pavement of the Tour Loop, has fat heart-shaped leaves.

Wild cowpea (*Vigna luteola*) is another twining vine with a raceme of yellow bonnet-shaped flowers and a three parted leaf. Cowpea has larger flowers and the leaf segments are lance shaped rather than triangular as in the snoutbeans. It also prefers wetter places. Look for cowpea among the reeds on the edge of San Antonio Bay.

The stems, leaves, and even parts of the flowers of **hairy stylisma** (*Stylisma villosa*) are densely covered with soft hairs, a protection against heat and evaporation in the dry, sandy areas it favors. To see the 1" white, funnel-shaped flowers, you must look before noon. They spread across the ground and clamber in the shrubby oaks at the head of the Heritage Trail and in sandy clearings along the Tour Loop.

EPIPHYTES

Epiphytes are plants that grow on other plants but are not parasitic. An epiphyte merely uses its host plant as a convenient place to sit in the sunshine. On the Aransas, only two species of flowering plants belong in this category: **Spanish moss** (*Tillandsia usneoides*) and **ball moss** (*T. recurvata*).

Since these plants do produce small flowers, they cannot be true mosses. (In fact, they are bromeliads, a predominantly tropical group.) Both species are composed of tangled masses of thin stems and leaves. They are silver-gray from a snug covering of waxy scales which prevent water loss but can be raised to absorb water when it is available. Beneath the scales the plants are quite green and carry on routine photosynthesis.

The long stems of Spanish moss hang in swaying festoons, usually from live oak branches. For a few hours after a summer rain, the pale lavender flowers can be seen among the stems. The short, rigid stems of ball moss form a fist-sized mass that sits astride a branch. Its small purple flowers bloom at the ends of wiry pedicels sticking out several inches beyond the leaves. These remain on the plant for months, so clumps of ball moss almost always have numerous protruding stalks. The minute seeds of both species are wafted to new perches by wisps of fluff.

A fascinating micro-community of insects, arachnids, millipedes and other small creatures lives in the moist, shady depths of moss plants. These clumps are favorite foraging sites for small passerine birds, and many birds and some rodents line their nests with the tough fibrous strands of dead moss.

You can see both kinds of moss in the live oaks on the Heron Flats and Big Tree trails, and ball moss is common in tree branches bordering the ramp to the Observation Tower.

PARASITES

Parasitic plants not only grow on other plants, they put roots into the host's tissue and obtain some or all of their nourishment there.

On the Refuge, **mistletoe** (*Phoradendron tomentosum*), grows mainly on mesquite and netleaf hackberry. It is not common in the area of public access, but there are small bunches in the hackberries over the picnic table at the alligator observation site across from the Visitors Center. The evergreen clumps of brittle, green branches and thick yellow-green leaves are easier to spot in the wintertime on leafless trees.

Mistletoe flowers are inconspicuous, but the round, translucent white berries which appear in the wintertime are well known. Seeds wiped from the bill of a bird that has fed on the sticky berries give mistletoe a start in a new spot.

The dodders are more evidently parasitic. They have neither green color nor leaves, and they look like loops of pale yellow string tangled through the branches of their host. Dodders sprout from seed and develop a root system, but they have no chlorophyll and to survive, a young dodder must be near enough to a host plant to twine into it. Then it puts fibrils into the host's tissues, severs its own connection with the ground and thereafter lives entirely on nutrients absorbed from the host. Each kind of dodder parasitizes one or a select group of plants. **Spreading dodder**(*Cuscuta indecora*), the most common one on the Refuge, can be seen in mats on the branches of marsh elder along the outer ridge of the Heron Flats Trail. Its clusters of white flowers appear in late summer. Although the host plants must be weakened by these parasites, they do not usually look disabled.

EXTRA SPECIALS

Botanists, like birders or butterfly collectors, delight in new, rare or especially appealing species. The Aransas Refuge harbors a reservoir of such botanical treats. We briefly mention a few that have pleased us.

- **Saltmarsh morning-glory** (*Ipomoea sagittata*): an occasional twiner on sea ox-eye on the tidal flats. The huge ($3^1/2$") rose-purple trumpets open early and wither by noon.
- **Meadow-beauty** (*Rhexia mariana*): a plant from the east, reported here for the first time in the Coastal Bend. The showy, 2" pink flower has four petals and eight curved yellow anthers.
- **Sundew** (*Drosera annua*): ground hugging, coin-sized rosettes of paddle-shaped leaves covered with red hairs. Sticky droplets on the hairs catch small insects which the plant consumes.
- **Bladderwort** (*Utricularia biflora*): submerged leaves of this plant are fashioned into unique traps that capture and digest tiny aquatic creatures. Bladderworts occur in Thomas Slough.
- **Ladies tresses** (*Spiranthes vernalis*): the only native orchid on the Refuge. Occasional shin-high stalks in roadside ditches are topped with a symmetrical spiral of small white flowers.
- **Woods wine-cup** (*Callirhoe papaver*): relatively huge wine-cup, with petals spreading over 2" and finely toothed on the tips. An eastern species.
- **Purple pleat-leaf** (*Eustylis purpurea*): the Refuge's finest native iris. This $1^1/2$" royal purple flower on a thin, knee-high stalk blooms in early summer between Dagger Point and the Tower.
- **Bluebells** (*Eustoma exaltatum*): 2" indigo flowers on knee-high stems with satiny blue-green foliage. In bud, the petals are twirled into a sharp spiral. Occasional on Heron Flats Trail.
- **American cupscale** (*Sacciolepis striata*): a species from the southeast not previously reported from the Coastal Bend. An uncommon grass of moist swales with panicle of asymmetrical, inflated flowers.
- **Woe-vine** (*Cassytha filiformis*): resembles a giant dodder. This pale green to orange vine snakes through live oak and red bay, at intervals curled around and attached to branches. Occasional on live oaks at the Tower and around the Tour Loop.
- **Passionflower** (*Passiflora foetida*) low-twining vine with tendrils and three-lobed leaves. The male and female floral parts and a lavender wreath of wavy, hairlike segments stand up on a stout central pedestal. Lacy bracts enclose the green fruit but drop off as it matures to orange red. One vine known on Heron Flats Trail.

Nonflowering Plants

The only trait common to this conglomeration of plants is that they do not have flowers, and so never produce either fruits or seeds. They reproduce by simple cell division or by spores. Many do not have ordinary roots, stems or leaves. Even lacking such conventional botanical attributes, they manage the basic life functions. Some carry on routine photosynthesis. Others absorb nourishment from living or dead hosts. Though they lack bright petals, not all kinds are drab, and many of them have peculiar and interesting life cycles.

These plants are low on the evolutionary tree, but they have a high ecological impact. Marine algae are a mainstay in the food web of the bays. The bacteria and fungi are important in recycling nutrients and providing the tons of detritus that feed the smallest of creatures and, by devious branches of the food web, many larger ones as well.

We will mention only a few members of five conspicuous groups of nonflowering plants: algae, fungi, lichens, mosses and ferns. *Non-Flowering Plants*, by Shuttleworth and Zim is a well illustrated introductory guide to this portion of the plant world.

ALGAE

During the fall and winter, rafts and flocks of waterfowl dive, dabble and graze in the shallows of San Antonio Bay, harvesting bushels of plant material every day. Two species comprise the bulk of the birds' fare. **Widgeongrass** (*Ruppia maritima*) is actually a flowering plant. Its flowers are tiny and the plant, which is rooted in the bottom and entirely submerged, resembles a thin-leaved seaweed. Many acres of shallow bay bottom are covered with widgeongrass until the waterfowl mow it down, eagerly consuming fruits, branches, leaves and even the roots.

The second plant utilized by waterfowl, **seahorse tail** (*Cladophora delicatula*) is a filmy alga that grows profusely throughout the summer and is available by the ton when the birds arrive. Cladophora often attaches to widgeongrass stalks and the two plants are eaten together. Coots and diving ducks often bob to the surface with long streamers of Cladophora in their bills. By the time the birds leave, the once luxuriant submarine meadows are virtually barren, but a warm season of growth reconstitutes them.

Bushy, olive to purple-green growths of the alga, **sea bush** (*Gracilaria verrucosa*), are attached to the muddy bottom and on oyster reefs in San Antonio Bay. Many of these fleshy textured plants are blown onto the shoreline where they turn bright lilac. Beach fleas seek food and shelter beneath these rotting algal masses and you might see a willet or sanderling adroitly flip a bit of Gracilaria to uncover a meal.

In portions of the tidal flat and the brackish pool communities, where there are extreme variations in moisture, in temperature, and in salinity, rooted plants do not grow at all. But these open stretches of silty sand are often coated with a thin, slick film of **blue-green algae** (*Lyngbya sp.* and *Microcoleus sp*), hardy plants quite important to the ecology of the bayshore. The mucous-covered mats retard evaporation and the bluegreen algae not only carry on photosynthesis, producing green matter and oxygen, they also engage in a peculiar activity called nitrogen fixation which increases the fertility of the soil and the water.

The ponds that constitute Muskgrass Slough between the middle and outer ridges on the Heron Flats Trail support dense tangles of **muskgrass** (*Chara spp.*), a many celled alga with the joints of its long stems marked by rings of leaf-like structures. When the water evaporates, the depressions are lined with thick mats of dying muskgrass, brown at first, but bleaching nearly white in the sun. When the pond refills, the subterranean portions of the stems quickly revive and regrow. Shorebirds search the foliage of muskgrass for crustaceans and insects, and the fresh growth is a favored food of ducks.

The commonest alga in Thomas Slough is **pond silk** (*Spirogyra sp.*). In early spring, its thin green threads grow at the bottom, but, as the season progresses, large verdant swirls of detached algae cloud the water. As it matures, pond silk rises to the surface where it forms bubbly, yellow-green mats. In late summer, the mats become a brown scum covered with blisters of gas from the decomposition of the now dead algae.

The mass eventually sinks and disintegrates to become part of the bottom detritus. You can observe pond silk from the Big Willow foot bridge.

Coontail (*Ceratophyllum demersum*) is actually a flowering plant, but its minute flowers are seldom observed. The rootless, submerged stems with their rings of thin leaves resemble muskgrass, but coontail is dark green while muskgrass is yellow-green. A dense growth of coontail clogs Thomas Slough at the head of the Rail Trail.

FUNGI

All fungi lack chlorophyll; they absorb their nourishment from living or dead organic matter. A few species cause disease, but the bulk of them is involved in decomposition, the breakdown of plant and animal remains that is crucial for the release of nutrients in both terrestrial and aquatic communities. Some of the larger kinds support insect microcommunities and several species are important seasonal food for mice, squirrels, javelinas, wild hogs, white-tailed deer and wild turkeys.

Mushrooms, puffballs, yeasts, mildews and sundry "molds" and their spores are everywhere, especially in the soil. Fungi are by far the most abundant and diverse of the nonflowering plants, but most kinds are microscopic or nearly so. *The Audubon Society Field-Guide to North American Mushrooms*, by Lincoff, is a well-illustrated reference to most local species.

Mushrooms

The Aransas Refuge supports a varied array of mushrooms and puffballs, general names for the two main groups of large fungi. But the growth of most kinds is fickle and fleeting and their distinguishing traits are subtle, so we will mention only a few conspicuous species.

The best time to see mushrooms and puffballs on the Aransas is in late summer or fall, a few days after a good rain. Look for mushrooms in the leaf litter on the edges of live oak mottes and around tree stumps. Puffballs often occur on sparsely grassed sand. One of the delights of fungi is that they can pop up unexpectedly most anywhere, so be alert wherever you roam.

Typical mushrooms release spores from gills, the radiating plate-like structures on the underside of the cap. The giant among Aransas species is the **green-spored lepiota** (*Chlorophyllum molybdites*) which has gray-green spores.

Clusters of these mushrooms appear on the roadsides after heavy spring rains. The flat white cap, up to almost a foot across, stands on a sturdy 6" stalk.

On a moist day you may encounter the silky, gray-brown 2-4" caps of **meadow mushrooms** (*Agaricus campestris*) along the Big Tree or Dagger Point trails. The gills start out bright pink, becoming rich chocolate brown as the spores mature. **Fawn mushrooms** (*Pluteus cervinus*) occur in the same habitat, but are more widely scattered. The 3" caps, soft brown and slightly sticky, usually grow beneath a cover of yaupon or oak branches. The fresh white gills turn salmon-pink when the spores ripen.

Cool fall days induce from the deep sand along the Dagger Point Trail one of the real gems among Aransas mushrooms--the **emetic russula** (*Russula emetica*). Watch for the flat topped, rose-pink caps among the leaf litter; they sit on stout white stalks and may be 3 inches across. If you find one, others are likely to be nearby.

Inky-cap mushrooms (*Coprinus spp.*) are common on the Aransas, but they are impulsive, springing up suddenly and disappearing in a few hours. Most have long slender white stalks and egg-shaped white caps that darken and flatten as they mature. A hallmark of the group is the rapid disintegration of the cap into a glutinous black mass. Though they are capricious, the picnic area is a likely place to watch for inky-caps.

After fall rains, clusters of **jack o'lantern mushrooms** (*Omphalotus olearius*) growing on tree stumps and buried wood where oak and bay have been mowed, are often spectacular. The cap is burnt orange and the orange gills pale to yellow as they blend into the stalk. Mature caps have down-curved edges and a deep depression in the center. It takes a close look in a really dark room to see the ghostly

green luminescence of the gills--an appropriate trait for a pumpkin-colored mushroom that grows at Halloween time.

The Aransas Refuge harbors several toxic mushrooms, including the extremely potent **destroying angel** (*Amanita bisporigera*). This is one of the many poisonous mushrooms that are a beguiling snow white color and lack distinctive traits. If you merely admire and pass on, they can do you no harm.

Boletes

Another group of mushrooms, the **boletes** ("BOH-leets", *Boletus spp.*) releases spores from an array of pores on the undersurface of the cap. These squatty mushrooms have bulbous stalks and caps that resemble doorknobs in size and shape. The cap of the common **delicate bolete** (*Boletus sensibilis*) is tinted like a ripe peach with a bright yellow pore surface below. Boletes are most common in live oak leaf litter.

During wet fall months, the **old man of the woods** (*Strobilomyces floccopus*) bursts sporadically from the leaf litter in the oak-bay forest community. The white cap of this hoary bolete is studded with blackish scales and hairy tufts and the stem is roughened with scales.

Shelf Fungi

The semi-woody caps of **shelf fungi** (*Polyporus spp.* and *Fomes spp.*) also release spores from a pored undersurface, but they do not have stalks; the caps grow directly from logs and tree trunks, often in overlapping clusters. Tiers of the orange-and-yellow banded fans of **sulfur shelf fungus** (*Laetiporus sulphureus*) grow commonly on live oaks. These and other shelf fungi can be found on the willows and live oaks along the shaded portion of the Heron Flats Trail.

Puffballs

Puffballs are distinguished by having a dense mass of spores enclosed in a parchment-like cover. Eventually the cover ruptures and a cloud of dark spores is released. These fungi usually appear following rains in dry, open sandy areas, but the fruiting bodies linger for weeks. Most puffballs are low-growing and globular, but the related stinkhorns are columnar.

White puffballs (*Lycoperdon spp.*) appear along sandy trailsides. They grow from pea to golf-ball size; some are smooth but most kinds have a warty or spiny surface. Some develop a pore at the top when the spores are ripe and if you press the fruiting body gently, a cloud of dark spores will spew from the hole. From such forced exhalations we get the name puffball.

The **earthball** (*Scleroderma bovista*) has a smooth, straw-colored outer skin. When the earthball matures the top quarter of the tough skin rips open to reveal a powdery mass of purple-brown spores. Raindrops and wind quickly disperse the spores, leaving empty, jagged edged urns.

Earthstars (*Astraeus hygrometricus*) have a thick outer skin over the papery spore case. As the fungus matures, this skin darkens and splits into segments that open into a star shape when the weather is wet and curl back over the spore case when it is dry. Spores are released through a pore in the center of the papery ball, and the drab, deflated spheres with their rim of stiff petals remain on the ground for weeks. Earthstars are common along the east side of the road between Dagger Point and the Tower; they favor one or two year old burns.

Stinkhorns

Stinkhorns are a peculiar type of puffball. They develop in egg-shaped capsules underground and then send up one or more tubes on which the spores are suspended in a smelly slime. The spore filled slime sticks onto flies that are attracted by the foul scent, and it is spread when the insects alight somewhere else.

The **common stinkhorn** (*Mutinus caninus*) is ankle-high. The tapered, spongy tube is salmon colored and capped with a layer of green-brown slime. The tube only lasts a day and is most commonly seen on sandy sites after fall rains.

Even the cinnabar color of the ankle high **columnar stinkhorn** (*Clathrus columnatus*) is easily missed in its grassy habitat. The central stalk is split into three segments which rejoin at their tips in the mass of greenish, fetid spore material. The odor of columnar stinkhorns is attractive to at least one animal besides flies; feral hogs avidly gobble these fungi up.

Stinkhorns are seldom abundant, but the **netted stinkhorn** (*Dictyophora duplicata*) is one of the most ephemeral fungi on the Refuge. At some unknown signal, the 5" white stalk rises rapidly from its subterranean bulb. A wrinkled greenish spore head develops atop the stalk and a delicate white, net-like veil spreads downward from the head to encircle the upper half of the stalk. The spectacular structure lasts less than a day. Watch for it on damp fall days in the oak-bay forest community. The sight may well be a once-in-a-lifetime experience.

LICHENS

Most of the body of these compound plants is fungal tissue but there is an enclosed layer of algal cells. A lichen ("LIKE-en") may be viewed as a fungus that has enslaved an alga to produce carbohydrates for it by photosynthesis. The combination is successful. Lichens are tough enough to survive every extreme of the coastal envrionment except prolonged submersion in saltwater or dry, shifting sand.

Typically, lichens are attached to a firm substrate which limits them on the Aransas Refuge to tree trunks and branches. A watchful eye will perceive that lichens are quite common on most of the trees along every trail; hackberries and live oaks support especially luxuriant growths. Lichens are epiphytes, not parasites.

Several species of **foliose lichens** (*Physcia spp.*) contribute to the gray-green patina on the chunky bark of live oak trees. As you walk up the Tower ramp you can closely observe the mineral gray **shield lichens** (*Parmelia perforata*) that grow in leaf-like layers on the oak branches. One tangled mass of **golden lichen** (*Teloschistes flavicans*) droops from a tree branch along the shaded portion of the Heron Flats Trail.

MOSSES

"Moss" is a one of those generalized words taken over from common language by science and sharpened in meaning to limit it to a specific group of plants. "Spanish moss" and "ball moss" are epiphytic flowering plants; lichens are frequently called "tree moss", and many people refer to marine algae as "sea moss". Here we consider "true moss"--plants which fit that botanical designation.

True mosses are delicate and low-growing, but always green. They lack true roots and stems and cannot easily draw water into their tiny leaves. Reproduction requires at least a film of water, so mosses grow successfuly only in moist habitats. This severely limits the occurrence of mosses on the drought-prone Aransas Refuge.

Where on the Refuge might an immobile, continually thirsty plant find the right combination of partial sunshine and dependable moisture to eke out a living? Only in the bark crevices of the larger live oak trees. That is where to look for the most common species of moss on the Aransas, **treemoss** (*Leucodon julaceus.*).

Tree moss forms green cushions on favorable live oak limbs on the Big Tree and Heron Flats trails and beneath the Observation Tower. Station #10 on the Heron Flats Trail marks a growth on a low live oak trunk that is convenient for close examination. You can kneel there and look through your magnifying glass at the diminutive forest of green leaves (they may be curled up if conditions are very dry) and stalked, golden spore capsules. Then you will recognize a true moss the next time you see one.

FERNS

Shifting sand, withering summers and occasional seawater overwash make the local environment a hostile one for ferns. Only about half a dozen of the approximately 100 species of ferns recorded from Texas occur in the Coastal Bend and none of them is widespread. Four kinds of ferns have been found on the Aransas Refuge; two of these grow in the area of public access.

Water clover (*Marsilea uncinata*) is well named for its long-stalked four parted leaves. Colonies of water clover are known from muddy overflows at several windmills in the interior of Blackjack Peninsula.

The smallest fern species in Texas, **mosquito fern** (*Azolla caroliniana*) would hardly spread across your thumbnail. During the summer, many plants form extensive floating mats which turn red as the the plants die in the fall. Water fern is spread from one freshwater site to another on the feet of the gadwall, teal, coots and gallinules which feed on it. On the Aransas Refuge water fern occurs consistently only at Tule Lake and it appears sporadically at Thomas Slough.

Resurrection fern (*Polypodium polypodioides*) is so named because it withers into a brown mound when dry and quickly unfurls its green fronds following rains. This is an epiphytic species that grows on large, well shaded live oak branches, usually accompanied by mats of tree moss. Resurrection fern is rare on the Refuge. It is known from a few live oaks near the Big Tree Trail and should be looked for along the shaded part of the Heron Flats Trail.

The wiry stems of **bracken fern** (*Pteridium aquilinum*) send a spray of olive-green fronds to chest-height. A colony of bracken fern growing on the dam at Big Devil Bayou and another near Johnson Mill are the first of this species reported from the Coastal Bend.

◊

Appendix A   Vistors Center Slope

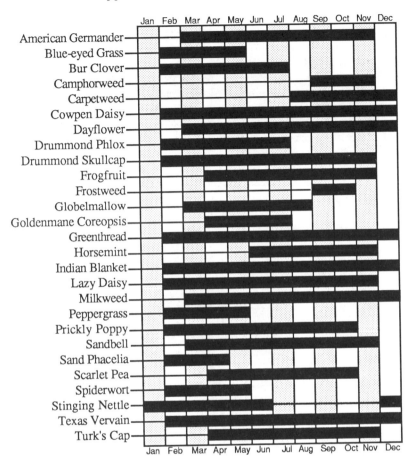

Summary of Flowering Plants 1985-86

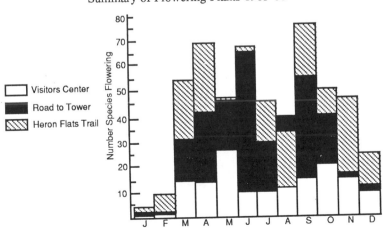

Appendix B   Road to Tower Part 1

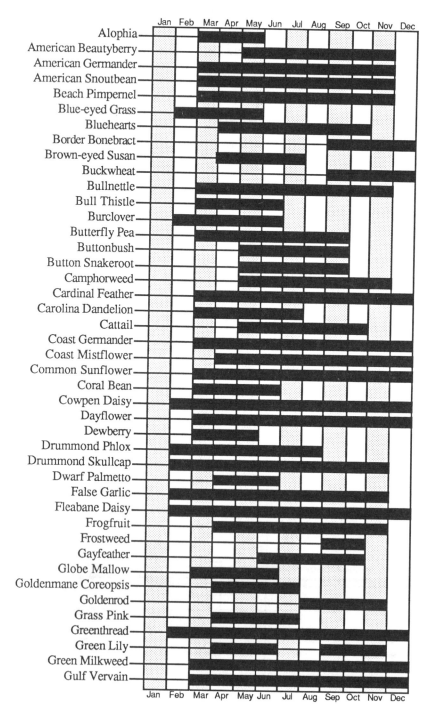

Appendix B Road to Tower Part 2

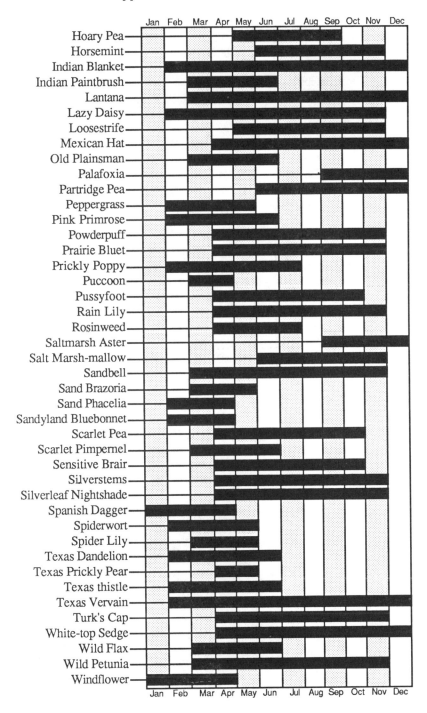

Appendix C   Heron Flats Trail Part 1

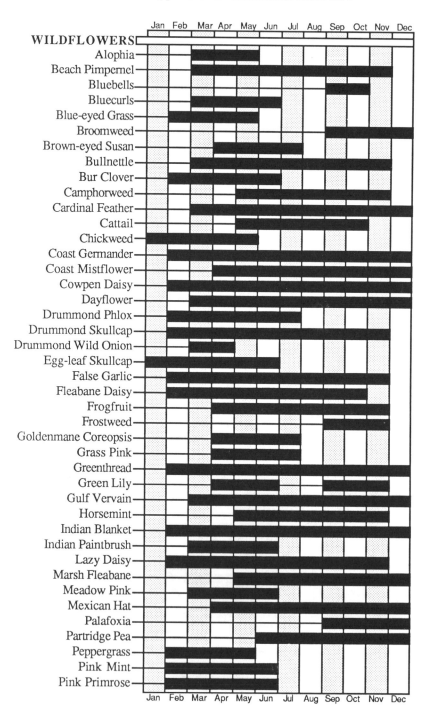

Appendix C   Heron Flats Trail Part 2

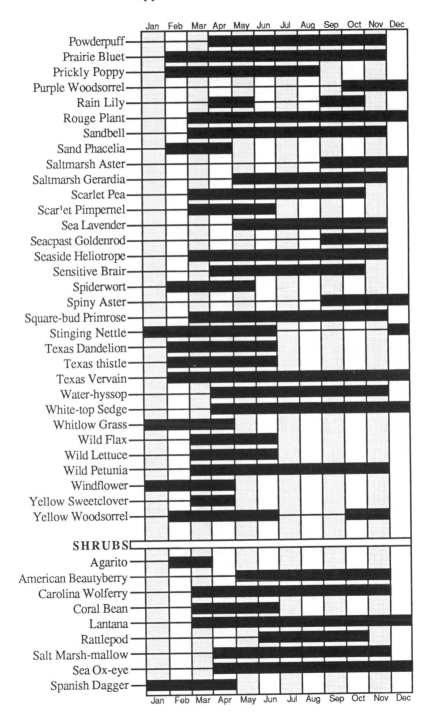

Appendix C Heron Flats Trail Part 3

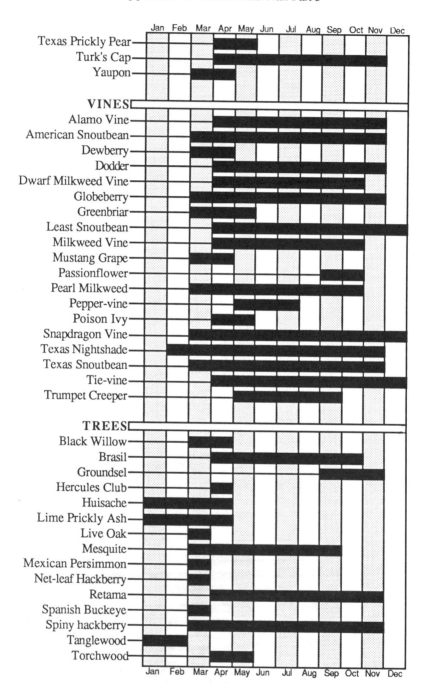

INDEX

sulphur
- clouded 217
- cloudless 217
- orange 217
- orange-barred 217
- shelf fungus 275

sulphur-winged grasshopper 226
sundew 270
sunfish
- bantam 208
- bluegill 208, 210
- longear 208
- redear 208, 210

sunflower
- coast 260
- common 260
- silver-leaved 260

Swainson's hawk 177
swallow
- barn 182
- cliff 182
- rough-winged 182
- tree 182

swallow-tailed kite 177
swallowtail
- eastern black 217
- eastern tiger 217
- giant 217
- palamedes 216
- pipevine 216

swamp rabbit. 151
swamp sparrow 185
swan, whistling 186
swift
- chimney 182
- white-throated 182

sycamore 142

tanglewood 240
tasajillo 245
teal
- blue-winged 128
- cinnamon 129
- green-winged 129

tern
- black 169
- Caspian 169
- Forster's 169
- gull-billed 169
- least 112
- royal 169

terrapin, Texas diamondback 193
Texan crescent 218
Texas blind snake 196
Texas bluebonnet 255
Texas brown snake 197
Texas coral snake 201
Texas dandelion 258
Texas diamondback terrapin 193
Texas garter snake 197
Texas horned lizard 112, 195
Texas leaf-cutter ant 228
Texas nightshade 267
Texas prickly pear 245
Texas rat snake 200
Texas scarlet snake 112, 199
Texas snoutbean 268

Texas spiny lizard 194
Texas thistle 254
Texas toad 191
Texas torchwood 240
Texas tortoise 193
Texas vervain 253
thistle
- bull 254
- Texas 254

thrasher
- brown 183
- long-billed 186

three-square bulrush 141, 261
tick
- gulf coast 233
- lone star 233

tidewater silverside 208
tie vine 267
tiger beetle 216
tiny bluet 249
toad
- Couch's spadefoot 191
- eastern narrow-mouthed 191
- great plains narrow-mouthed 191
- Gulf Coast 191
- Hurter's spadefoot 191
- Texas 191

toadflax 254
tonguefish, blackcheek 208
topminnow, golden 209
topminnow, golden 208
torchwood, Texas 240
tortoise
- Texas 193

tree cricket 226
tree huckleberry 239
tree sparrow 186
tree swallow 182
treefrog
- green 189
- squirrel 189

treemoss 278
tricolored heron 166
tripleawn, Roemer 264
tropical fire ant 229
trout, speckled 208
trumpet creeper 244
turkey vulture 178
turkey, wild 121, 134
turk's cap 243
turtle
- common snapping 193
- Mississippi mud 193
- ornate box 193
- red-eared 193
- spiny softshell 193
- yellow mud 193

upland sandpiper 170

variegated fritillary 217
veery 186
vervain
- Gulf 253
- Texas 253